D1476120

JOHN FRANKENHEIMER

A CONVERSATION

JOHN FRANKENHEIMER

A CONVERSATION

WITH CHARLES CHAMPLIN

DIRECTORS GUILD OF AMERICA

ADDITIONAL RESEARCH AND TEXT BY
Lisa Mitchell

FILMOGRAPHY BY
Karl Thiede

BURBANK, CALIFORNIA

A Riverwood Press Book

Production and typeset by Michael Bifulco
Design and layout by Packy Smith

Published by Riverwood Press, an imprint of Red Circle, Inc.,
Burbank, California/Nashville, Tennessee.

ISBN 1-880756-13-3

Manufactured in the United States of America

PHOTO ACKNOWLEDGEMENTS

The publishers wish to thank John Frankenheimer, Critt Davis, Karl Theide and Mark Haggard for the use of the illustrations appearing in this book. Special thanks to producer Martin Manulis for the pictures on pages 21, 32, 33, 34, 35 and 38.

We acknowledge with thanks the cooperation of the following: Turner Pictures, Inc.; United Artists; MGM; 20th Century-Fox; Embassy Pictures; HBO World Wide Pictures; Universal Pictures; Warner Bros.; Cannon Pictures.

Jim McHugh deserves special mention for opening his entire Frankenheimer archive to help us find the right photographs for both the front and back cover as well as the beautiful photo of JF used as the frontispiece. Also, thanks with proper credit due the following photographers and their photos: Jim McHugh—Frontispiece, p 194; Allan Grant—p 75, 76, 78, 82; Vincent Rossell—p 80, 84, 87, 130, 131; John Bryson—p 90, 91, 92, 93, (bottom l & r), 94; Serge Moritz—p 124, 127, 128, 140, 142, 144; Christopher Casler/HBO Pictures—p 164, 165; Cliff Lipson/HBO Pictures—p 186 (l & r), 187; Erik Heinila/HBO Pictures—p 188, 190, 191; Christopher J. Berkey/HBO Pictures-- p 192 (both); Doug Hyun/HBO Pictures—p 196, 197 (all); Doug Hyun/Turner Pictures—p 200, 202, 206 (all), 207 (all); Jim McHugh/Turner Pictures—p 204, 205, 208.

Contents

Preface   vii

Introduction   1

Early Days   3

Tackling New York   11

You Are There   18

Danger   20

Climax   21

The Young Stranger   27

Playhouse 90   31

The Young Savages   47

Birdman of Alcatraz   53

All Fall Down   63

The Manchurian Candidate   67

Seven Days In May   75

The Train   81

Seconds   91

Grand Prix   97

The Extraordinary Seaman   103

The Fixer   107

Interlude with Bobby   113

The Gypsy Moths   117

I Walk the Line   121

The Horsemen   123

The Impossible Object   131

The Iceman Cometh   133

99 and 44/100 Per Cent Dead   137

French Connection II   139

Black Sunday   147

Working with Dino   153

Prophecy   157

The Challenge   161

The Rainmaker and others   165

The Holcroft Covenent   167

52 Pick-Up   171

Dead-Bang   177

The Fourth War   179

Year of the Gun   181

Short Takes   183

Tales From the Crypt   187

Against The Wall   189

The Burning Season   195

Andersonville   201

Videography   213

Filmography   227

Sources   230

Index   233

Preface

The Directors Guild of America Oral History series records the career achievements and personal insights of pioneers in the fields of film, television and radio. This volume of interviews with John Frankenheimer conducted by Charles Champlin was commissioned in 1993 by Directors Guild of America Special Projects, headed by National Special Projects Officer Selise E. Eiseman.

An esteemed film/TV historian, as well as longtime friend of John Frankenheimer, Charles Champlin not only brought a unique perspective and relaxed openness to the interviews but, with judicious editing, also shaped the text into its present form, resulting in an informative portrait of one of the foremost television directors and film makers of our times. From its modest beginnings as an oral history, the present volume has been enriched by a marvelous collection of one-of-a-kind photographs, and augmented by sidebar material and captions researched by Lisa Mitchell. This book is a valuable addition to reference collections, and will be enjoyed by film fans and historians alike.

In addition to John Frankenheimer and Charles Champlin, who worked for two years on this project, and Lisa Mitchell, we also wish to thank the following individuals who contributed their time, talents and resources: research assistant Josh Ryan; Ron Simon and Sean Johnson at the Museum of Television and Radio in New York; Olivia Nagel of John Frankenheimer's office; Packy Smith and Sheila Roman of Riverwood Press; the Margaret Herrick Library of the Academy of Motion Picture Arts & Sciences; and typists Alex Kustanovich, Hamilton Underwood, and David Lurvey.

—Adele Field, Oral Histories Editor
Directors Guild of America

INTRODUCTION

John Frankenheimer is a member of that small but important generation of Hollywood film makers who began their careers and learned their trade largely in New York, in the volatile, glorious days of live television. Those days lasted hardly a decade, from the dawning of commercial television in the early years of postwar to the late fifties, when tape and color arrived and live television virtually disappeared (taking with it a spontaneity and a kind of daring that were central to its achievements).

"We didn't know what we couldn't do in live television," Frankenheimer once recalled, "so we went ahead and did it."

There were actually relatively few directors who moved from live and taped television to prominence in the world of features: Sidney Lumet, Franklin Schaffner, Delbert Mann, Robert Mulligan and Frankenheimer himself are chief among them. Frankenheimer's personal experiences, occasionally hilarious to look back on although nerve-wracking at the moment, provide an invaluable and thus far mostly untold history of the formative years of the television medium, seen from within.

Beginning as an assistant director, Frankenheimer worked on the *You Are There* series hosted by Walter Cronkite and *Person to Person* with Edward R. Murrow, and then as director on many of the dramatic anthologies *(Danger, Studio One, Climax, Ford Startime, Producer's Showcase)* that also introduced a whole new generation of young actors, including Paul Newman, Jack Lemmon, Eva Marie Saint, Joanne Woodward and scores of others.

Ultimately Frankenheimer was recruited to the west coast to help launch *Playhouse 90*, the weekly hour and a half dramatic anthology which set new standards of form and content for the young medium.

He directed his first film, *The Young Stranger*, in 1956, and his subsequent credits include *All Fall Down, The Man-churian Candidate, Birdman of Alcatraz, Seconds, Seven Days in May, The Train, Grand Prix, French Connection II* and *Black Sunday.* More recently Frankenheimer has returned to television: to the adventurous world of cable television, directing *Against the Wall,* a drama drawn from the tragic Attica Prison riot of 1971; *The Burning Season,* based on the life of Chico Mendes, martyred trying to save the rain forests; and *Andersonville,* an epic-sized dramatization of the infamous Civil War prison.

The interviews for this oral history were conducted in Los Angeles, over a period of nearly three years, from mid-1992 to early 1995, as part of the Directors Guild of America Oral History Series. The series, launched under the general editorship of David H. Shepard in the mid-1970s, continues now under the guidance of Selise Eiseman, head of Special Projects for the Guild, and Adele Field, her associate who administers the Oral History Project.

I owe very great thanks to John Frankenheimer for his candor and the pleasure of his company during many hours of remarkable conversation. To his assistant, Olivia Nagel, great appreciation for her combing of the Frankenheimer archives for pictures and clippings. The tapes, including the sound effects of crockery at lunchtime, were transcribed by Alex Kustanovich, David Lurvey, Hamilton Underwood and Josh Ryan. I am grateful to them for their patient deciphering. I am particularly appreciative of the work of Lisa Mitchell for researching and writing the supplemental material under deadline pressure. I thank Peggy Champlin for her sharp-eyed proof-reading of the history. Far from least, I am indebted to Selise E. Eiseman and Adele Field for their support.

Charles Champlin.
Los Angeles
April 1995

A family portrait taken at their summer home in Bayshore, Long Island, 1937. From left, brother Richard, mother Helen Sheedy Frankenheimer, sister Jean and John, age 7.

John, to set the scene, I'd like to go back to the beginning — where you were born, what your father did, your early life.

I kind of thought you'd want to do that.

So you're ready, right?

I've been looking back and remembering a lot of things. I was born February 19th, 1930, in New York City. My father was a stockbroker, thirteen years older than my mother. He was thirty-five when I was born, my mother was twenty-two. My mother was Irish Catholic, first generation Irish. Her maiden name was Sheedy. I think Ally and I are related. I was their first child, and they'd been married a year.

My father had gone to Yale, graduated in 1914, served in World War I in the Medical Corps, as a kind of hospital officer. He was first lieutenant when he got out. His father was the lawyer for "Our Crowd"—that group of wealthy New York Jewish families that Stephen Birmingham wrote about.

My father was never religious in any sense. His father was prominent in the Ethical Culture movement. My father's family owned a very upscale haberdashery place called Kaskle and Kaskle and my father had become president of it at a very young age. When they sold out to Knox Hats he made some money and went into the stock market. He became a limited partner in a brokerage firm and was not hurt really by the '29 Depression. But his partner absconded with a lot of the firm's money in 1932. So we moved from Manhattan to Long Island, a little town called Malba, between Whitestone and College Point.

We lived very comfortably. I went to a private school called Foxwood. I was quite shy, quite introverted. My father encouraged me to partake of all sports, particularly tennis. He had tried to make the Yale tennis team but he never had. So he really pushed

Prophetic 17 year-old JF with chums Wesley Carpenter and George Beck.

tennis. He had me take a lot of lessons, starting when I was eleven. I was entering and playing tournaments from the time I was twelve. I was ranked when I was thirteen in the under fifteen class, and I was ranked continually for a number of years. I won quite a few tournaments. I played in the National Junior Championships in 1946.

I went to a Catholic military school—La Salle Military Academy, at Oakfield, Long Island. I graduated from there in 1947 as valedictorian. As I did in tennis, I had this kind of fanatic drive to want to excel, at everything. I don't know what it meant from a Freudian standpoint, Chuck, and I couldn't be less interested. The point is that

"I was always a very introverted child and I recall finding great escape in films. I remember as far back as being. . . seven years old, going to the movies every Saturday. . . I have always been terribly interested in films and it was not something that happened to me in later life."

"Soon after he discovered that his acting was 'terrible—stiff and nervous,' John Frankenheimer decided to become a director. He was a twenty-year-old undergraduate at Williams College at the time, and his first directorial chore was Noel Coward's Design For Living *— a production that by his own admission was 'one of the worst-staged plays ever done at Williams. I had about as much right to direct it as entering myself as a jockey in The Kentucky Derby. It was an appalling fiasco—the leading actor tripped over a couch, fell flat on his rear end, and everybody forgot their lines.'"*

—C. Robert Jennings

John (standing third from right), with his Williams College tennis team, circa 1950.

I did very well at school. And I could have gotten into just about any college I wanted to. I wanted to go to Williams because my father had gone to Yale and I didn't want to go there. But when I got to Williams I really hated it. I really, really detested it.

There was a very kind of Establishment feeling at Williams—the guys who'd gone to Deerfield, Andover, Exeter, prep schools like that. All those guys were much better prepared for Williams than I was. I just couldn't seem to adapt to the place, and I didn't seem to fit in. I went into a fraternity, but that didn't work for me, either. I still felt alienated.

I'd been deeply religious, really deeply religious. I had wanted to be a priest and that continued through my first year at Williams. In my second year I began to break away from the Catholic church. I also started to get very interested in the theater at Williams. And after feeling alienated from the whole place, I suddenly felt terrific. I had a great, great feeling of belonging.

I was terrified because I still didn't know what I wanted to do with my life. I just knew what I didn't want to do. And what I didn't want to do was to come out and become one of that mass of people that were going into advertising and insurance, and jobs like that. I just didn't think I could fit into it. I'd spent my freshman summer working at an insurance company and hated it. I knew I couldn't do that; it would be horrendous for me.

But I was very, very interested in literature, both English and American, in poetry, in drama, in photography. And maybe, now, what I wanted to be was an actor. I met tremendous resistance from my father. It was the last thing in the world he wanted his son to be. Because not only was everybody in that line of work a homosexual, they made no money, which was even worse, if possible. It was impossible for him to imagine that this son he'd paid all this money to have educated and who played such great tennis, was going to end up as an actor. But nevertheless he and my mother both said, when they realized it was inevitable, "Well, we've done everything we can to dissuade you from it, but if that's what you want to be, that's what you want to be. You're going to have to find out for yourself what it's really like."

So in my junior year I went into summer stock. I was part of a group that was supposedly the rebirth of the University Players at Falmouth on the Cape. The Players was the theater which Henry Fonda, Jimmy Stewart and Josh Logan and a lot of others were part of in the early '30s. An Irish playwright-director named Denis Johnston was our director. And he was a very good, very good director. He gave me a lot of encouragement as an actor.

I was in all the plays and starred in quite a few of them, including *Voice of the Turtle*. Around that time the Korean War broke out. I realized that I was going to be drafted, which I didn't want. I'd been given credit for two years of ROTC because of my military school, and my freshman year at Williams I'd taken the third year of ROTC but then dropped out of it. I got back into it. When I graduated in 1951, I did two things. I got a commission as a second lieutenant in the Air Force, and I married a girl from Bennington.

We went to Washington and she got a job as a school teacher and I worked in the Aeronautical Chart and Information Service of the Air Force, a horrible place, but I played the lead in the American Theater Wing production of *Blue Moon* down there, and continued my acting studies at American University.

Then, by one of those strange quirks that change your whole life, I was in the mail room and I read this announcement that the Air Force was forming a motion picture squadron out in California, and that anyone with any experience in acting or directing or anything to do with film should apply directly, without having to go through channels. Well, I don't have to tell you how rare it is in the military not to have go through channels. It's beautiful.

I wrote this long letter with a rather imaginative resume of all of the things I'd done. And I was accepted! So in 1952 Joanne—her name was Joanne Evans; two of my wives have been named Evans—Joanne and I went to California. She found a job teaching at the Lookout Mountain school, and we lived over on Fountain Avenue and Crescent Heights, in a very nice apartment for a $110 dollars a month.

I was stationed at the Lockheed Air Force Base. The major who was running the film squadron was an ex-special effects guy from Warner Bros. When I reported in, he said, "Listen, we've got a hell of a problem. Most of the guys signed up for this thing to stay out of Korea. They don't know a damned thing about film." I didn't want to tell him I don't know anything either. But as an old studio hand, he knew a

On stage in one of several Williams College plays John acted in or directed. Meriam Rauss is the leading lady (above).

"I had men in that squadron who had absolutely no interest in photography. . . so I'd let them go to lunch starting at nine-thirty in the morning and I would just film the whole thing myself—light it, operate the camera, and edit the film. Of course I made some terrible movies, but I did learn what I was doing, at the Government's expense. . ."

Frankenheimer, third from left. . . inspired by Eisenstein.

lot. He said, "We don't have a lot of assignments, so what I'm trying to do is dream up things to keep them from going to Hollywood and bouncing checks and generally getting themselves in trouble. What I want you to do is take a group of them out to this asphalt plant on Vanowen, and make a movie about asphalt."

I didn't say anything. You learn not to say anything in the military; you just do what you're told. The major said, "I know it sounds stupid, but that's what I want you to do. It'll keep them busy and give them some training."

I took my guys out there and they set me straight right away. "Lieutenant," they said, "we don't really want to make this movie. What we really want to do is go into Hollywood and fool around and pick up some girls."

That's what they'd been doing and that's what they did. One young black guy stayed with me and we decided we wanted to learn how to make movies. We knew nothing about cameras but we had all the directions and we taught ourselves. The Air Force had terrific 35mm equipment in those days but nobody knew how to use it. I would take cameras home on weekends and learn how they worked by shooting home movies.

The enlisted man and I exposed a lot of film on the making of asphalt. I'd seen Eisenstein's film on the creamery. It's a classic short on this dairy in the Soviet Union, and it's absolutely magnificent. So I did my rip-off of that with the asphalt plant. We showed it to the major and he liked it a lot. So we cut it together, again a kind of do-it-yourself thing, but it turned out to be damned good.

I did a lot of movies, including some real Air Force sponsored stuff. And after I'd been at it about six months, the major said, "Listen, I have another one of those harebrained assignments for you, because your guys are getting into a lot of trouble again and they need work. There's a ranch out in Northridge where a guy has registered cattle. Do you know anything about cattle?"

I said, "The only cattle I know anything about are cows we passed in the parkway in my parents' car." He laughed and said, "Well, you go out there and do a movie about registered cattle. This guy has some kind of a chain letter operation. He controls the bulls and sells the calves to investors. They get the proceeds when the calves are sold. But the guy charges them a rental fee to feed the cows, and the whole thing sounds like a total scam, but the guy is charming. Go out and see him."

I did. He had a big spread out in Northridge called Harvey Howard's Registered Cattle. My guys couldn't get out of this one because they had no way to get back to Hollywood. So the first day we were all out there, about twelve of us, filming the cows like mad. A Cadillac convertible drove up and two very sharp looking guys went in to Harvey.

"I shot a whole short subject about my auto-mobile. I guess that was the forerunner of Grand Prix."

7

EARLY DAYS

On the second day I heard voices raised and I saw the Cadillac convertible take off in a cloud of dust. Harvey came over to me and said, "You know who that was, tearing out of here like that? Those were my writers for my television show."

Harvey had explained to me that in addition to his registered cattle thing, he had a television show on Channel 13. It was called *Harvey Howard's Ranch Roundup*, and he used it to advertise his cattle. He was very proud of it.

Harvey said, "Now you seem like a bright young man. Do you write? I need new writers for the TV show. I thought you might like it."

I said, "Well, Mr. Howard, I do write, as a matter of fact." That wasn't quite accurate, I'd always wanted to write, but I never had.

Harvey said, "I'll pay you $50 a script." I was making $350 a month as a lieutenant, so $50 a week was more than double my salary.

I said, "You got yourself a writer."

"What I want you to do," Harvey said, "is write my introduction. I introduce Country and Western acts. I have the cows with me and I talk about the cows, and then I introduce the music."

I went down to the Beverly Hills Public Library and looked up everything I could about registered cattle. I wrote a set of intros for him and he loved 'em. He said, "This is the best stuff I've ever had. You come on down to the show, I might want to make changes when I get down there."

In those days the station was just a group of nice looking Spanish buildings in Hollywood. Harvey had the cows out in the courtyard. This was the first time I had ever been in a television station. There were two cameras. One of them was on Harvey and one was on the cows, and the director was drunk.

Harvey said, "Look, this guy is drunk.

I'm not going to have some drunk direct me. You go in there and direct."

I said, "But I don't know what to do."

"There's nothing to do," Harvey said. "Just cut between me and what I'm talking about. Then you put another camera on the music and you just photograph that. It's very simple."

And that's what I did. I wrote and directed *Harvey Howard's Ranch Roundup* for about twelve weeks. At which point the FCC came to us and said, "You guys are off the air. In an hour show you are allowed to have forty-eight minutes of show and twelve minutes of commercials. You guys are twelve minutes of show and forty-eight minutes of commercials." And that was that. But I owe this guy, Harvey Howard, a tremendous debt, because the experience really convinced me that directing was what I wanted to do. I didn't want to be an actor anymore. I wanted to direct.

But you were still a second lieutenant in the Air Force.

Yes, and I *liked* the Air Force. I was actually very happy in the Air Force. And I was terrified of getting out and having to get a job, especially since I only had a fool's dream of what I wanted to do. For a time it seemed attractive to stay in the Air Force and take that pension. But I knew that to get promoted you had to be a rated officer. General [Curtis] Lemay, for whom I'd done a lot of photographic work, wanted me to stay in the Air Force. I told him I'd had a lifelong sinus problem.

But he said, "I want you to become a pilot. But what I need you to do is go up high in one of the planes and come down quickly and see what it does to your sinuses. If it's terribly painful we can't ask you to do it."

Not long after that conversation, I was making a film about an aerial gunnery

Frankenheimer, second from left. . . "we knew nothing about cameras but. . ."

meeting in Yuma, Arizona. I hadn't been able to get in a plane and get the opening shot I wanted for the opening titles, which was the aerial approach to the place. I bugged some of the majors and threw Lemay's name around and finally a guy said, "There's a new F94E here, and the test pilot is going to take it up for a couple

of turns before the Air Defense Command people arrive. You can shoot from it if the pilot agrees." The pilot was Colonel Chuck Yeager and he said, "If you're on flying status, great." I was, and I bolted my camera in place and sat behind him. He took off and got me my shot, beautifully I might add. We were just circling when

Yeager got a radio message: "Air Defense team here early. Must see performance immediately, they're rushed for time. Maximum effort."

Yeager turned around and said, "You poor son of a bitch." Then he kicked the thing straight up in the air. And we went up, to about 45,000 feet. Then he turned it over and down we went. The only thing I had sense enough to do was press the automatic trigger on the camera, because I blacked out.

Now that's something to tell your children and grandchildren.

Even the anti-climax. I came to just as Yeager was doing rolls right over the air base, at 500 feet. We landed and I puked all over the place. I thought they might give me a medal, but as I climbed out of the plane, a master sergeant was standing there with a bucket and he said, "Clean it up, Lieutenant."

What happened was that the dive made my sinuses hurt terrifically. I couldn't think of going into pilot training, which is why we're talking here today.

And having broken the sound barrier you were back to wondering what to do when you took the uniform off.

So I was. Then through an ex-actress named Sally O'Neil and an agent named Al Rockett, I met John Ford. He was going to make a picture called *The Long Gray Line*, which he eventually did. Because of my military background, he thought he could use me as a gofer. That was thrilling. I'd already started interviewing for other jobs out there, but the idea of working for Ford was incredible.

But about three months before I got out, Ford went into the hospital. I went to see him and he said, "Look, I have a cataract problem, and I don't know what's going to happen. I can't guarantee you any kind of a job, and I know you're getting out of the service. If I were you and if I were starting out today, if I were twenty-one, twenty-two, twenty-three years old—you're twenty-three?—I'd get into television. That's what it's all about."

I took his advice. I went to see people at NBC and CBS here. At NBC they offered me a page's job, maybe. They showed me applications from people with Ph.Ds who were eager for those jobs. At CBS they said they could use me as a parking lot attendant. ABC didn't have a network office here yet but I went to Channel 7 and found I could get a job as a construction coordinator at $100 a week.

But this is how fortune can work in your life. At the air base, in addition to my motion picture squadron, there was a television squadron, with a group of guys I got to know fairly well. One was Patrick O'Neal, the actor. Another was Jack Shea, who'd been an assistant director in New York, and Jack took me over to see a show at the NBC studio on Hollywood Boulevard, in what had been a theater. *The Dennis Day Show* was being done there. John Rich was directing and Arthur Penn was the assistant director. I stood in the control room during the broadcast show and I thought it was the most exciting thing I'd ever seen in my life. And, even more than before, I knew what I wanted to do.

I got out of the Air Force June 30th, 1953. I wasn't loaded with money, but since both Joanne and I had been working, we'd saved about $1,000, maybe a little more.

We flew back to New York at government expense. They had to take you back whence you came. In those days the planes, the DC3s, stopped in Chicago. It was my first transcontinental flight.

When we got back to New York, Joanne and I realized that we don't want to be together anymore, and we started proceedings to dissolve the marriage. I moved into a hotel in the 40s, a terrible place. But it was in New York and I wasn't paying much for it. I started job-hunting, going to all these places and trying to get in to see people. A lot of them I've seen since, like Steve Krantz.

Steve Krantz of Fritz the Cat *fame, husband of Judith?*

Right. Steve was managing director of the NBC owned and operated station in New York. He was very nice to me, but he didn't have anything.

Nick Dunne—Dominick Dunne—had been a couple of years ahead of me at Williams. He'd been my junior advisor in fact. Apropos of nothing, he was a superb actor at Williams. His performance as Eddie Fuselli in *Golden Boy* was one of the best I've ever seen. Stephen Sondheim was there, too, a year ahead of me. The college musicals were pretty darned good.

Anyway, Nick Dunne was the stage manager for *Robert Montgomery Presents* for NBC in New York. And he wasn't too overjoyed to see me. In fact nobody I knew who was working was too overjoyed to see me, because they all felt if they helped somebody it might eventually jeopardize them.

There was a lot of insecurity going around.

I feel as if my whole life in this business has been having to deal with rejection. I think everybody's is. And the rejections started right then, very early. I mean, nobody wanted to know about my availability. The marriage was breaking up and I was running out of money. I thought, well, what do I do? I figured that maybe I should go back to the west coast and take that job as a senior coordinator at ABC.

I was actually on my way to get the plane ticket, and I had to go past 52nd Street and Madison Avenue, where CBS was. I knew nobody at CBS. It was about four o'clock on a very hot afternoon. I went in and asked where the employment office was. I went up, I think to the third floor. I filled out the usual application and the girl said, "What do you want to be?" I said, "I want to be an assistant director."

From the other side of a partition, a voice said, "Send that lunatic in here." I went in and a guy in his late thirties, early forties, was sitting behind a fan, because the building was not air-conditioned. His name was Richard Stanley. He was head of employment for CBS—of secretaries, clerical employees. He said, "I just wanted to see what kind of a fool would come in on a day like this, and ask for a job like the one you asked for. Because first of all you're in the wrong building, and second, because that's an impossible job to get."

I sat down and he started telling me all of his problems, like the fact that he was up all night because his apartment isn't air-conditioned, and the office was no better. Then he said, "Look, there's a guy you *should* talk to. His name is Hal Meier and I'll call and see if he can give you an appointment."

I can't remember what I did last week, but I remember all of this very, very vividly. Stanley said, "It's after five and they close at

5:30. It's down at 15 Vanderbilt in Grand Central Station. Can you get them a resume today? The secretary'll make an appointment for you."

It was a sweltering day in New York and I couldn't find a cab. To get the resume, I ran from 52nd to my crummy hotel on 44th and got back to the other office, soaked in sweat, just as it was closing. Miss O'Neill, the secretary, looked at me and said, "Mr. Meier can see you in three weeks." I don't know what gave me the nerve, but I said, "That's no good for me. I'm going back to California; I have to see him sooner than that." She looked at me again and said, "Oh, all right, how about tomorrow at ten?"

I was there, and Miss O'Neill said, "Look, he's very busy. If he doesn't spend much time with you, don't think he's being rude."

I went into his office and he looked like Lloyd Nolan, a bit formidable. He glanced at the resume and said, "I'll be god-damned. You were in the 1352nd Photographic Squadron. I was in the 1352nd in World War II!"

What were the chances of that?

Meier spent a long time with me. He showed me a huge pile of applications. "All these guys have theater experience, some of them have movie experience. What makes you think you can do the job?"

I said, "Well, it's really very simple. You know what I've done, you were in the same squadron. These guys have terrific experience, but they've never been in television. I've at least got my feet wet, so that puts me a little bit ahead."

He laughed and said, "Yeah, somehow I don't think you'll get lost in the crowd. Look, I know you've heard all this, but believe me, I will call you. Don't bother to call me."

I believed him. I was down to the last $200 of my mustering out pay. I went back to my fleabag hotel and waited by the phone. It didn't have any message service and I didn't dare go out. Nothing happened. Finally I called Miss O'Neill and said I'd be at my parents' house. I was about out of money. It was very uncomfortable staying with them, but at last Meier called. He said, "We're promoting one of our assistant directors to director for the summer, so I have an eight-week job for an A.D. I can't guarantee you anything more than that. Are you interested?"

I said, "Are you kidding?"

Meier said, "You start tomorrow."

Strangely the man they promoted to director was Robert Ellis Miller, and luckily for me, Robert Ellis Miller stayed a director, so I stayed an assistant director.

Even with the Air Force experience and all of Harvey Howard's cows behind you, it must have been slightly intimidating to plunge into the high-powered world of CBS.

Oh, wasn't it, though. And what complicated things a lot was that there was tremendous resentment at CBS because I got this job. They had always thought that somebody would be promoted from within. The president of the CBS television network was named Jack Van Volkenberg, and the rumor got around that I was related to him, which I wasn't. There was terrific hostility about that. But the fact was that I was a good assistant director. An assistant director's main responsibility was to talk to the cameraman and set up the shots for the director. A close-up, a two-shot, "Around to the right," "This is what we want here," and so on.

I had a good camera eye. It's something I seem to have been born with. Fred Coe once wrote me a note saying: "Talent is doing easily what other people find difficult." Setting up shots was always easy for me. As a matter of fact, I had no wish to become a director then. I was a terrific assistant to the directors because I wasn't trying to take their job. I was really trying to help them. I was happy being an A.D. I had some wild times.

I remember working on a *Person to Person*. If you remember, Murrow would be in the studio and we would do remotes from people's houses. You'd have Murrow's voice on a speaker and we would transmit the pictures back to the studio.

This night we were doing Tallulah and she had just had breast surgery. Had them raised or augmented or realigned, whatever it was. She was very proud of the results. We were in rehearsal and she came and sat on my lap with her breasts fully exposed. And that great Murrow voice came over the speaker and said, "John, please get our guest off your lap and get her tits covered up if you will."

Maybe one of the greatest nights of my life was when we did a remote from Ethel Waters's house in Brooklyn. I'd seen her in *Member of the Wedding* and loved everything she'd done. After everybody left I stayed and we talked and she sang until six o'clock in the morning. I was in tears.

I did a remote from Benny Goodman's house and Benny played for me afterwards. I mean, extraordinary memories.

It was an exciting time because the possibilities seemed limitless. There was a lot going on.

In late 1953 when I went to work at CBS as an associate director, there were a lot of live television dramas being done. The biggest one that CBS had at that moment was *Studio One*, which was being directed alternately by Franklin Schaffner and Paul Nickell. It was everybody's ambition to do something like that. There was *Suspense*, which Bob Mulligan was directing. There was *The Web* on Sunday night that Herb Hirschman directed. On NBC the very prestigious *Philco Playhouse* was produced by Fred Coe, with Delbert Mann as one of his directors. Back at CBS there were *Omnibus* and *Kraft Theater*. Sidney Lumet was directing at CBS, as you know, and I became his assistant director.

I gravitated toward the dramatic shows because that's where my interests were. I was a good associate director.

You've said assistant director and associate director. Was there a distinction or were the terms interchangeable, or was there a rank involved?

Basically you were called an associate director in television. An assistant director was really what you were, but technically you were an associate director. I guess it was to differentiate the job in television from the job in film.

Because the A.D. in film definitely means assistant director.

Right. The associate director in television was in motion picture terms really the cinematographer. My job was to get the shots for the director. I didn't light them; my job was to work out where the cameras should be, to keep them free so they could get into position for the next shot. In other words, we'd have to keep ferrying them back and forth—and without getting in each other's line of sight.

I was also responsible for the timing of the show. I loved it. I was very happy being an associate director. I was doing two dramatic shows a week. I was doing the *You Are There* show as Sidney Lumet's A.D. on Sunday afternoon, which meant I would work the rehearsal with him on Saturday, then do the show on Sunday. On Monday I would do a soap opera, *Guiding Light*, in the morning just to fill in because they were letting the regular associate director direct

"What I remember as an actor was that Johnny had such an eye for composition with the camera. He was always taking the camera and shooting 'through' things—like the curve of an umbrella handle. I remember one shot of an iron bedstead that had been moved out on the floor so that the camera could be behind it, shooting through the head of the bedstead onto the scene below. And you knew, because it was live, it had to be moved back again by the stagehands while the show was going on. His eye for the camera has always been quite fabulous . . . He's also a great cook!"

—Betsy Palmer

the show. Then Monday afternoon I'd go to the *Danger* rehearsal and Tuesday night would do the show. Wednesday and Thursday were my days off and on Friday I would do *Person to Person* with Murrow. I also did the commercials for *Danger*. I was making about $400 a week in 1953.

I learned a lot from Lumet. I learned a great deal from the bad directors I worked with, too. I find you learn even more out of

Walter Hampden, James Dean and Betsy Palmer in "Death In My Neighborhood" for *Danger,* which aired August 25, 1953. Frankenheimer was associate director.

the bad movies than the good movies. And what I learned I applied to trying to get better shots for the directors, and trying to arrange so that we had our best cameramen for the most difficult shots.

I know men and women who've spent their whole careers in the industry being very happy and content as A.D.s. It's a highly skilled job. But you didn't stay an A.D. very long.

No, and it's kind of weird and convoluted how my life changed.

One of the most prestigious shows on CBS at the time was *You Are There.* Walter Cronkite was the host, Sidney Lumet was the director and Charles Russell the producer. The commercials, for an insurance company, were done from another studio, and I was assigned to the commercials as an assistant director. As the assistant director, I was on the phone all the time with Lumet's A.D., a man named Mel Ferber. We became quite friendly because we were on the phone so much. One night I got a call from Ferber at home. He said, "Look, I'm leaving. They're going to make me a director. Would you be interested in being the A.D. on *You Are There?*"

Well, of course I would. I met Lumet and Charles Russell, and they liked me, and I became Lumet's A.D. I was Sidney's assistant for about seven months. Then he left the show to go do it on film. They were going to start putting it on film, but in the meantime, there were going to be thirteen more live shows. And the guy they brought in to replace Sidney Lumet was not a good director. He just wasn't. His name isn't important in this history. He's a very nice guy, but he just was a terrible director. And indirectly that led to the next stage of my life at CBS.

Coincidentally with Sidney's move to film, I was working as an A.D. on *Danger. Danger* was the opposite of *You Are There* in terms of quality and prestige. The fact was they assigned all the directors they wanted to get rid of to work on *Danger,* which was an anthology mystery series that went on at ten at night. They would put a director on the show and he'd work for three weeks or so, then they'd throw him out.

In those days there were only the two networks, NBC and CBS. And the contracts were really slave contracts. They signed you as a director for $180 a week. It was for six years, with a raise of $20 a week each year. They had a firing clause that called for only two weeks' notice. If you got a commercial show, you got a commercial fee. The price went up, but your base salary was $180 a week.

Actually I was making $400 a week as an A.D., which today I suppose would be as good as $4,000 a week, because I was also doing those commercials. I was doing the Ipana toothpaste commercials on *Danger.* Dick Stark was the host on the show and he liked me. And the directors knew that if they gave them to me, I'd make sure they had the cameras to do them, because I was in charge of the cameras. I was much in demand, and you got $100 for the commercial. It seemed fabulous.

I suspect your pals from Williams, starting in the insurance trade in the early 1950s would have been glad for $100 a week.

Ah, yes, that did occur to me. But the real point was that I loved doing what I was doing and I was good at it.

Now, the assistant director's job on a half-hour dramatic show was to go to the run-through in the rehearsal hall the day before the shoot. The director gave you his shots and you wrote them in your script. "Close-up on Champlin...Two-shot on Champlin and Frankenheimer...Panning shot," whatever. Your job was to get those shots on the monitor for the director to look at.

The sets in the rehearsal hall were actually strips of tape on the floor, with makeshift furniture in place. You would confirm to the director that the shots would work, but it was also your job to say a shot wouldn't work, if you *really* thought it wouldn't. You gave the director the benefit of the doubt.

One week I went in to do the show with a director I'd never met. He was very big—

six three—and very elitist, very superior, very condescending to me and the actors. And the actors were all the good young actors: Mark Rydell, John Cassavetes, Harry Guardino, Mark Richman, Ben Gazzara, quite a crowd.

The story was about American POWs in a German concentration camp. They're supposed to escape. And the action included a knife fight between Mark Rydell and Cassavetes. The first thing that happened to me when I walked through the rehearsal hall was that Mark Rydell ran up to me—we knew each other from a lot of other shows—and said, "This guy's crazy, crazy, crazy! He's lettin' Cassavetes use a real knife. You gotta stop him!" That was only the beginning.

As the rehearsal went on, the director said, "Camera one, close-up of Cassavetes, here." I said, "But—" He said, "You don't say anything. Just write down what I tell you to write down."

I wrote it down. But then I said, "Look, I can't let this go any further. You've got a wall over here and you're asking to shoot a close-up right through the wall. It can't be done."

He said, "You just write down what I tell you to write down. I don't want to hear any more from you."

The next day when we were in the studio on the sets, he of course started screaming, "Where did this wall come from?" I said, "Yesterday you were standing on it."

Well, it was total and utter chaos. Utter chaos. I have never before or since been involved in anything quite that chaotic. Nobody had a clue what anybody else was doing. The director was screaming about how awful we all were. Some of the cameramen wanted to hit him, and the actors were screaming back at him. I mean, it was *awful.*

To make a long story short, we had a 32-page script and at the end of the normal blocking time, which was six hours, we were on page 12. And we still had like 20 pages to go. Then we were supposed to do a complete run-through, then the dress rehearsal, then break for dinner, then come back and do the show on air—live, of course.

We didn't do the run-through and we were still only on page 24; we skipped the dress rehearsal and continued the blocking and got to page 30. Then we had to break for dinner. We never got all the way through the blocking.

And the show would be going out live. Those really were the days.

Tell me about it. We broke for dinner. You can imagine the chaos. No, you *can't* imagine the chaos! The cameraman didn't know what was happening, the actors didn't know what was happening.

I got the cameraman aside and told him the plot of the show.

"How we're going to shoot this I don't know," I said. "But when we get to this point in the script, we'll just see who's got a shot and pray for the best. I don't know what this guy's going to do. He's very, very unstable."

At this time I'd met again a girl that I'd known in college. She was absolutely and exquisitely magnificent. I fell wildly in love with her after my freshman year. I'd worked all that summer at the insurance company in New York so I could take her out when she came down to the city. She stayed with us and I took her to 21 for dinner. The dinner was $29 and I was making $28 a week at the insurance company. Then she dumped me for the captain of the Army football team.

Now I'd met her again just about three days before this episode of *Danger*, which was in February of 1954. I had invited her to watch the show, and then we were going

to go out and have some dinner. I bought a new suit for the occasion and I changed into it during the crazy break between dress and air. She arrived, looking fabulous. I put her back in the client's booth behind the control room, so she could watch all that and also see everything on the floor.

We did the show out of CBS Studio 55 on 55th Street at 9th Avenue. It was an old movie theater and the control room was up where the balcony used to be. (Ironically, I did my next to last television show there a few years later, "The Browning Version," with John Gielgud.)

The set for the *Danger* show was the concentration camp courtyard, with a big fence and a guard tower and a German sentry. The camera was supposed to pan along and discover the guard tower, then look through the barbed wire and, as the searchlights came on, see a man running across the courtyard, escaping. This was a long ambitious shot, especially for early television. I'll never forget it. It was on camera two. The other cameras had nothing to do at that point, and the cameramen, not thrilled with the director, were keeping kind of loose and pointing the cameras every which way.

We didn't have zoom lenses in those days. We had turrets with four lenses on them: long, wide-angle and so on. The show's format was that we came out of black and there was a dagger stuck in the wall. The stage manager twanged the dagger. You said, "Dagger, Tony," and Tony Mottola, our guitar player, did a great "Boing!" and the announcer said, "Danger!" and we were away.

I did all that stuff on camera three. The first shot of the guard tower, as I said, was on camera two. Now we're about to come up on camera two, and I remember saying to the technical director, whose name was Vernon Gambell—God, that name just came back to me—"Ready to come up on

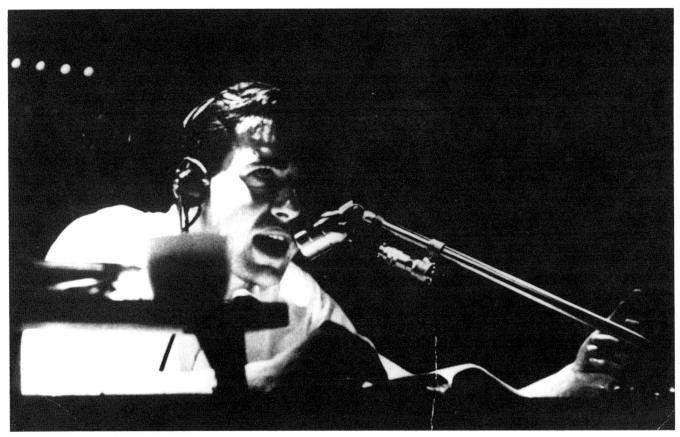

Directing a live television show.

two." And suddenly the director screamed, "One! One! Take one!"

Now camera one was on his long lens and because he didn't have a shot at the moment and was keeping loose, as I said, he was pointing directly at the control room. And suddenly I looked at the monitor and there was was a close-up of *me* behind the glass, being transmitted to thousands of living rooms.

Where the viewers were as startled as you were.

But not as terrified as I was. I remember thinking, "Oh, my God." But somehow I kept calm and I said, "Vernon, take two." Needless to say he couldn't hear me, I mouthed it, but he saw my lips moving. And he took camera two and we started the shot.

Now the director stood up and screamed, "Take anything! Save me, save me!" And he threw up all over me. The production assistant was an ex-prize fighter named Ron Sobol. I said, "Ron, get this

son-of-a-bitch out of here." Ron decked the guy with one punch and they pulled him out of the booth.

I said, "Guys, we've got to shoot this thing like a game of the week." I'm trying to get the vomit out of my face; I can't read the script, I can't read anything. "We're just gonna cut like we're following the ball," I said. "I have no idea how we're going to do it. But I'll tell you when to come in, and we're going to try it."

Well, we got it on. I mean, it wasn't a masterpiece, but it went from beginning to end. Afterward my date and I went back to my apartment and I changed my suit and we went out for a cup of coffee.

The next day I was called into the senior vice-president's office, who was Hubbell Robinson. And with him was a very tall gentleman named Lewis Stone, who was head of talent—directors and everybody else. (It's awful to think back on it. Robinson died in his fifties of alcoholism and Stone committed suicide about ten years after this meeting.)

Hubbell said, "We heard what you did

"I remember sitting up for nights figuring out how I'm going to block this, how I'm going to have this fellow move from here over to there, and this man move from there to there, and of course when we got on our feet and started doing it we didn't do any of those things at all. It took me quite a long time to get rid of that *feeling of panic that I really didn't know how to stage a scene beforehand. It took many years actually, because I'd always think 'It's not going to happen today for you, that thing that happens won't happen.' Well sometimes it doesn't but sooner or later it does again."*

last night. We apologize for what happened. We just want you to know that we're very, very grateful."

I said, "You know, it's some kind of schizophrenic life, going from the best show on this network, which is *You Are There*, to the worst." I was full of the confidence you have at age twenty-four and I said, "I don't mean to be presumptuous, sir, but I could direct this show better than the guys you've got doing it." And Robinson said, "That's exactly why we called you in here. That's what we want you to do. Only not this show. We want you to direct *You Are There*."

I said, "I don't honestly know if I can do it." Robinson said, "We think you can." "Well," I said, "Let's look at the other side. In the first place I would lose some money because I'm doing some commercials as well as being an A.D. now. In the second place, suppose I can't do it. I see these directors being thrown out of this network left and right, and there's no place for them to go. They're out on the street. The only other place I could go would be NBC and they wouldn't take me if I'd been fired from CBS."

We talked for an hour. Hub Robinson and Lew Stone said I was a young man with a tremendous future in television directing, and they thought I should really take the job. I said, "I'll make a deal with you, and that is if I screw up I get my old job back as an A.D." They agreed.

YOU ARE THERE

My first *You Are There* was in November, 1954. It was called "The Plot Against King Solomon." You remember the format of *You Are There*? It was a reenactment of history, and historical personalities were interviewed by CBS correspondents like Walter Cronkite, Ned Kilmer, Eric

Sevareid, Charles Collingwood, guys like that. Cronkite was the host. For example, if we were doing Columbus, which we did with Lorne Greene as Columbus, there would be a dramatic scene with Columbus and the king and queen of Spain. The king and queen would exit, the correspondent would say, "Señor Columbus." He would turn to the camera and meet the correspondent. It was a very good show, with great actors.

That first *You Are There* I did was the episode with Solomon having to threaten to cut the baby in half, at which point the true mother comes forward and says, "Give the baby to the other woman, but don't cut the baby in half," which told Solomon that this was the real mother.

I cast it with actors with whom I've worked before as an assistant director— Shepperd Strudwick, Marty Brooks, Katherine Barker and an ex-girlfriend of mine from Bennington, and other actors I knew and was comfortable with.

The script was written during the blacklist. But as an assistant director you didn't come in contact with the blacklist, because casting wasn't part of my job. I'd heard about it, of course, but this was the first time I'd had to deal with it. I found that what you had to do was call a certain extension at CBS—you never knew who was on the other end—and you gave the whole list of actors you wanted for the show. They would write it down and an hour or two later someone would call back and say, "Champlin yes, Frankenheimer no," right down the list. There was no appeal, all decisions were final. You never knew where it was coming from, and you could never hire the actor.

The script was by a woman named Kate Nickerson. I'd been the A.D. on a lot of shows that were written by this Kate Nickerson, and I'd always said, "Wow, she is some terrific writer. Well, she was, or he is.

Kate Nickerson was Walter Bernstein, who later wrote *The Front* for Marty Ritt.

Of course: that was the era of the phony names and the fronts.

Yeah, all of which I was told, now that I was a director. Abe Polonsky was somebody else, and Albert Maltz was somebody else. They were all writing for *You Are There* under assumed names, which is why the show was so good.

So now you're on your maiden voyage, so to speak, as a director.

Yes, and I don't mind telling you I was panicked. The thing that worried me was having to move the actors, staging the scenes. So I stayed home. By this time I'd married the girl who'd come to that nightmare show I told you about. We got married September 22nd and I started the Solomon show just before Thanksgiving. We had a very partially furnished apartment. We had a couch and a table and a mattress and that was about it.

I was scared to death. I was telling myself, "I know all the technical stuff but I'm never going to be able to tell these actors where to go." I remember kneeling on the floor with a plan of the sets and all these different colored pins, trying to move the actors from here to there. There were so many pins, and they all seemed wooden to me. I'd mark up my script with colored pens. Not good. Then the moment came, as it always does, when I had to go to that first reading. I was really terrified. The actors were all glad to see me and thrilled that I was directing. I was twenty-four, the youngest person in the room by far, except for the ex-girl friend from Bennington.

We read the script through, and Charles Russell, the producer, talked to me about cuts, because we were long. Then he said,

"See you at the run-through."

Now we had to get up from the table and begin the staging. Harold Clurman wrote at length about how he dreaded that moment. I know what he meant, to this day I know what he meant.

It's so comfortable around the table, talking about the script, theorizing about the characters, discussing the scenes. I wasn't bad at that, and I found I had some pertinent things to say about the script.

But finally there's that awful moment of truth. I had all these complicated things written in my script about who goes where. Then suddenly Strudwick went over there, and Marty Brooks went over here, and Margaret Barker went over there. It all worked, and they did it. None of my pins were relevant any more. I never used them again. What I did was stage the scenes with the actors' help, and then figured out how to shoot them, which is what I've always done since then. It's made me a great advocate of rehearsal, which I still am.

The ice was broken. We staged the rest of the script and I figured the camerawork myself, for the first time. Incidentally, Joe Papp was my stage manager.

The amazing people who came out of live television.

Absolutely. Joe Papp and Kenny Utt were the two stage managers. Kenny Utt won the Academy Award for producing *Silence of the Lambs*. And Joe Papp, rest his soul, we know from all the magnificent work he did with his *Shakespeare in the Park*, and all the writers and actors he encouraged over the years.

The two of them and the whole crew— this tough, seasoned crew—broke their butts for me. If a shot didn't work, they made it work. They wanted to make it good for me.

I decided to go for it, because I knew that

"I learned a great deal about cutting in live television because, after all, the live television director certainly had the final cut. . . Some directors preplanned all of their shots before they started rehearsals. I didn't. I would rehearse and work with the actors for about a week and a half, and then I would decide how I wanted to shoot the show. What we were in essence doing was, on the air, functioning as film editors—I mean deciding what was going to be in close-up, what was going to be in two-shot, what we were going to dissolve, what was going to be in master shot and so forth. And also the experience and the confidence

if it wasn't good I could go back to what I'd been doing before. I knew that my visuals were my strongest suit, and as I remember, the show looked wonderful. Hub Robinson and Charles Russell loved it. They said, "Look, what we want you to do now is alternate between *You Are There* and *Danger,* which we want to improve." I said, "Does that mean my next stop is the street?" As I told you, that was the reputation *Danger* had, as a kind of jumping-off place to nowhere. They said, "No, no, we're trying to get the show back to the prestige it once had." That sounded fine to me.

DANGER

We're talking forty years ago, of course, but my memory is that Danger *was, or became, a first-rate show.*

The executives turned out to be very serious about wanting it to be better.

My first show had Paul Newman as the lead and James Gregory as the heavy. Paul got $300 for the show, I got $250 and Rod Serling got $250. The whole budget was $17,000. Jimmy Gregory was in one of the first television shows I ever directed, the first movie I directed and the first movie I ever produced and directed.

I did three more *Danger* shows, including one with John Cassavetes that was really a stunner, where we went outside and shot. Walter Bernstein had written an article in *The New Yorker,* about a Puerto Rican man who got in to the United States illegally and began to spread smallpox until it became an epidemic. This was the subject of the show ("No Passport for Death") we were going to do. It was written by Frank De Felitta, who later wrote *Audrey Rose* for Bob Wise.

I cast John Cassavetes as the immigrant and Miriam Colon as his brother's wife. Leo Penn, Sean's father, played the cop who was looking for him.

What happened was that in rehearsal the dialogue didn't sound so hot. So I said to Cassavetes, "We should do this in Spanish and put subtitles on it." And we did four scenes in Spanish, and you'd only do something like that in those days if you were very young, and crazy. But the next thing was even crazier.

The guy was supposed to be trapped in a building by the police, and there was to be a chase through the building. Now, the studio we were using was at Seventy-third Street and First Avenue. Behind the studio was an alley, and across the alley were some brownstone tenements. And I don't know how the idea came to me but I said, "Wow, wouldn't it be great if we could put the immigrant on the roof, where he threatens to jump off and does—we'd throw a dummy off—and we catch him in a firemen's net, and that's it."

It was crazy, but the script really needed something big. But it had never been done, playing part of a live dramatic show outside the studio. Ball games and horse races, yes, but never a dramatic show. I didn't even tell the powers that be at CBS what I was going to do, because I was pretty sure they'd have said no.

I worked it out that we'd have Cassavetes on the roof, Leo Penn down below. Close-up of Cassavetes, close-up of Leo Penn, close-up of Cassavetes. And when Cassavetes says in Spanish, "I'm going to jump", we would cut to Leo Penn, who yells, "No!, No!" Then we'd cut to a long shot and they would throw the dummy. The dummy would land in the net and Cassavetes would run down the stairs, where we'd have another net. He would climb in the net and we'd cut to him. Which if you stop to think about it is totally insane.

you gain in yourself—I don't see how you can get that any other way but working. You can't get it discussing it. You can't get it in school. You can't get it sitting around swimming pools, talking about the great movies you are going to make."

—John Frankenheimer

". . . producer Martin Manulis says (Frankenheimer) is the most talented director for his age (33) and weight (170) I know."

—C. Robert Jennings

What happens if he can't make it down the stairs? What happens if he trips? What, what, what? And what we had to do was, during the commercial, to unscrew the cameras from their big bases in the studio, hand carry them—they weighed a ton—out to the alley and put them on tripods so we'd be ready for the second act in a half-hour show.

At the dress rehearsal it was a nightmare, because it was the first time we'd tried it in the dark. We'd done the blocking by daylight. But now it's dark, and no one can see where the eff they're going. And they didn't get the cameras attached to the tripods.

Cassavetes was up there and yelled "I'm going to jump;" we cut to Leo Penn. They threw the dummy right over the net onto the roof of the next building, and there were people on the stairs so Cassevetes couldn't get down to the ground.

It was a terrible mess. The producers—David Heilweil and his wife, Eva Wallace—said, "My God, this isn't going to work." I said, "It's going to work." This was an hour before the show was going to go on the air, and I have to tell you I wasn't as confident as I tried to sound.

To this day I don't know how it all came together. We got on the air and the first half went fabulously well. We went to black and then to commercial, and we rushed outside. And it had started to snow. It was snowing in New York City.

The guys got the cameras screwed on the tripods in good time and we came out in the first shot, and it was just magic, a beautiful shot of the snow falling and the building looming up behind it. Cassavetes yelled, "I'm going to jump" and they threw the dummy. We had guards in the stairwell keeping it clear for John and the people inside said they'd never seen anything like Cassavetes hurtling down the stairs. Talk about adrenalin! The dummy

hit a clothesline and took the clothesline with it into the net. We cut to Cassavetes in his net. Perfection!

The network had never seen anything like it, and the letters rolled in. A few of them, I have to tell you, said, "When are they going to stop using this phony snow on TV shows?"

CLIMAX

After the show I got a call from Martin Manulis, who was the biggest producer at CBS at that time. He'd done *Suspense,* he'd done a lot of stuff, and now he was doing a big series of specials called *The Best Of Broadway,* with huge stars doing Broadway plays.

Producer Martin Manulis.

I went up to his very, very plush Fifth Avenue apartment, met him and his wife, the actress Katharine Bard. He was very elegant, and he told me how much he loved the shows I'd done. And he said, "I'm doing a production of 'The Guardsman,' with Franchot Tone." And it was going to be directed by Alfred Lunt, who'd done it on stage and as a movie with his wife Lynn Fontanne. Manulis said, "I want you to do the camerawork for Alfred Lunt."

Well, I was 24 years old. And you have a certain chutzpah at that age that you probably don't have at any other time in your life. And I said, "It's a great honor to meet you, Mr. Manulis. But I don't do camera work for anybody, not for Alfred Lunt, not for Alfred Hitchcock or anybody else. If I'm going to direct the show, it means I direct it." I said, "I have great respect for Alfred Lunt, but he should do his own camerawork. Thank you very much for having me up here, but I'm just not the person for the job." He was very charming and I left.

With some thought that you had burned a bridge behind you?

Could be, but with my 24-year-old confidence, who worried?

By this time I'd just been married as I said. Carolyn had been a Phi Beta Kappa at Cornell, and we were going away for a weekend in Connecticut and a side trip to Williamstown, Massachusetts. I wanted to show her my rooming house and other historic landmarks.

Now the moral of the story is that when the industry wants to find you, it finds you.

No one except my wife's mother knew where we were going for the weekend. And, to the best of my knowledge, no one knew my wife's mother's name. But, we're at this inn in Connecticut and it's eight in the morning on Saturday, and the phone rings. It has to be a wrong number, I tell myself. We were invisible. Wrong.

The voice on the other end said, "John, it's Jerry." This was Jerome Hellman, my first agent, with the Ted Ashley office.

Jerry was Sidney Lumet's agent and when I wanted an agent myself I figured Lumet's agent had to be pretty good. It turned out to be a very smart move because I found out years later that Hubbell Robinson had come to Jerry to beg him to talk Lumet into coming to California to direct *Climax*. But Lumet was having marital problems and was deep into analysis and couldn't leave New York. So Hellman recommended me, Robinson said okay and thus the phone call.

Jerry said, "Let's not get in to how I found you. It's too complicated. The thing is, the biggest dramatic show CBS has on the air right now is *Climax*. It originates on the west coast and they're in deep trouble with it. The reviews and the ratings have both been terrible.

"Bretaigne Windust has been producing, but the show's a disaster. They're sending Martin Manulis out to take over, and he wants you as the director."

Jerry said, "It means getting on a plane to California tomorrow night and starting rehearsals on Tuesday. Can you do that? They'll pay you $850 a show."

I said, "I'm on the plane." Manulis met me at the airport and we flew out together. It was his fortieth birthday. I was just twenty-five. We got on the plane and he said, "Here are two scripts we're doing. This is the next one." It was the worst script I ever read; to this *day* it's the worst script I ever read. I said, "Martin, they can't do either one of these scripts." He said, "I know; it's the kind of garbage we've been doing." We joked about it.

And here you were, bound for Hollywood for the first time since your Air Force days, and earning big money.

"John Frankenheimer's direction is superb. Out here from New York only a short time, his work in this shows that he will soon be one of the coast's important directors."

—Milton Lubin
The Hollywood Reporter (6/27/55)
review of "To Awake at Midnight" (Climax)

"John Frankenheimer's direction was a king-sized asset as he brought out the varied hues of emotions involved in the turbulence of a boy's world. It was one of the finest Climax hours yet seen."

—Daily Variety (8/29/55)
review of "Deal A Blow" (Climax)

A *lot* of money. The next morning I had a call from Bill Dozier, an old friend from CBS, who later produced *Batman* and *Bewitched* and who was then head of programming.

Manulis had said he was using an interim producer on the first show. I said, "I hope you told them an interim director, too." He said, "Don't worry; I've taken care of it." I should have known better. Anyway, Dozier said, "You're directing *Climax* two weeks from now, and that's the script." I said, "But Uncle Bill, this is the worst script I ever read." He said, "I don't care what it is. It's going on the air. Your job is to make it look better."

My wife and I went to my aunt's place in Palos Verdes, while I faced the fact that the next day I had to start rehearsals on the worst script I ever read. It was called "South of the Sun." Manulis had in fact refused to produce it.

They'd already cast it. Margaret O'Brien, Jeffrey Hunter, Edward Arnold, Thomas Gomez and Natalie Schafer. It took place in a hotel in Acapulco, one of those stories where you're not quite sure who did it. I think it turned out to be the Natalie Schafer character. It made no sense. It was *really* a terrible script.

I didn't know quite what to do. I'd never directed an hour show. I needed a place to live, so the next morning before rehearsal I drove around and rented the first furnished apartment I looked at. It was the Sunset Lanai on Sweetzer and it's still there.

We rehearsed, and the script was so bad that even the good actors, which not all were, could do anything with it. So I hired a friend of mine from New York, Robert H. Harris.

One of the great character actors out of the live television era. I watched him a lot.

Yes, and a wonderful guy. I created a role

CLIMAX: "Bail Out at Forty-Three Thousand" aired December 29, 1955.

Lee Marvin (above) starred as a pioneer pilot testing devices which would enable fliers to bail out of jet bombers at more than seven miles above the earth. The Martin Manulis production, broadcast live on CBS, also starred Charlton Heston, Richard Boone and Nancy Davis.

"John Frankenheimer's direction has an excellent quality and he sustains the suspense well. Charlton Heston is standout in a uniformly fine cast. . ."

—Daily Variety (1/3/56)

Producer Martin Manulis tells the story of trying to get John Wayne for the Climax *episode about Louella Parsons. Wayne flatly refused to appear on television. Then Miss Parsons told the producer that she would personally telephone Wayne—and within minutes, Wayne himself called Manulis and agreed to do the cameo.*

as a private detective for him. He was trying to find out who did what. I found a way to design the set so the lobby was over here and the bar was over there and you had a terrace over here. And I did the whole first twenty-eight pages of the script on one camera, without ever cutting once, bouncing everything off Robert H. Harris's face. I don't know if it had ever been done before.

He could hear what everybody was saying. We used this huge depth of focus shot with Harris in the foreground, or dollying past Harris and picking him up on the other side, all that kind of stuff. You knew he was in the background, or the camera came around and he was in the foreground and the others were in the background.

There was a fountain in the middle of the courtyard. And we wrapped that camera cable around that goddamn fountain four times, so in the end the camera could hardly move at all. Then we unwound it. That cameraman, Bob Stone, won the Emmy five years in a row with me. He was the best cameraman that CBS had, and that was his baptism of fire. He'll never forget it.

Did the viewers—and the critics—know what they were seeing?

We got raves for the thing. There were articles written about the appearance of a whole new style. "The new look of *Climax,*" one of the reviews said. Forget the fact that the script didn't make any sense. It was "Take camera four" for half an hour, and nobody'd seen that on live TV.

I still thought the thing was terrible and that I'd be right back on the plane to New York. But they loved it. And from then on I did a *Climax* every other week for two years.

I did "Pale Horse, Pale Rider" by Katherine Anne Porter with Dorothy McGuire and John Forsythe. I did "A Portrait in Celluloid," which was written by

Rod Serling. Jack Carson won an Emmy for it. We won the Emmy for best show both years. I did "Sailor on Horseback," a bio of Jack London, with Lloyd Nolan. In that one I did a fight scene live with a subjective camera for each actor. Two cameras right next to each other. I did a lot of innovative things. And we hired a lot of good actors— Wendell Corey, Akim Tamiroff, Teresa Wright, MacDonald Carey, Ruth Hussey, Victor Jory, Joanne Dru, Walter Matthau, Charlton Heston, Richard Boone, Lee Marvin, Nancy Davis Reagan and so on.

At one point, Manulis wanted to boost the ratings and he came up with the idea of "The Louella Parsons Story." He figured that she and we could blackmail all the stars in Hollywood to be in the show, and that's what happened. Teresa Wright played Louella, and we got everybody to come over and do their plugs. John Wayne, Rock Hudson, Susan Hayward, Jack Benny, George Burns, Joan Crawford, everybody. My only specific remembrances of the show are that I never got over how tall John Wayne was, and how nice he and Rock were.

One of the crazy shows we did on *Climax,* "Flame-Out on T-6," was supposed to be taking place at the North Pole. Richard Carlson, Sidney Blackmer and Jack Warden were in it. We wrapped dry ice in the mufflers they wore across their mouths so their breath would condense and make it look cold. They had to be careful not to burn their mouths on the dry ice.

I'd seen Sidney in *Come Back Little Sheba* and a lot of other things. In our show he was the heavy, a madman. He had to go to pieces in the last act, laughing fiendishly and running around from set to set. In the rehearsal room he couldn't find his way from set to set. And he made a classic remark. He said, "You know what live television is? It's summer stock in an iron lung."

During the *Climax* years there weren't yet any color television sets in the United States, but CBS made us do every third show in color. We didn't get any extra time and the lighting was twice as difficult. Also the cameras were twice as bulky.

Actually, as an A.D. I'd kind of been in on the ground floor of color television. CBS and NBC were both experimenting in color and they both wanted to get the FCC approval for their system because only one standard would be adopted. CBS had a system invented by this mad Hungarian genius, Dr. Peter Goldmark, who also invented the LP record. This was a color wheel with the primary colors on it that spun in front of the camera. It used regular-sized cameras. It was a good system. The RCA system involved much heavier cameras.

What happened was that the RCA system won, and on a given day in the Fall of 1954 they were going to go on the air and say this is the first color show on television. CBS decided to go one up on them and do the first color show with *their* system.

So no one would find out about it, we were doing it from a studio on top of 485 Madison Avenue. Mike Wallace was the emcee. I remember we had Bil and Cora Baird's puppets. The whole studio was about the size of this dining room. We went on the air at five o'clock on the day NBC was going on at eight o'clock. Jerome Shaw was the director and I was the A.D. Bill Paley stepped in front of the camera and said, "I'm William Paley, chairman of the Columbia Broadcasting System, and this is the first television show ever broadcast in color." And there it was. It's another of my memories, along with having been an A.D. on *See It Now* with Edward R. Murrow the night he nailed Senator McCarthy.

CLIMAX: "The Louella Parsons Story" (3/8/56) was adapted for television by Whitfield Cook from Parsons' autobiography, *The Gay Illiterate*.

THE YOUNG STRANGER (RKO, 1957).

"Deal a Blow" was the first show of the second season of Climax. *It was a triumph. That year, in the Spring of 1956, Bill Dozier took over as head of RKO. He'd liked 'Deal a Blow,' and I don't think it was just nepotism. He really loved the show. He bought it for RKO and hired me to direct it. It was retitled* The Young Stranger, *and it became my first movie."*

One of the *Climax* shows I did was written by Bill Dozier's son Robert Dozier. It was called "Deal A Blow." When Manulis met Helen Hayes's adopted son James MacArthur in New York, he suggested we put James in the story, although he'd never acted then.

Jamie came out to Los Angeles and lived with me for about a month and a half while we did the show. I talked to him about acting, taught him how to act, taught him how to do the show. And he went on live and did it.

You can't even call the television years an apprenticeship for the movies. It was a postgraduate education, a doctorate that simply isn't available to young people any more.

But I have to make it clear to you again that it wasn't an apprenticeship. I never thought of it that way. I didn't want to be a movie director. Television wasn't a means to an end. It *was* the end. As a matter of fact, we thought we were doing better work than they were doing in the movies. Charles Vidor was a prominent movie director. His wife was watching the first *Playhouse 90* and half-way through she went to him and said, "Charlie, you better come look at Channel 2, because they're doing this tonight and they're going to do it every week." It was a very fulfilling time.

Later on I turned down a lot of movies. I turned down *I Want to Live*, which was probably a mistake, and a lot of other stuff, because I had a terrible time doing *The Young Stranger*.

I loved live television, but tape ruined it, because the executives at the networks wanted more outside stuff. What they really wanted us to do was make A movies on C budgets. We directors looked at each other and said, "Hey, if that's what we're going to do we should get paid for it, and we

shouldn't have to do it in such a short shooting schedule."

Well, you still had a lot of television ahead of you, of course, but it must have seemed that you had a real foothold in movie Hollywood.

It didn't seem like much of a foothold at the time. It was a triumphant time for me, yes, except for the movie. I hated doing it. Jamie McArthur starred in it, as he had on television and the movie got very, very good reviews.

But it was an unhappy experience. I didn't really feel at ease in that environment. The cameraman I had had been under contract at Metro for years, and didn't want to do the stuff I wanted him to do. He influenced the way the rest of the crew reacted to me. We had two weeks' rehearsal and a twenty-five day shooting schedule, and I was told that if I didn't finish the film in twenty-five days, the lights get turned out. So we finished in twenty-five days.

It sounds to me as if at that time the Hollywood old-timers weren't dead keen about having you upstarts from television moving in on their turf.

Absolutely right. I sure wasn't welcomed with open arms.

I don't remember The Young Stranger, *I confess. What was it about?*

It was autobiographical, about a young kid whose father is a movie producer. The kid is provoked in a movie theater. He punches the theater manager. The manager brings charges against him, but finally the kid is exonerated. It's a nice, little story about a boy and his father. But, as I say, I didn't like the experience of making it at all.

Were you working mostly on sound stages?

Opposite page (l to r): *RKO producer Stuart Millar, James MacArthur, writer Robert Dozier, Frankenheimer and Kim Hunter.*

"I was panic-stricken on my first day at the studio. I had two weeks rehearsal before shooting, the way I did in television. This was a mistake. We rehearsed in continuity, and the actors began to use one scene to get into the other. When we shot the film out of continuity, they were lost and had to start all over again."

Top right: *Whit Bissell as a vindictive theater owner confronts Kim Hunter, James Mac-Arthur and James Gregory in a key scene from* The Young Stranger.

Middle right: *MacArthur and Gregory, the sympathetic cop.*

Below right: *James Daly as a film producer who thinks that he is being a good father just by providing his son with material benefits.*

Below left: *Kim Hunter as a weak mother who has grown apart from her son and is not quite sure how to deal with his father.*

"... [The Young Stranger] *is one of those unusual surprises Hollywood occasionally produces. Not the least remarkable thing about the movie is the youth of the four men most responsible for it. Producer Millar is 27, director Frankenheimer, 26, writer Dozier, 25. Promising lead actor MacArthur is 19.*"
—Time Magazine (1/28/57).

"Director John Frankenheimer rates high praise, both for tying the story together with force and cohesion, and for his use of the live camera as an instrument of dramatic construction. He missed few bets to build tension by the skillful employment of his tools, and by avoiding the arty and the cliche."
—Daily Variety (2/18/57)

Frankenheimer, shown at left on location for The Young Stranger, *was assigned a crew that obviously did not want to work with a "television" director. They treated him so badly and gave so little cooperation that he became bitter about the whole experience and decided to return to television.*

"In the current rash of juve delinquency dramas, this is the first which can be recalled as giving the youngster's side of it. . . John Frankenheimer's direction was a king-sized asset as he brought out the varied hues of emotions involved in the turbulence of a boy's world."
—Daily Variety (8/29/55)

James MacArthur, Kim Hunter, and first time feature director Frankenheimer.

Mostly. We shot some exteriors around L.A., in Bel Air. Which reminds me of a funny story.

I was a member of the Radio and Television Directors Guild, which I had joined for $25. In those days it cost $1,500 or $2,000 to join the Screen Directors Guild, and my salary for the picture was $12,500. They came to me from the Screen Directors Guild. I said, "No, under Taft-Hartley I can do one picture without joining." They were very incensed. I said I wanted to wait to see what happened. And I also said, "We have the rights to tape, and you guys are going to need us. You're going to have to take us in."

They said, "No, no, no, never."

Now, there was a scene in the movie which takes place in a movie theater, and the only place the location manager could find to shoot was the screening room of the Screen Directors Guild. So there I was, shooting in the Guild's screening room for a week, and not a member of the Guild. That really bugged them, especially Joe Youngerman, who was executive secretary of the Guild. We kidded about it years later, because the very next year the Screen Directors Guild took in all of us from the Radio and Television Directors Guild, and I saved $2,000.

But then it was back to television, and in a big way.

CBS was planning to do an hour and a half weekly dramatic show. It had never been done. They'd had ninety minute specials, but never weekly dramatic shows at that length. They were going to call it *Playhouse 90* and they wanted Manulis to produce it and me to be the chief director. It was to begin in 1956.

So I did the first *Playhouse 90* and the last *Playhouse 90* and every third show in-between from 1956 to 1960, more than fifty shows altogether. I did one every three weeks during the season, with two days off, for three years. I don't know how I did it, but I did. I had the same unit all the time; same A.D., same script girl, same crew.

The first one was "The Forbidden Area" from a Pat Frank story with a script by Rod Serling. It aired October 4, 1956.

It was about the Russians planting a spy over here and Strategic Air Command planes beginning to blow up at certain altitudes because of a so-called vacuum bomb. The cast was Charlton Heston, Diana Lynn, Victor Jory, Vincent Price, Tab Hunter, who was the Russian spy and very good, too, and Whit Bissell. Whit was practically a regular on every show I did for a long time.

As my second show, I was supposed to do "Requiem for a Heavyweight." I worked on the script with Serling, cutting it to the right length. It was much too long. Then CBS took it away from me and made it the second show in the series. Ralph Nelson directed it and won the Emmy for it. I think the second show I did was a thriller, "Rendezvous in Black," with Franchot Tone and Boris Karloff. Karloff was a wonderful actor, and wonderful to work with.

I get carried away going back into all of this. Sometimes it gets difficult to remember a lot, but then it all starts coming back.

PLAYHOUSE 90: "The Forbidden Area" aired October 4, 1956.

Above: *Charlton Heston and Diana Lynn get advice from JF during rehearsals for "Forbidden Area."*

Martin Manulis produced the first Playhouse 90, *starring Tab Hunter, Diana Lynn, Charlton Heston, Victor Jory, Vincent Price and Charles Bickford. Also in the cast were Jackie Coogan and Jack Palance. Frankenheimer said "So I did the first* Playhouse 90 *and the last* Playhouse 90 *and every third show in between. . ."*

". . . and the closeups were handled like a carefully orchestrated symphony beaten into willing submission by a TV Toscanini. Credit for a lot of this, maybe most of it, must go to John Frankenheimer, one of the brilliantly equipped directors of this plainly maturing medium. His job—he was the Toscanini herein—was managed to a superb, rising pitch of excitement."

—Jack O'Brian
New York Journal-American (10/5/56)
review of "The Forbidden Area" (Playhouse 90)

Cornell Woolrich's "Rendezvous in Black" was adapted for the Manulis production of Playhouse 90 *and became Frankenheimer's second directoral effort for that series. The*

cast: (standing, l to r) Boris Karloff, Tom Brown, Elizabeth Patterson and Franchot Tone, (seated) Viveca Lindfors and Laraine Day.

PLAYHOUSE 90: "Rendezvous in Black", October 25, 1956.

I've never been a guy who likes to look backwards; you've got to keep going ahead. But if I start thinking about it, I suddenly realize that I did a lot, I really did, and I worked with some incredible people.

I think of "The Last Tycoon," written by Don Mankiewicz, and "The Comedian" by Rod Serling. In all Serling and I must have done ten shows together. He was one of the most stressed-out people I ever knew. Nothing was working for Rod unless he was right at the edge. But God, what titles: "Requiem," "Patterns," "The Velvet Alley," "To Wake at Midnight," on and on.

There was another one, "A Town Has Turned to Dust," that was supposed to be the first show of the second season. It was about the murder of a black boy named Emmett Till in Mississippi.

I remember the story. I worked on it for LIFE *magazine in New York. He was sup-*

posed to have whistled at a white woman. The man or men who killed him were never convicted.

That's right, and the story was supposed to be what happened to the men who killed Emmett Till. But the insurance company and the other sponsors wouldn't let us do it. It got pulled. We had to put in "The Death of Manolete" with Jack Palance, which was a disaster.

Serling rewrote the Emmett Till story later, as a period western, set in 1870 or thereabouts. Same title, "A Town Has Turned to Dust," and essentially the same story. Rod Steiger played the sheriff who protected the killer and gave his tacit approval to the lynching. Then he gave this speech, an apologia to the town, and somebody says, "What are you going to do, Harvey?" He says, "The right thing, the right thing." Then, in the script, he turns and walks into his office in the jail. The camera holds outside and you hear a gunshot, Boom.

Four days before it was to go on the air, the insurance company let it be known that the ending was totally unacceptable. Nobody on a show sponsored by the Prudential Insurance Company of America was going to commit suicide. Well, you can imagine: we yelled, we screamed, but all to no avail. CBS said, "Either you change it..." But there was no "either," so we changed. Billy Shatner was playing the heavy, who was supposed to be killed by Steiger. We changed the script so that in the gun fight, he gets off a last shot as he lies dying and Steiger is mortally wounded. But he lives long enough to make his last speech of apology to the town. Rod was very good in the part, and so was Shatner. So was a girl named Fay Spain, and of course Jimmy Gregory, the ubiquitous Jimmy Gregory who was in so many shows I did. It's a very good show; it came off well.

"John Frankenheimer's mounting of 'A Town Has Turned To Dust' was simply superb. . . Mr. Frankenheimer's staging was the directorial art at its most effective. . . His handling of the crowd scenes, his superb use of sequences of total silence, and his uncannily judicious employment of close-ups truly strengthened Rod Serling's intent. . ."

—Jack Gould
New York Times (6/21/58)

PLAYHOUSE 90: "A Town Has Turned To Dust" aired June 19, 1958.

Above: *Rod Steiger, William Shatner, Fay Spain and James Gregory make up the cast of "A Town Has Turned To Dust." The drama, originally called "Aftermath," was considered too hot to handle by the sponsors without some rewriting. Martin Manulis and CBS-TV programming chief, Hubbell Robinson, Jr., urged Rod Serling to rework the story without watering down its message. According to Variety (6/25/58), ". . . the result was certainly worth the effort."*

The cast of "The Last Tycoon" (pictured right) included Viveca Lindfors, Jack Palance and Lee Remick (seated), with John Hudson, Peter Lorre, Keenan Wynn and Reginald Denny (standing). "The Comedian" won the Emmy for the Best Dramatic Program of 1957.

Produced by Martin Manulis, adapted by Rod Serling from a story by Ernest Lehman and starring Mickey Rooney, the show became a classic. The cast (pictured left) included Constance Moore, Edmond O'Brien, Rooney, Mel Torme and Kim Hunter.

PLAYHOUSE 90: "The Comedian" aired February 14, 1957.

PLAYHOUSE 90: "The Last Tycoon" aired March 15, 1957.

"...Last week Manulis said as soon as the teleplay on F. Scott Fitzgerald's The Last Tycoon *is finished, he will submit it to Humphrey Bogart and Lauren Bacall. So Bogie said yesterday he's 'very interested' in 'Tycoon' as his first TV activity when he returns to work. 'Johnny Frankenheimer is a fine director, and Manulis is a good producer,' comments Bogie."*

—Dave Kaufman
Daily Variety (10/9/56)

(Bogart died January 14, 1957, three months after this item appeared).

"The Last Tycoon" is obviously another show you remember with considerable pride.

We did "The Last Tycoon" here in California. Jack Palance played Monroe Starr, Lee Remick played Cecilia. She was nineteen and, God, so beautiful. Robert L. Simon was her father, Brady, the studio executive. Viveca Lindfors played Cathleen, Keenan Wynn was the businessman from New York, Peter Lorre played the old director and Reginald Denny was the writer. John Hudson played the young writer she falls in love with. Manulis produced it.

We didn't try to improve on Fitzgerald. We stopped it where he stopped it. We left it with Monroe Stahr in his beach house knowing he was dying and we closed with a shot of Palance. I think the narrator says that Fitzgerald died before he finished the book. Some of the best dialogue in that show is not Fitzgerald, it's Don Mankiewicz. Jack Palance was superb. I remember that the night before the show he slept in the office because he wanted that office to be so much a part of him.

"The Comedian" was a tour de force. The basis was a magazine story by Ernest Lehman, which Serling adapted. Mickey Rooney was brilliant. He's one of the most talented guys I ever met. I don't think there's anything he can't do. He had the performance from the first reading. From there he kept changing it and the big job was to get him back to what he had.

Sometimes the shows didn't work. "The Death of Manolete" didn't work because we couldn't do the bull-fighting sequences very well. Suzy Parker didn't work as the girl and there was other miscasting. But Jack Palance was very good as Manolete. The film clips didn't look right, though. We were in over our heads. It just looked fake.

". . . Casting Jack Palance in the role of the Hollywood genius had seemed to be casting directly against type. . . But Palance managed an amazing sensitivity for someone seen far more frequently in brutally physical roles, and the rest of the cast were deployed with equal perception by the amazingly young and successful John Frankenheimer. Some- *one tell Sheldon Reynolds he's no longer properly to be described as a 'wunderkind', while there are younger, wunderkinder around such as 26-year-old Frankenheimer, TV's best director.*

—Jack O'Brian
New York Journal-American (3/15/57)
review of "The Last Tycoon" (Playhouse 90)

35

PLAYHOUSE 90

I did one thing of William Faulkner's, "Old Man." I did a lot more of Jack London. I'd done the biography on *Climax* with Lloyd Nolan, as I told you.

Clifford Odets adapted "Clash By Night" for television himself. What happened was that we bought the rights to the play and Manulis hired a writer to adapt it. But he really messed it up. So I called Odets at home and said, "There are big problems in the adaptation and I don't want to screw up your play." He said, "Come on over and we'll talk about it." He served lemonade and we talked and eventually spent a week working on the script. I even got *Playhouse 90* to pay him. He met Kim Stanley, who was in it and had a long affair with her and directed her in the Paddy Chayevsky film *The Goddess.*

Were you doing tape by then?

No that was all live. Tape didn't come in until 1958. Then when tape did come in, at first, we had to do whole sequences on tape. You couldn't cut it, so you'd do a tape insert. I did a show called "Bomber's Moon" with Robert Cummings and Marty Balsam, about a bomber pilot. I did all the stuff inside the B-17 the day before and used them as tape inserts. We had a nine-second roll cue. You had to start the tape nine seconds before you wanted it on the screen. Nine seconds is an eternity. It was a nightmare because you obviously had to hit it just right. With film it was a four-second roll cue. On "Days of Wine and Roses" I shot the AA meetings the day before.

In every television show and picture we've discussed you've been very much involved with the script. You obviously have no doubt that the script is everything. In the beginning is the word, still.

Without the script you're doomed. I think of all those terrific writers from live

PLAYHOUSE 90: "Clash By Night" aired June 13, 1957.

Above: *Lloyd Bridges, E.G. Marshall and Kim Stanley.*

television: Robert Alan Aurthur, Sumner Locke Elliott, Horton Foote—we did his "A Little Bear." J. P. Miller ("Days of Wine and Roses") Roger Hirson, Paddy Chayevsky, Reginald Rose, Tad Mosel. And don't forget the producers: Fred Coe, John Houseman, Herbert Brodkin, Martin Manulis. That's a good poker hand to draw to.

You didn't do many shows with Fred Coe. But he and Manulis seemed to be, what, the most influential producers in your television years. How did they compare?

With Coe, I did the equivalent of five shows because "For Whom the Bell Tolls"

Veteran character actor Marc Lawrence remembers the director's unique rehearsal style: "He used his own face as the camera, pushing it into our faces, in and around us, most of the time. Although it looked and seemed ridiculous, Frankenheimer felt it was helpful for the actors to be familiar with that closeness, as well as it was for the director to observe the performances. Actors trained in Stanislavski technique were sometimes told, 'you're acting too generally, not specifically,' or 'play it moment to moment,' and other little verbal notes to those who understood—or pretended to. Those possessing improvisational equipment were more at ease with the tension generated on live, non-audience shows."

was in two parts. Of those five shows, arguably four of them are the best things I ever did in television. You'd have to add "The Comedian" and "The Last Tycoon" to the best list.

But let's start with Manulis. Manulis was a charming man. He was a guy who had a tremendous gift for organizing things. He was able to produce—on a *weekly* basis—*Climax* for two years and *Playhouse 90* for two years, and he could do it terribly, terribly well. As I've often said, it took three men to replace him—Coe, Herbert Brodkin and John Houseman.

Manulis had a tremendous gift, in a strange kind of way, for facing reality. He would say, "Okay, if we can't get So-and-So, we'll get So-and-So, and somehow the show will go on." He had a way of making people do very, very good work, of making them do things they didn't think they could do. He had a great sense of humor, which I think saved the day in many cases.

He had a wonderful way of dealing with executives, of running interference for me. He was an awfully good producer. God knows I did an awful lot of shows with him, seventy-odd, it must have been.

Fred Coe was the best producer I ever worked with. His contribution was enormous, just enormous. First on script, secondly on casting and third just in sharing with me his vision, his idea of what the show should be.

I had tremendous respect for Fred Coe artistically. He really knew what was good. He came to *Playhouse 90* with these incredible credentials, mainly the *Philco Playhouse*. I realized also that he was used to working with other directors, and he had a very close relationship with certain people like Delbert Mann, Vincent Donohue and Arthur Penn.

And so we were starting from scratch, and we were at the beginning like two fighters sizing each other up, because I had a pretty good reputation and he had a pretty good reputation, and both of us had reputations for being very independent. But we developed that rare thing, a relationship in which he brought out the best in me, and I think I brought out some of the best in him.

He challenged me tremendously. I remember a scene in "The Days of Wine and Roses" which was, if I do say so myself, brilliantly shot. He used to call me Pappy, and after he looked at the camera run-through he called me into the little announcer's booth where he sat with his monitor.

He had this southern acccent and he said, "Now, Pappy, I think this scene between Piper [Laurie] and Cliff [Robertson], when he decides he's going to go out the window, I think it's absolutely brilliantly done. Some of those camera angles are just absolute inspiration. The trouble is, Pappy, I just don't understand what the fuck the scene is about. You got to simplify it. You've got to tell the story."

He said, and I'll never forget it, that, "The camera comes so easy for you, and you come in with these great shots, but sometimes they don't push the story forward, and that's what you've got to do." I never forgot it.

So I changed it. I just simplified the scene, and Fred said, "Now that looks more ordinary, and I understand it. And *now*, what can we do to make it look like it looked before, with all those angles." So we lit it differently.

He was incredible. Script points that had to be made, crucial things like that. What Coe didn't know how to do, he didn't know how to play the executive suite as well as Manulis did.

When we ran into budget problems on "For Whom the Bell Tolls," he wasn't there to support us. Fred had a drinking problem even then, which later killed him. When

PLAYHOUSE 90: "The Days of Wine and Roses" aired November 2, 1958.

Cliff Robertson and Piper Laurie.

"As we look back on the kines of Playhouse 90 *days, we can readily see the lack of camera movement in its frozen techniques. But it was Frankenheimer's personal charm that made you feel it was constantly in movement."*
—Marc Lawrence

PLAYHOUSE 90: "Winter Dreams" aired May 23, 1957.

Above: *Featured in the cast were (l to r) Dana Wynter, Phyllis Love, Darryl Hickman, Joseph Sweeney, Robert Simon, Mildred Dunnock, and John Cassavetes.*

"The 90-minute course proved too long for F. Scott Fitzgerald's 'Winter Dreams' of his favorite theme, the doomed love of a poor, ambitious lad for a rich, spoiled girl. Even his undoubted writing skill, ably adapted by James Cavanagh, couldn't hold back an increasing irritation and boredom with Fitzgerald's world of determinedly bright and unhappy misfits. But the evident skill, taste and care with which the story was staged and acted was a credit to all concerned. As a demonstration of sheer technical virtuosity, 'Winter Dreams' should stand as a model."
—Daily Variety (5/27/57)

things got rough on "For Whom the Bell Tolls," he got drunk and ended up in Florida with his ex-wife, and we couldn't find him.

After we did Faulkner's "Old Man," Fred wrote me a letter. I think I quoted to you from it. Basically it said, "Dear John, Talent is doing easily what other people find difficult. Genius is doing what talent finds difficult." It was an incredible compliment, especially getting it from a man like Fred Coe.

If we'd stopped our relationship after "Old Man" and "Days of Wine and Roses," it would have been historic, that relationship. But we went on to do "For Whom the Bell Tolls" and "Journey to the Day." "Journey to the Day" is good television, but not great, and "For Whom the Bell Tolls" has its moments, but it was flawed.

I can't imagine how you did it at all within the technical limitations of television in those days. But that must have been a big part of the excitement of the live television days—working with so much great material, and producers, and writers, and performers.

It was a wonderful experience. I don't say learning experience because I never wanted to be anything but a television director. I loved doing live television. I worked with some of the greatest actors there were: John Gielgud, Jack Lemmon, Jack Palance, Diana Lynn, Helen Hayes, Dorothy McGuire, Eva Marie Saint, Kim Hunter, Kim Stanley, E.G. Marshall, Rod Steiger. The list goes on.

Dana Wynter was perhaps the most beautiful girl I'd ever seen. She did "Winter Dreams" for me, from a typical Scott Fitzgerald story: the poor boy and the inaccessible girl he ends up with and then leaves. Cassavetes played the boy, and Darryl Hickman was in it, and Vivian Nathan, whom I kept using a lot. Dana did "The Violent Heart" for me, too.

"I remember during an on air show—for instance, a Playhouse 90— *I would lose four to five pounds in perspiration. I'd have to take my shirt off and just wring it out at the end of one of those things."*

—John Frankenheimer

"Someone once compared doing live television to doing summer stock in an iron lung. I think that about says it."

—JF

"Winter Dreams" was the one where the Cassavetes-Wynter kiss got you into trouble.

I'd forgotten about that, but you're right. We lost some affiliates on that kiss. I think we cost CBS the Bible Belt.

You used a lot of theater people in the live television days.

You had to. They could remember the lines and they could do it from beginning to end, and they knew there was no time to mess around.

What happened if an actor blew a line, or were they all so good it didn't happen?

They were awfully good. But once in a while there were problems. I was doing a *Climax* show about the discovery of the Stone of Scone by the Scottish Nationalists. Sir Cedric Hardwicke was in it. He was a dear friend and I used him a lot. "No Stone Unturned," as it was called, was a very wordy script and he had all the exposition.

"Dear fellow," he said. "I shall never remember all these lines."

I said, "Cedric, of course you will."

He said, "Never. It's page after page after page."

I said, "I never worry about you. I'll shoot it all in close-up."

Cedric said, "You'll regret it."

We got on the air and things were going fine. Then, partway into his longest speech, suddenly Cedric's lips were moving but there was no sound. It took me a couple of seconds to realize what was happening. There was nothing wrong with the equipment. The old devil was telling me he'd blown his lines. As quickly as I could I killed the audio and turned on the speakers in the studio and fed him his lines. I turned the audio back on and he said, "and furthermore" or whatever the line was and he went on as if nothing had happened that was *his* fault. I suppose the viewers thought the network had goofed for a minute.

When you think back over the years of live television, what do you think the great lessons were for you?

Technically, I learned tremendous things. We were our own cameramen in live television. And about cutting. After all, the shows were live, so there was no question about who had the final cut. Everything had to be pre-cut, pre-arranged, cut on paper, so that we knew every shot, and how cameras were going to be released. Timing, pacing, actual experience. Not talking about doing the job, *doing* the job.

Probably the one thing I got out of live television that was more important than anything else was confidence, the feeling that I could probably *do* anything. I had so many emergencies; so many things went wrong that I had to fix in a hell of a hurry.

And you didn't have to wait for Charles Champlin or Cecil Smith or Jack Gould to review it to tell you how you did. You knew how it did. The time was marred by the blacklisting, of course, but it was still a great, creative time.

Someone once asked me, "How were you able to do such quality stuff then, compared to what television does now?" The answer is that most people didn't own a television set in those days. Owning a TV set was a kind of elitist thing, and we had an elitist audience. It's comparable to playing to a cable audience today.

Playhouse 90 went off the air for a while. At that time I did the Hemingway specials at CBS. It was called *The Hemingway Playhouse* and Gordon Duff produced them. I did two of them. I'd done "For Whom the Bell Tolls" as a two-part *Playhouse 90* with Jason Robards as Robert Jordan and Maria Schell as Maria, Nehemiah

When Hemingway saw the production, he described it as "ringing true, adding that costumes and general atmosphere 'were splendid and absolutely in contrast to the movie version which was Abercrombie and Fitch out of Helena Rubenstein.'"

—Daily Variety (4/1/59)

BUICK ELECTRA PLAYHOUSE: "The Snows of Kilimanjaro" aired March 25, 1960.

Above: *Seated from left, Robert Ryan, Brock Peters, Ann Todd, Mary Astor and the director. Standing from left, Janice Rule, Clancy Cooper, scriptwriter A. E. Hotchner, James Gregory, Liliane Monterecchi, Norma Crane and Albert Paulson.*

"The best thing I've ever done, anywhere, was a TV adaptation of The Snows of Kilimanjaro. *We had a director on it. . . who* really *knew his business."*

- Robert Ryan
Films And Filming (8/61)

Persoff, Maureen Stapleton as Pilar, Steven Hill, Sydney Pollack, Milton Selzer and Vladimir Sokoloff as the Gypsy, the role he played in the movie.

Persoff played Pablo and won an Emmy and a Peabody award.

At CBS I did "The Snows of Kilimanjaro" with Robert Ryan and "The Fifth Column," which was Hemingway's only play, with Richard Burton, Maximilian Schell and Sally Ann Howes.

"The Snows of Kilimanjaro" was quite something. Ryan, Janice Rule, Ann Todd, my old favorite Jimmy Gregory, a hell of a cast. It was done well after the invention of tape, but we had to do it live on tape, rather than tape it. There's a big difference. Ryan agreed to do it on the understanding that we were going to tape it out of New York. But we found out that Fox owned the rights to the movie and wouldn't give CBS the right to tape it. So we did it live from California.

To do the flashback scenes was enormously difficult because you had a man dying of gangrene in the jungle and his whole life is flashing before him. How to do it?

I had a very, very talented art director named Burr Schmidt. We had the jungle set absolutely real. Then we put Ryan's bed on a turntable, although you couldn't see that it was. We put a camera on the turntable as well and when he began to hallucinate we pushed close into his face with the camera and the turntable moved but you got no feeling of movement because he and the camera moved together.

We built the flashback sets out of white paper, and he got up out of his bed and walked into the flashbacks. It was very effective.

It was during that show that Mike Curtiz, who'd directed *Casablanca* and a zillion other movies, came over to CBS to be a television director. The president of

PLAYHOUSE 90: "For Whom The Bell Tolls"
aired March 12 and 19, 1959.

"For Whom The Bell Tolls" was the longest (3 hrs) and costliest ($500,000) drama yet to be presented on television. Though the show was taped, twelve minutes ran live, blizzards and shell explosions had to be created and fifteen horses had to be shod with rubber shoes that would not slip on the studio floor.

Top right: *JF and Kenny Utt, here JF's A.D., but later to become the Academy Award Producer of* Silence of the Lambs, *setting up one of the many shots using live horses. Actor Steven Hill is standing behind the director.*

Middle right: *Maria Schell (left) and Frankenheimer are discussing a particular scene during one of the rehearsals as Jason Robards, Jr. listens.*

Below right: *Eli Wallach (left) and Robards listen to the director as he sets up a shot during the taping.*

Below: *The director watches on a monitor as a scene unfolds during one of the tapings.*

PLAYHOUSE 90: "Journey To The Day" aired April 22, 1960.

Above: *The director sets up one of the group therapy sessions in a rehearsal for "Journey." From left, Vivian Nathan, Steven Hill, JF, Janice Rule, Mike Nichols, Mary Astor and James Dunn.*

Right: *JF, cameraman Bob Danne and dolly grip Grant Wilson are preparing to shoot the above scene.*

"John Frankenheimer was the man. He was the most exciting director around. He inspired us all."

—Mark Rydell

43

PLAYHOUSE 90

CBS brought him to the set to watch a TV director at work. I was on the floor blocking the show, which is a crazy time to begin with, and here were these paper sets and the camera on the turntable. Even for me it was crazy.

Curtiz came over and looked at me and said, "Young man you are crazy, you are an insane young man." And he announced, "I cannot do this," and he walked out and CBS never saw him again.

It was during this time that I did "The Browning Version" with John Gielgud and Margaret Leighton. Superb actors.

Then *Playhouse 90* came back with four specials and one of them was "Journey to the Day." It was the last *Playhouse 90* I did. It was in black and white; color was coming in but to that point only for special things.

We watched your kinescope of "Journey to the Day," and I thought it was an astonishing piece of work. A look at a number of very unhappy but in most cases very sympathetic people who were in group therapy. A remarkable set of performances, including the one by Mike Nichols in a very straight role. Not a laugh in a carload. It must have been one of the first dramas to look at group therapy.

Fred Coe, the producer, came up with the idea and Roger O. Hirson wrote it. It really was a terrific cast: Vivian Nathan; James Gregory, who as I've said was in the first movie I directed, the first movie I produced and directed and the last television show I directed; Steven Hill, who went off to Israel and became a Hassidic rabbi; Peter Votrian; Mary Astor; Helen Cleaves, who was later in *The Manchurian Candidate*; Mike Nichols, who by the way had never acted in a straight drama before; and Janice Rule. The critics said of Steve Hill, "Where'd they find this terrific Brazilian or Argentinian actor?"

DUPONT SHOW OF THE MONTH: "The Browning Version" aired 4/23/59.

Above: *Sir John Gielgud.*

"John Frankenheimer's direction of this fine David Susskind-Talent Associates production was artistically meticulous enough to survive a tendency towards insufficient lighting in certain sequences . . . and one or two rough mechanical maneuvers."

—Daily Variety (4/27/59)
review of "The Browning Version"

"John Frankenheimer. . . was so long the 'child prodigy' of the TV industry that the joke was he would be 29 until Jack Benny was 40. . ."

—Burt Prelutsky

How was the show done?

Live on tape. The beautiful thing was we had two and a half weeks of rehearsal, then were four days on the set. I just wanted the actors to be free, and we'd try things and see if they worked, and if they did we kept them.

Janice Rule's performance is terribly moving. How do you work with an actress to get a performance like that? To what extent can she take the script and run with it, and how much of it came out of discussions?

At that time my wife and I were separated. She'd made several suicide attempts and been diagnosed as a manic-depressive. Four weeks after the show she had to be institutionalized. So I had been deeply involved with mental illness since I was married to someone who was ill. Janice and I had begun seeing each other and we went to several mental institutions together and observed behavior. So her performance, all the performances, came out of discussions, and rehearsal.

She was one of the best actresses I ever worked with. When I saw her on stage in *Picnic*, I thought she was the most beautiful girl I'd seen. And imagine who her three understudies were: Kim Stanley, Joanne Woodward and Sandra Church.

Jerry Goldsmith did the music for "Journey." He did sixty shows for me.

After the two and a half weeks of rehearsal, you're on the set for four days. How did that break down?

We would tape it all in one day, obviously. We would have run-through, run-through, run-through and then we'd tape. I think we taped it act by act, the same way we'd do a live show.

Every camera shot was written out beforehand during rehearsal, by me and the assistant director. When we got to the set on a Monday, we'd go through it with the actors, shot by shot. The actors had a chance to use the props. Then Tuesday we'd start to block it, shot by shot. I'd have a rolling television monitor on the floor. I'd be right next to the cameramen and they'd be talking to the A.D. over headphones, and if something didn't work, I'd be there to fix it.

We'd do a scene, stagger through it. We'd do that all day Tuesday and into Wednesday morning. Wednesday we'd do a run-through, then a run-through with costumes later in the day. There would be extensive notes and then a dinner break. The cast would go home and I'd stay with the crew. We'd come back and discuss all the technical problems we had and try to fix them.

One cameraman would say, "Hey, every time I go over here, the boom's in the shot; we gotta move the boom back." Another cameraman would say, "I got a terrific problem when she moves there and there," and so on.

Thursday morning we would presumably fix all the problems and then have a technical run-through. Then we'd do the first dress rehearsal, from maybe twelve to two, an hour break and then we'd do a second dress rehearsal from three to five-thirty. There'd be an hour of notes, and we're on the air at six-thirty. Live for New York. Four cameras, usually three cranes and a pedestal.

You directed Ingrid Bergman in her first television outing, Henry James's "Turn of the Screw," I think. How was she to work with?

Magnificent. Hubbell Robinson signed her through Kay Brown, who was her agent

"There are probably few chillers more difficult to dramatize satisfactorily than Henry James' novelette, Turn of the Screw. *. . . yet for all the difficulties, adaptor James Costigan, producer-director John Frankenheimer and star Ingrid Bergman did a remarkably good job in bringing (it) to television. . . Frankenheimer's direction was brilliant in his handling of the actors and his construction of the mounting suspense."*

—Daily Variety (10/22/59)

and who'd been Selznick's story editor all those years. By then she was with MCA. Robinson assigned James Costigan to write it and me to direct it. Then he said, "You're going to have to come over to Goteborg with me and talk with Bergman. It's her debut and she's nervous and she knows you only by reputation. We also stop in Paris and see Costigan." This was 1959 and I was twenty-nine.

We reached Goteborg and took a cab down to the wharf. Lars Schmidt, who was still her husband then, met us in a speedboat and took us, Kay Brown, Robinson and me, through the very choppy waters of the North Sea to the island where they lived. And there was Bergman, waiting to greet us. She was thirty-seven or thirty-eight, I think, and she looked fabulous.

She said, "You must be very tired from your journey. We have a custom here and perhaps you'll like it. Why don't you take a sauna and then we'll talk."

The geography was that the sauna was just off the pier at the North Sea and the house a bit further inland. So we're sitting in the sauna talking and suddenly Bergman comes in in a robe and she took off a robe and there she was naked.

I felt all sorts of things happening to me and I thought, "My God, you're going to be a disgrace." So I said, "Excuse me, I think I'd like a swim." So I bolted out of the sauna and dove into the North Sea, which was *freezing* cold.

When I got out of the water you couldn't tell if I was a man or a woman. I went back into the sauna but in five minutes I was in trouble again. I made four trips into the North Sea that afternoon.

Years later, when she was doing Golda Meir in Israel and was already very ill, a friend of mine who knew the Goteborg story met her and asked if she remembered the afternoon. She smiled very cryptically and said, "Yes." But that's all she would say.

NBC FORD STARTIME: "Turn of the Screw" aired October 20, 1959.

Above: *The director with Ingrid Bergman.*

How was "Turn of the Screw" done?

That was done in color on tape, not live. Again, we had to do whole scenes; you couldn't cut. In those early days of tape, you couldn't shoot a close-up or a medium shot.

We had two and a half weeks of rehearsal and four days on camera. I had all I could do to deal with Ingrid because it was her first foray into television. Then the little English girl we'd hired turned out to be all wrong. We let her go and used Alexandra Wager, Michael Wager's daughter.

It was really difficult. The heat in the studio was tremendous because of the light needed for color television. Nobody had color sets then, so I muted all the color. I wanted everything muted except for the little girl's red shoes and the red roses. I heard later that the idea was regarded as a huge failure because the people complained to NBC that there seemed to be something wrong with their sets.

"If only that it brought Ingrid Bergman to television in her first dramatic role. . . 'Turn of the Screw'. . . amply justifies itself. Its virtues, however, went beyond her presence. . ."

—Variety (10/28/59)

Somewhere in the archives, I read that you very nearly got to direct Breakfast at Tiffany's.

I almost did, and it was another of those rejection experiences that do seem to be a fact of life in the industry.

What happened was that while I was doing Hemingway's play "The Fifth Column" at CBS in New York, I had a call from two producers I knew, Martin Jurow and Dick Shepherd. They had bought *Breakfast at Tiffany's* and they wanted me to direct it. They had Marilyn Monroe in mind to play Holly Golightly, and she had approved me. Naturally, I said I'd love to do it.

We got Sumner Locke Elliott to write the screenplay, but his screenplay didn't work. The producers asked me what we ought to do. I said, "I think the guy that can do it is George Axelrod." They hired him for a lot of money and he and I really worked closely on the screenplay. It turned out very, very well.

Then somehow—I was naive in those days and I never got to the bottom of this—somehow, overnight, the producers went to Switzerland and cast Audrey Hepburn. But Hepburn and her then husband, Mel Ferrer, had never heard of me. So Paramount paid me off and the producers hired Blake Edwards. That was the first time I'd lost to Blake Edwards. The *coup de grâce* was losing to Blake on *Days of Wine and Roses* later. I've since gotten to like him very much; he's a lovely guy. But I wasn't president of his fan club back then.

And I was out. But I mean really out. At that point, I was like a blacksmith after the invention of the automobile: I was a live television director and there was no more live television. I didn't have a job.

I was supposed to have done *Tender Is the Night* for [David O.] Selznick. I'd become Selznick's protégé in a way. He'd seen a lot of the television I'd done and wanted to meet me and we got together in 1956. After that he'd have a kinescope of every show I did sent to the house and he'd critique it. He'd tell me what was good and what was bad.

I'd go up to the house—Jennifer [Jones] was off at one of her ashrams in India—and we'd have dinner and talk until three or four in the morning. I learned an awful lot from him. He had two sons, but he was a bit alienated from them, and I think I might have been a kind of third son he wished he had.

He told me stuff about the technical aspect of making movies that I use to this day. He helped me cut *The Young Savages*, he helped me cut *Birdman of Alcatraz*. But finally, when I went on to make *The Manchurian Candidate*, I wanted to make it on my own, without Daddy. David was very upset about that and he said, "Are you going to let me see this movie or not?"

I said, "Yes, but I want to do it myself. You can see it, David, when I'm finished with it." I finished it and I sent him a release print about a week before it was going to open. In those days there were about a hundred release prints.

So my phone rang at three in the morning, and David said, "How many prints are made?"

I said, "David, it's three in the morning."

He said, "I don't care what time it is. You can't have this picture released like this. It's a disgrace. *How* many prints are there?"

I said a hundred.

He said, "We have to buy them all, every one of them! You've directed the worst scene you've ever directed in your life."

I said, "Jesus, David, which?"

He used to light a cigarette and take a long, whooshing inhale; the cigarettes finally killed him. I heard the whoosh, then he said, "You have a scene with James Gregory in a makeup chair, with the makeup man in the room, and Angela Lansbury

THE YOUNG SAVAGES (United Artists, 1961).

(Opposite page) Top: *The young savages of the film's title attempting to elude police in this "between-titles-and-credits" sequence.*

Bottom right: *The beautifully staged funeral sequence is prepared.*

Bottom left: *Neil Nephew, Stanley Kristien and John Davis Chandler terrify and threaten a potential witness.*

49

THE YOUNG SAVAGES

comes in and you have her discuss this very intimate dinner she's going to give for this senator and what she wants out of him and how she's going to use him. Don't you understand that you'd never have a conversation like that *in front of anybody?* How could you do that?"

I realize to this day that he was right; that's the terrible part. Angela would never have said that stuff in front of the guy. David went on for another half-hour, but there was nothing we could do. Up to that moment, it was the worst review I'd ever had.

As I said, I was supposed to do *Tender Is the Night*, which was one of my favorite books in college, with David. I wanted desperately to do it, and it seemed to be all set. It was an ideal cast. Jennifer was a given, of course, even though she was too old for it. We had an unknown English actor, whom you'd never have heard of then, Peter O'Toole, to play Dick, Jane Fonda for Rosemary and Steve Hill to play Abe North. We had a beautiful script written by Ivan Moffat.

Selznick actually got Fox to hire me, but then they decided they didn't want Selznick to produce it. They fired Selznick and brought in another producer, Henry Weinstein, whose job was to get rid of me. Up to that point he had been a ticket taker at the Westport County Playhouse. Fox said, "You will shoot the picture in thirty-five days and you will shoot the French Riviera footage in Palos Verdes." The whole thing smacked of disaster. The idea of doing the movie was to work with Selznick and, without him, I wanted out. I resigned.

Were you permanently settled in Hollywood then?

No, I was in New York, getting legally separated from my wife. Nothing in my life was going right at all.

Yet you got a second movie, The Young Savages, *fairly quickly. It came out in 1961.*

Yes, and getting to do it was in its way as bizarre as not getting the others. Harold Hecht asked me to direct the movie, but it had nothing to do with my real ability. He simply wanted to know if I could do it in thirty-five days, and I said I could. What had happened was that the production company of Hecht-Hill-Lancaster had got itself deeply into debt to United Artists. To get out of the debt they'd had to agree to do four very inexpensive pictures, with Burt Lancaster getting $150,000 instead of his usual price in those days of $750,000. He'd just come off *Elmer Gantry*, and the last thing on earth he wanted to do was this movie.

It was based on a novel called *A Matter of Conviction* by Evan Hunter. Hecht just wanted to get the movie over with. But that wasn't what I wanted to do at all. I convinced Hecht and his production manager that we could shoot the scenes on real locations in New York as quickly as we could do them on the back lot in Hollywood. It was about juvenile delinquents and I also convinced Hecht that the thing to do was cast some real juvenile delinquents.

I had to keep trading with him to get what I wanted. He wanted Paul Anka as one of the delinquents so he could sing the title song. To beat that idea I agreed to use a girl he also wanted in the picture. I wanted Lee Grant very, very badly, so I agreed to use Dina Merrill, whom he wanted in the picture. Ironically after the first day of shooting in New York I had to let Lee Grant go, and I hired Shelley Winters in her place.

The picture, incidentally, led to Sydney Pollack starting his career in Hollywood. I had done a live *Studio One*, which was written by Frank Gilroy and called "The Last Summer," and it had a mother and a

"...What makes this a good film? Simply, the direction..."
—Films and Filming
London (8/61)

Lionel ("Curly") Lindon, director of photography, listens as Frankenheimer directs Burt Lancaster and Edward Andrews in the funeral scene just before they confront the victim's mother.

son and a beautiful, unobtainable girl. Vivian Nathan was the mother, Dennis Hopper was the son and I needed the beautiful girl. I'd studied acting with Sandy Meisner at the Neighborhood Playhouse and I asked him for a suggestion. He recommended a young woman named Claire Griswold who'd just graduated from the Playhouse. She was engaged to a guy still in the Army named Sydney Pollack.

When I did "For Whom the Bell Tolls" the next year, she called me and said, "Do you think you can possibly use my husband in anything?" They were married by then. I met him and I liked him, and I used him in that one and other shows later. He's a very

good actor. He was teaching at the Playhouse, too. When I was doing "The Turn of the Screw" with Ingrid Bergman, I hired him to coach the kids in the show. It was the first time he'd done any directing.

Now I'm doing *A Matter of Conviction*, or *The Young Savages*, as it came to be called, and I hired Sydney again, to coach the delinquents, who'd never acted before. He started in New York and then came to the Coast with us. Lancaster liked him and between us we helped him get his first directing job at MCA. All the rest of it Sydney has done himself.

Actually, Lancaster and I did not get along during the filming of *The Young Sav-*

The real-life case of a New York gang murder of a crippled boy, Michael Farmer, and some other well-publicized teenage slayings involving Puerto Rican youths, became an obvious springboard for The Young Savages. *Bosley Crowther of the* New York Times *(5/25/61)* faulted the script—adapted from Evan Hunter's novel, A Matter of Conviction—for overshadowing the youngsters' story with the personal conflicts of the assistant district attorney.

Above left: *Telly Savalas in his first film role as Gunnison, the policeman who is determined to get the young killers off the street. This was the first of five films Lancaster was to do with Frankenheimer.*

Above: *Stanley Kristien, Shelley Winters and Lancaster.*

Left: *Frankenheimer discusses the above scene with the actors. Winters plays a former girlfriend of the prosecutor (Lancaster) and the mother of one of the accused murderers. She tries to convince her son to tell the truth.*

"If it's violence you want, The Young Savages *has it."*

—New York Daily News (5/25/61)

ages. I thought he was very good in the movie, but we just didn't get along. He hated the idea of doing the movie. He'd just bought *Elmer Gantry* and he was about to do *Birdman of Alcatraz.* He was working with the writer of *Birdman*, Guy Trosper, and he resented being called to the set do a scene for *our* movie.

I'd read the Thomas Gaddis book and I'd always wanted to do *Birdman* on *Playhouse 90.* In those days I was arrogant enough to think I could do anything. How I'd have handled the birds I've no idea, but the whole thing became academic because the Bureau of Prisons told CBS they would get no cooperation at all. Then Burt's company acquired the rights, and his star power got the picture off the ground.

I'd told Harold Hecht, who was producing *The Young Savages* and was going to produce *Birdman*, that I'd love to do it. He teased me along by saying he and Burt would discuss it. Then halfway through the film Burt and I had an argument and I wouldn't back down and it ended badly. Hecht said, "You just blew any chance you ever had of doing *Birdman.*"

They hired an Englishman, Charles Crichton, who had done *The Lavender Hill Mob* with Alec Guinness.

So I cut *The Young Savages* together and did all the usual post-production stuff and went back to New York.

I'd hardly gotten back to New York when Hecht called me and said, "Look, there's a problem with the picture."

I said, "There's no problem with the picture. Don't screw around with it, just release it the way I cut it and there'll be no problem."

"No, no," he said. "We've got a real problem with the picture and you've *got* to come back out and fix it."

Well, by then I was separated and the last thing I wanted to do was go back to California, because there was a chance I could get stuck with an alimony-child support thing I was immune to in New York. So I said, "Okay, I'll come out for a weekend under an assumed name. Get me a ticket as John Michael, which is my middle name. I'll come out and look at the picture but basically I guarantee you there's nothing wrong with it."

This was November of 1960 and I had a date to go to the Giants football game that Sunday with a woman I'd started seeing named Evans Evans. And the whole trip happened so fast I forgot to tell her I was going to California. It's a wonder she forgave me, but we got married a little later and we've been married a long time.

When I got to California, Lancaster, Hecht and Guy Trosper were at LAX to meet me. Burt said, "I knew you'd never come if I called you, so we got you out here under false pretenses. But I loved what you did with the movie. I saw it last week and I think it's brilliant. We're getting rid of the director on *Birdman* and we want you to direct the picture."

Crichton didn't have another big success until *A Fish Called Wanda* many years later.

Birdman of Alcatraz

BIRDMAN OF ALCATRAZ (United Artists, 1962).

Birdman *must have been a terrific challenge in every way.*

It was, and one of the reasons was because I'd had no preparation. I said I didn't want to take another guy's job. Burt said he was gone; they were going to replace him and wanted to replace him with me. They'd even worked out the details with my agents at the Morris office. So I checked in to the Chateau Marmont and read the script.

I told Lancaster "This script is four and a half hours long. It's called *Birdman of Alcatraz* but they don't find the birds until page seventy-five." Burt and Trosper said, "We had the picture timed, and it comes out to a little over two hours and fifteen or twenty minutes. And that's what we're going to shoot. Take it or leave it."

So on Monday I went to work, and on the second shot I fired the cameraman and

Burt Lancaster and Frankenheimer confer on the confining set that helped the director shoot *Birdman of Alcatraz* (1962) in continuity. The film inspired John L. Scott to write in the *Los Angeles Times* (7/4/62) that "John Frankenheimer's incisive direction is his best to date for the large screen."

brought in my own cameraman, Bernard Guffey. We got no cooperation at all from the Bureau of Prisons. We couldn't film at Alcatraz and had to build that.

We shot the whole thing in continuity, right from the beginning. Because it was all in such a confined space, you could do it in continuity. And Burt's aging process had to be very carefully choreographed, which made the continuity vital.

Burt had a full head of hair, so we had him play the younger Robert Stroud with his own hair. Then as he aged we shaved his head in the classic pattern of male baldness and used gradually thinning toupees, which were brilliantly conceived by a guy named Bob Schiffer.

Working with the birds was very, very tough. I found out that there's no such thing as a trained bird, only a hungry bird. And we just had to wait, and wait, and wait. Late in the movie we found a wonderful

guy named Ray Berwick, who really was able to train the birds to some extent and we re-did a lot stuff we'd already done.

But the movie was nothing but problems, and finally we were going to film the exterior of Alcatraz. There were rumors that the guards had orders to fire if we got too close, because the Bureau of Prisons felt so strongly about, or against, the film. I couldn't believe it, because it would have been terrific publicity for the picture, and we weren't living in Nazi Germany, for God's sake.

Still, everybody was very nervous. The producer, Harold Hecht, was notoriously tight on below the line costs—production costs—and his production manager, Gil Kurland, went right along with him. They rented a horrible boat, with a single engine, for us to shoot from. Lancaster insisted that Hecht go along with us on the boat, to be sure that I didn't go completely berserk and

 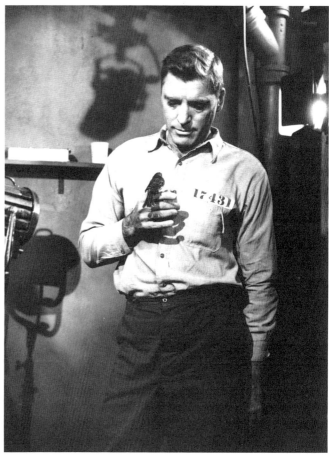

Lancaster as Robert Stroud, a man who spent more than fifty years in Federal prisons.

Birdman of Alcatraz *takes about the knottiest premise ever given a story-teller—make a story out of a man who spends 43 years in solitary confinement!—and turns it into an exciting, engrossing, unique film experience. . .*

But where is the 'audience identification' with a murderer. . . who spends his whole adult life in prison? Well. . . Identification is not with externals but with interior life of mind and spirit. . . In some sense almost every man feels himself imprisoned unjustly.

. . .Whether the film story is completely accurate is as immaterial as questioning Zola's attitude about Dreyfus. The dramatic legend . . . is superbly handled in (Guy) Trosper's screenplay, Frankenheimer's direction and the portrait of Stroud enacted by Burt Lancaster."

—The Hollywood Reporter (6/18/62)

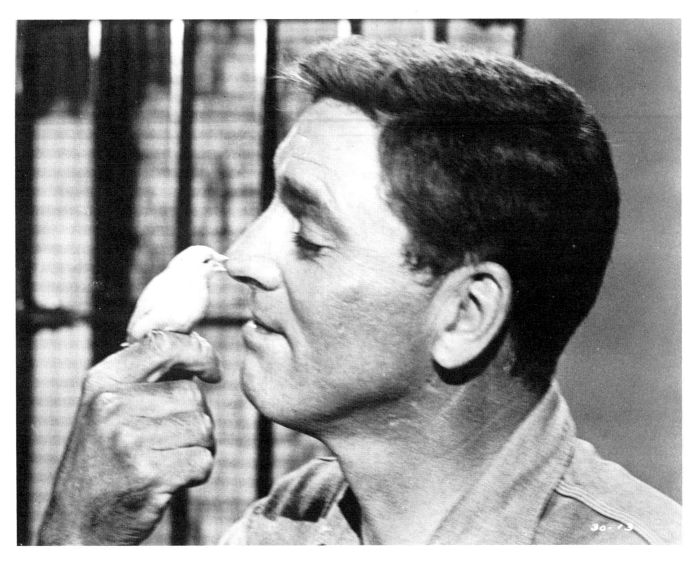

"Some of the most poignant sequences in the film deal with Lancaster and his birds, starting when he discovers and nurses back to health an injured sparrow, and continuing through his breeding of canaries and writing a 'Digest of Bird Diseases'."

—Los Angeles Times (7/4/62)

try to land on Alcatraz or something equally bizarre. I think Burt thought I might really try to do something like that.

So now we are on the water, filming Alcatraz, and the engine conks out. The tide is bringing us closer and closer to the island. Hecht is not only seasick, he is screaming that we're all going to die.

I said, "A, we are not going to die, and B, if you're so concerned about living, why didn't you rent us a boat with two engines?"

And at that moment, I'm damned if the guards didn't start shouting over their loudspeakers, "Film company, if you come any closer we are going to fire." They didn't know our engine had conked out. But at the last minute, they got the engine running again and we moved off.

There were a lot of good people in the picture—Neville Brand, Betty Field, Thelma Ritter. And Telly Savalas. In *The Young Savages*, I'd wanted a wonderful actor named John Randolph to play Lancaster's detective sidekick. But I got a call from United Artists saying I couldn't use him because he was a Communist. UA was supposed to be a studio that had no blacklist, but they blacklisted Randolph—ten days before we were going to shoot. Then the casting director, Joyce Selznick, said, "I want you to meet this English teacher from Forest Hills High School."

I said, "Listen, I'm about to direct a movie with one of the biggest and most difficult stars in Hollywood. This guy has to be his sidekick and I want an actor with a mile of credits and a lot of experience, not an English teacher from Forest Hills."

I couldn't shake her, and finally I met him. It was Telly. I hired him and he was wonderful in the movie. We cast him in *Birdman*, and the picture really made his career.

Lancaster was sensational in the movie, of course, and this time he and I got along,

Lancaster with Neville Brand, who plays his longtime prison guard.

Telly Savalas as a fellow inmate with Lancaster.

Thelma Ritter and Lancaster. Ritter played Stroud's domineering mother who persuaded Mrs. Woodrow Wilson to have her son's death sentence commuted.

JF rehearsing Ritter and Lancaster.

Lancaster with Betty Field, who portrayed the fellow bird-lover he marries.

Something For The Birds: *Burt Lancaster and Telly Savalas were both nominated for Academy Awards for their performances in* Birdman of Alcatraz. *Lancaster lost the Best Actor Oscar to Gregory Peck for* To Kill A Mockingbird; *Savalas saw Supporting Actor honors fly to Ed Begley for his role in* Sweet Bird of Youth. *In the Best Supporting Actress category, Thelma Ritter was competing with Angela Lansbury—also up for work in a Frankenheimer film* (The Manchurian Candidate).

"Birdman of Alcatraz *was something I'd wanted to do when I was doing live television. As a matter of fact, at one time we owned the rights at CBS and the Bureau of Prisons said to the network, 'If you do this, we'll never cooperate with anything again on anything that you* might want to do.' As I look back at it, it was a godsend that we didn't try to do that show live—I mean, the birds would have been up in the rafters as soon as we finished the first commercial.*"
—John Frankenheimer*

"There are few actors, and Lancaster is one of the few, who can portray credibly a combination of physical force and intellectual stature."
—The Hollywood Reporter (6/18/62)

Both Frankenheimer and Lancaster hoped that the film would aid Stroud's release, with Lancaster actively lecturing on behalf of the real Birdman's parole.

"Often in an actor's tour-de-force portrayal, the power and the guidance of the director is forgotten . . . but in Birdman of Alcatraz, I shall always remember John Frankenheimer's masterful direction—it's 'Oscar' quality!"
—Jonah Ruddly
London Daily Mail

Karl Malden listens as the director makes a point. Malden received critical praise as Shoemaker, the stringent Warden who relentlessly worked towards keeping Stroud imprisoned.

Opposite page: *Actress Evans Evans, soon to be Mrs. John Frankenheimer, accompanies the director to the Acapulco Film Festival, in 1962, where* Birdman of Alcatraz *was one of the featured films.*

except that I kept saying, "I know we're long." And everybody would say, "No, no; we're fine."

I cut the movie together and I told the guys it was ready. So they asked me to book a projection room and I got one for 3:30. This was at the old Columbia Studios on Gower. Hecht said he had a cocktail date at the Brown Derby on Vine at 6:30.

"And a dinner date after that?" I asked him. Yes, he had a dinner date.

I told him to cancel the cocktail date *and* the dinner date.

The picture really *was* four and a half hours long, which is what I told Hecht it was going to be. He and Lancaster and the writer looked at it and said, "My God, this is terrible. You have to cut it."

I said, "You can't cut it. The way it's written he doesn't find the birds for an hour and twenty-five minutes. He's got to find the birds in the first fifteen to twenty minutes."

They said, "You'll have to edit it."

I said, "The way the script is constructed, I can't. You're going to have to rewrite it and re-shoot it. You'll have to go to UA and get the money." Only Burt's star power would've persuaded UA to put up the extra million-plus, but they did, because they wanted a continuing association with him.

Lancaster had been offered a part in *Judgment at Nuremberg*, and he didn't know what to do. I said, "You go do *Judgment* and we'll re-write the script." That's what we did. Then we went back and re-shot the whole first part of the movie. As it happened, Burt now had to wear a toupee over his own hair. There's not a frame of the movie in which you see Burt's own hair. But the result was the movie you see.

I was never allowed to meet the birdman, Robert Stroud. Lancaster finally saw him after the movie was completed. And Stroud himself was never allowed to see the movie. He died without having seen it.

ALL FALL DOWN (MGM, 1962).

Above: (from left) Novelist James Leo Herlihy, whose book was the basis of the screenplay by William Inge (2nd from left), Eva Marie Saint and Frankenheimer.

You'd have thought my own little chronicle of rejection might be over, but not so. When I did "Days of Wine and Roses" with Fred Coe on *Playhouse 90,* Jack Lemmon wasn't available, so we cast Cliff Robertson. After we did a *Playhouse* live at six-thirty from California for the East, we'd go someplace to look at it when it was rebroadcast here at nine-thirty.

Martin Manulis, with whom I'd done maybe a hundred television shows and with whom I was very friendly, asked me to watch the "Wine and Roses" show at his house. I did, and he loved it. He'd just signed a contract with 20th Century-Fox and he said, "My God, I'd like to make this as a movie, with you. Do you think we could get it?"

I said, "I don't know if Fred Coe wants to do it, and I don't know if J.P. Miller will sell it to you. But I'll try."

I went to Miller, who distrusted Manulis. But I said, "No, no, no, he's wonderful." So he sold it to Manulis, and we were going to do it with Lemmon. But when I came back from shooting exteriors on *Birdman,* I found a note from Manulis under my door. saying, "Before you read this in the trades tomorrow, you're not doing the movie. They've hired Blake Edwards." Strike Two! I've never gotten over it; it's colored my relationship with Martin ever since. I'd brought the movie to him, and he hadn't fought for me. I'd worked with Lemmon on *Playhouse 90.* In fact, we'd done one of the most successful *Playhouse 90s* of all, "Face of a Hero," with John Houseman producing.

But then Houseman, with whom I'd done that *Playhouse 90,* called me and said, "Dear boy, I've just signed a three-picture deal with MGM. I have three projects and you can do any one of the three you want." One of them was *Two Weeks in Another Town.* I forget what the second was, and the third was *All Fall Down,* the James Leo Herlihy book. William Inge had written the screenplay. I loved it and that's the one I chose to do. I started it right after *Birdman.*

Meantime, you're working with the hot, young Warren Beatty.

Looking back on it, *All Fall Down* was probably one of the two or three best movies for me. It was a terrific movie to make. Wonderful cast: Warren, Brandon de Wilde, Angela Lansbury, Karl Malden, Eva Marie Saint, with that script by William Inge and Houseman producing. It was the second picture I did with the cinematographer Lionel Lindon, and he was very good.

Inge was a lovely man, really a chronic depressive, always concerned about his talent and everything else. He was so delicate, you always felt, My God, you have to protect him.

Evans, my wife to be, played the bar girl in the film. Inge knew her because she'd created the role of Flirt Conroy in his play,

Madame Spivy, former nightclub-owner-turned-actress, receives instructions from John Frankenheimer.

"All Fall Down is an absorbing melodrama of tenderness and violence that explores a young man's coming of age through the jolting knowledge that his idol is clay from the waist down. John Houseman's production, directed with verve and insight by John Frank-enheimer, has an exceptionally interesting cast, the kind of mixture that creates its own chemistry parallel to the values of the film itself."

—The Hollywood Reporter (3/26/62)

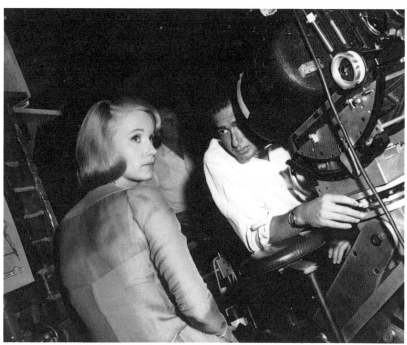

Eva Marie Saint with the director.

"Eva Marie Saint brings her uniquely ethereal characteristics to the part of Echo O'Brien. . . and in a sense All Fall Down is peculiarly her picture, for Echo's unguarded sensibility seems to be at the heart of the drama."

—Lionel Godfrey
Films and Filming (1966)

Dark at the Top of the Stairs, with Kazan, so he was friendly with her. John Houseman wanted Beatty from the start. Bill Inge knew him very well, having worked with him on *Splendor in the Grass*. Inge had also known him from Broadway, and he agreed that Warren was the one we should use. Warren was very hot.

The rest of it was pretty easy to cast. I think it was Houseman's idea to cast Angela Lansbury. I wasn't convinced she could do the American accent, but she certainly could. With *All Fall Down* and then *Manchurian Candidate*, I really made her Mother of the Year.

I worked with Karl Malden on *Birdman*, and I got him, Brandon de Wilde for the young boy and Eva Marie Saint, whom I really wanted to work with, as Echo.

You actually shot the film in Key West, didn't you?

I did the first part of the film in Key West, although we actually shot the last half of the film on the MGM backlot before we went to Key West. I won a big fight with MGM about shooting in Key West. They didn't want me to because they worried that they would lose control of the project—or lose control of me. I convinced them I could shoot it quicker on location than I could in the studio, and they bought it.

Houseman fought for me on it. He was a wonderful producer and we became life-long friends. I was living in a tiny rented house on Beverly Drive, out by the reservoir. One day I went to lunch at his house in Malibu, a gorgeous day.

I said, "John, you're so lucky to live out here." He looked at me in that way only he could look at somebody and he said, "Dear boy, luck has nothing to do with it. I live out here because I wish to live out here." I used that line later in *Grand Prix*. He said, "You could live out here if you wished." The rental agent for the Malibu Colony was

From left: Karl Malden, Angela Lansbury, Brandon de Wilde, William Inge, Frankenheimer, Warren Beatty and Eva Marie Saint at script readthrough.

coming to lunch, and after lunch she showed me a house that was available, and I rented it that afternoon. In the end, Evans and I lived in the Colony for thirty-two years.

It was a wonderful experience. Even in those days, Warren was very, very demanding of himself, wanting as many takes as he could get. We had a relatively modest shooting schedule, but Warren and I came out of it very good friends.

My pal from the Times, *Dan Sullivan, is doing a biography of Inge and he heard a story about your locking Warren in a jail cell. What was all that about?*

As I say, Warren and I got along terribly well on *All Fall Down*. And we were shooting in a jail, literally in a real jail in Key West and, just as a joke, I locked Warren in the cell on the last shot and wouldn't let him out. We all left and he languished there for about two hours. It wasn't an act of retribution; it was honest to God fun, and we're still good friends.

The sadness is that MGM dumped the movie. They promised Houseman they would take great care of it. But they had *The Four Horsemen of the Apocalypse* on their hands, and it died. They had all those big theaters booked, so they put our little movie in those big houses.

On the set of The Manchurian Candidate *is John Frankenheimer (standing under the light). Seated are Henry Silva, Madame Spivy, George Axelrod (the writer/co-producer) and Laurence Harvey. That's Sinatra standing with a pipe in his mouth.*

The Manchurian Candidate

At the same time George Axelrod, with whom I'd been working before I got shut out of *Breakfast at Tiffany's*, called me up and said, "I want to work with you a lot. Have you ever read a book by Richard Condon called *The Manchurian Candidate*?" I hadn't. He was living at Sixty-third and Madison and there was a bookstore across the street, so we bought two copies of the book and sat in separate rooms at his apartment and read it. That afternoon we called George's agent, Irving Lazar in California, and by that evening we owned the rights. We put up $5,000 apiece of our own money against a $75,000 purchase price. And we found out that almost every major studio in town had turned it down and that certain actors, like Robert Mitchum, had been approached unsuccessfully. But George knew Sinatra and had heard that he'd been interested in it. So as I started *All Fall Down*, he was working on the script and we were both trying to get Sinatra interested in acting in it.

You once said that your obituaries would undoubtedly lead off with the fact that you directed The Manchurian Candidate. *And here you were, ready to begin it.*

Yes, George and I were preparing it. But as I said the property had been turned down by every studio in town. But George got Sinatra, and once Sinatra said he wanted to do it, the rest was easy. United Artists backed it. George moved his family out to California and he and I worked on the script some more.

The question was, who would play Raymond? We tossed around a lot of names. Tony Curtis, everybody. We came up with Laurence Harvey, because Kennedy was president and he talked with that strange accent of his, so we thought we could get away with Harvey's English accent.

Sinatra wanted Lucille Ball for the mother. Having worked with Angela Lansbury on *All Fall Down*, I wanted her very badly. I'll tell you about that.

There are some interesting things about the making of the movie. George Axelrod and I had a "Go" movie, and we had a cast and a start date. But we knew it was a movie we couldn't make.

Couldn't make? Why not?

In the book—and we'd used it in the screenplay—Marco, the Sinatra character,

Below: *Frank Sinatra*

THE MANCHURIAN CANDIDATE (United Artists, 1962).

"John Frankenheimer's direction (is). . . exciting in the style of Orson Welles when he was making Citizen Kane. . *."*

—*Bosley Crowther*
New York Times (10/25/62)

Angela Lansbury (above with Laurence Harvey) was nominated for an Academy Award for Best Supporting Actress for her portrayal of the ruthless, scheming mother of Raymond Shaw (Harvey), who will stop at nothing to realize her Machiavellian ideals. Lansbury was actually only one year older than Harvey.

orders the execution of the mother and Johnny Iselin. And you find out that he had ordered them to be shot. We didn't want to make a movie where the hero solves the problem by ordering a murder. Totally immoral. What we had to do was rejigger the plot so that Marco didn't know how the scheme worked. We worked it so that Marco was questioning Raymond when Raymond was summoned by his mother. But Marco still didn't know the specifics of the assassination plan. His problem was how to find Raymond in Madison Square Garden.

Today they would call it an *hommage.* In those days we called it a rip-off. I ripped off Hitchcock's *Foreign Correspondent.* Joel McCrea locates the Nazis in the windmill because all the windmills are turning in one direction except the one where the Nazis are, which is electrically driven.

All the lights in Madison Square Garden went out, except one, which is the booth where Raymond was. Sinatra put two and two together, and ran to the light, and that was that. Thanks, Hitch.

For the coda with the Congressional Medal of Honor stuff, Axelrod took the wording right out of the citations for the actual Congressional Medal of Honor.

How was Sinatra to work with? Over the years he developed a reputation for being difficult.

He had a terrible reputation. I told Axelrod that I was afraid of him and that I had a big problem with him. The stories were so awful, that he kept whole crews waiting for hours, that he walked off sets, and so on, that I even told George, "I'm not sure I even want to make this movie with Frank Sinatra."

George said, "Dear boy, I've moved my whole family out here from New York to do this picture and I'm going to do this picture with you or without you. If it's without

"Every once in a rare while a film comes along that 'works' in all departments, with story, production and performance so well blended that the end effect is one of nearly complete satisfaction. Such is The Manchurian Candidate, *George Axelrod and John Frankenheimer's jazzy, hip screen translation of Richard Condon's bestselling novel. . . One of the brilliant achievements of the film is the way Axelrod and Frankenheimer have been able to blend the diverse moods, including the tender and explosively funny as well as the satiric and brutally shocking."*

—Vincent Canby
Variety (10/17/62)

you, we'll buy out your interest." But then he said, "If you've got a problem with Sinatra, why don't you make an appointment to go see him and thrash it out."

I'd met him just once before, when he was deciding to do the picture. George and I had financed our own trip to Miami, where he was singing at the Fontainbleu, to see him. We were financing a lot of stuff in those days, and I was paying a lot of alimony and it was tough.

We went to his suite and he opened the door, and there was that big grin of his, and he said, "God I love this project and I fought desperately to be able to do it." George took me aside and said, "You just keep out of his way and keep quiet the whole time you're here. I'll do the same

thing and we've got him."

We got him. So I made the appointment and went up to his house off Coldwater Canyon. We'd done the deal, but we hadn't even come to discuss the casting of Angela Lansbury yet, and I was about to raise all this other stuff.

I said, "Frank, I've got a couple of problems. One is that you have a reputation for treating directors badly, eating them alive, of keeping everybody waiting, of doing things in one take and refusing to do any more—"

Frank interrupted me. He said, "Look, let me tell you something, John. I really admire your work and I want to make this movie with you. Now let me explain a few things about myself. First of all, I'm an

"A pleasant surprise is Janet Leigh as a sweet, swinging N.Y. career girl. The actress only has two or three scenes, but they count. One especially, on a. . . train on which she picks up a semi-hysterical Sinatra, registers as one of the great love scenes since Bogart and Bacall first tossed non-sequiturs at one another in To Have and Have Not.

—Vincent Canby
Variety (10/17/62)

Frankenheimer directing Sinatra and Janet Leigh.

insomniac. I don't get to sleep until five or six in the morning. When we're not on location, if you could start at eleven o'clock or noon, the way they do in French studios, I promise you that I'll be there and I'll be on time."

I said, "You've got it."

"Now, as far as the one take business is concerned, I'm a performer, I'm an entertainer, not an actor. I'm better on the first take, honest to God. But if you want, I'll keep doing stuff as long as you want me to, but I'm telling you now, I'm better on the first take."

Then I said, "Frank, I feel very strongly about Angela Lansbury for the mother." He said, "I feel just as strong about Lucille Ball, and if you and I were to go to the mat with United Artists, I'd win because I'm making more money than you are." I said, "What about coming to see a rough cut of the movie I've just finished. If you don't like Angela Lansbury in it, I won't say another word." So he came over to MGM—on time—and watched *All Fall Down*, and when the lights came up, he said, "That's the lady."

He couldn't have been more cooperative, and the biggest problem he had wasn't his fault.

His big scene in the picture is his confrontation with Raymond when he holds up a deck of cards and they're all the Queen of Hearts. Marco has figured out the trigger, and he debriefs Raymond, de-brainwashes him. And Frank was incredible in his close-up. We embraced afterwards, he was that good.

But when I looked at the dailies the next day, the close-up was out of focus. The only thing that was in focus were the oak leaf insignias on Frank's shoulders. The assistant cameraman had made a mistake.

Going to tell Frank—he didn't watch the dailies—was the longest walk of my life. He was crushed; he almost cried. "My God,

"It was one of the best film experiences I've ever had. President Kennedy was supportive of the project and, when I told him what we were planning, he was most interested in the casting. . ."

—Frank Sinatra

Frankenheimer directing Barry Kelly and Sinatra.

Frankenheimer, who loses weight when he makes a movie, once described The Manchurian Candidate *as "a fifteen pound picture."*

The director in intense discussion with two of his main players, Angela Lansbury above, and Frank Sinatra below.

what can we do," he said. I told him the only thing we could do was re-shoot it.

We re-scheduled the shoot, but he had laryngitis so we couldn't do it. We re-scheduled again and he was so uptight about it he was physically sick to his stomach before we began. We did three or four takes, and none of them was really any good. We scheduled it again and did some more takes. But it wasn't there; he couldn't do it. So I finally said, "Screw it. I'm going to use the one that's out of focus." I put it in the movie, and it becomes Raymond looking at him, kind of brain-washing *him*.

I got the greatest reviews of my life for that shot. Critics called me a genius because I was using this brainwashed guy's point of view, by being out of focus on Sinatra. Now you know what really happened.

Had The Manchurian Candidate *actually been released before Kennedy was shot?*

Oh, yes. It had been released and played itself out. There were some distributors who wanted to exploit the movie and re-release it right after the assassination, but we said no.

Ironically, United Artists didn't have any faith in it when it was first released. They put all their ad money in *The Pride and the Passion*, which also had Sinatra, and Cary Grant and Sophia Loren. Our picture was a moderate success, and then the reviews came out, and they were classic, and it did some more business before it was played out.

There was quite a long time when it couldn't be seen at all.

There was. What happened was that, to appease Frank, because we had all the creative control, we gave him ownership of the right to re-release after seven years. That amounted to nothing in those days, because there wasn't any re-release after seven years. A picture played on television

Frankenheimer, Harvey, Sinatra and screenwriter/co-producer George Axelrod.

and it was over. Nobody knew about those ancillary markets.

Through their creative accounting, United Artists had us in a loss position all those years. They had cross-collateralized *Manchurian* against every other Frank Sinatra picture they did. So even though *Manchurian* had done fairly well, there were zero profits.

Now, lo and behold, along come cable and cassettes, and UA suddenly announces that they want to re-release the picture on video, et cetera. And Sinatra's lawyers and George's and my lawyers said, "No way. You put us in a position where we stand to make some money out of it, and we'll let you do it. Not otherwise." But through countless conversations they wouldn't do it. Finally a new management came into

play long enough to sit down and renegotiate as we had demanded.

Then Sinatra said, "I really believe in this movie and I want it to come out under the right auspices. I want it re-released in theaters." The UA guys said there was no way they would do that; it had been on television and it would be crazy to put it in theaters again. Frank said, "I'll tell you what. I'll put up two million of my own money as a guarantee that the picture is going to do okay, and I want the money spent on prints and advertising." Well, with that kind of a guarantee, UA gave it a big re-release theatrically, and the rest is history. Thanks to Sinatra, on screen and off. Frank steps forward in the crunch. We had one of the best relationships I've ever had with an actor and we remain good friends.

SEVEN DAYS IN MAY (Paramount, 1964).

Seven Days in May *is another of your films that has had a long afterlife, like* Manchurian. *How did it come about?*

I'd just finished *Manchurian*, and George Axelrod and I were both involved in the American Civil Liberties Union. At that time the ACLU had an idea it wanted to do a television show of some kind. They contacted George about writing it and me about directing it. They said it was going to be produced by someone named Edward Lewis, who was Kirk Douglas's partner in his production company.

George and I went to see him, and Eddie Lewis and I got along famously well. He called me a little later and said, "I don't know if this ACLU thing is going to happen. But I've just read a book I've liked, and I'd like to go into business with you. It's got a wonderful part for Kirk. If you go half, I'll go half."

The book, of course, was *Seven Days in May*, which was written by Charles Bailey II and Fletcher Knebel, who was a writer for *Look* magazine. We each put up half of the option money, the Kirk Douglas Company and me, which was quite a stretch for me in those days. Lewis to produce, I to direct and Douglas to play the general, James Matoon Scott.

We hired Rod Serling to do the script, and we each put up half of that, but we gave Serling points in the picture, so he did it for short money. Eddie and I went on to become partners and we made several pictures in later years.

The book became the number one best-seller in the country. We were sitting there with it, and we had Kirk Douglas, who was a big star at the height of his fame at that time. We brought in [Nathan E.] Ned Young, the blacklisted writer who co-wrote *The Defiant Ones*, to do a polish on the script.

Kirk was always going to play the gen-

"This was the film that really marked what I wanted to do in films and how I wanted to make movies. In other words, I wanted to initiate the project, I wanted to have full control, I never wanted to go back to being hired as a director again."

—John Frankenheimer

Opposite page: *Frankenheimer and Kirk Douglas.*

75

"*Seven Days could easily have been played for melodrama, but by playing it cool Franken-heimer and his big-name cast have . . . heightened its effectiveness . . . the role (of President) was wisely entrusted to Fredric March, a powerful scene being his personal showdown with (Gen. James M.) Scott, played with fanatical glint by Burt Lancaster . . . Frankenheimer—who knows the medium!—makes clever dramatic use of tele-vision sets to intensify his climaxes.*"

—Philip K. Scheuer
Los Angeles Times (2/5/64)

eral. But then he wanted Burt Lancaster in the picture, because they'd had such success together with *Gunfight at the OK Corral* and so on. He said, "I really want him in the picture," and I said, "Well, I don't." It got complicated because my new agent-managers, Freddie Fields and David Begelman, also represented Paul Newman and wanted him to play Colonel Cason.

Kirk kept harping on it and one day he called and said, "I beg you, beg you, beg you. I will give up playing the general and play the colonel and Burt can play the general."

I said, "Kirk, the colonel is a lousy part. The colonel turns in his boss; he's a fake." And Kirk said, "No, no, no, no, I'd be great at it." I said, "All right, but remember what you're saying, Kirk."

So I had to call Freddie Fields and get out of the commitment to Paul Newman, which I'm afraid has soured my relationship with Paul over the years.

For the rest of it, Fredric March was

"The performances are excellent down the line, under the taut and penetrating directorial guidance of John Frankenheimer."
—Variety (2/5/64)

Douglas with Martin Balsam.

Douglas with Ava Gardner.

(L to r): Balsam, George Macready, Douglas, Fredric March and Edmond O'Brien.

always our first choice for the President. Ava Gardner was given us by Ray Stark, thanks to the fact that his Seven Arts was a partner in the film and Ava was under contract to Seven Arts. We used her for a week. She was not in good shape and it was very difficult.

Marty Balsam I'd wanted to work with always. He'd been blacklisted at CBS. He could work at NBC but not at CBS. Eddie O'Brien I'd already done three big television shows with, including "The Comedian," for which we won an Emmy. He was a dear friend, and there was never anybody else we had in mind for the Southern senator but Eddie.

Fredd Wayne I'd seen in other stuff and wanted him. George Macready I thought was great in *Paths of Glory* and I wanted him very badly. Lancaster had hepatitis and couldn't join us until halfway through the shooting. Fredric March came in knowing every line. He was such an example to everybody, the best actor I've ever worked

with and the greatest gentleman. We became lifelong friends out of that movie.

It was a picture that went terribly well. We rehearsed for two weeks and shot it in fifty days. The only big problem was that, just as I'd warned him, Douglas realized more and more that the colonel was a lousy part, much inferior to Burt's. One day in his dressing room in his undershorts he launched a tirade at me, including the fact that I did not seem to know a major star when I saw one. I heard him out, there was nothing to be done about the part, and he never mentioned it again.

On the other hand, Lancaster and I became close friends during the making of *Seven Days in May*. I'd always admired him and on that film I really liked him. I think one of the best scenes I ever directed was between Burt and Fredric March in the President's Oval Office, when Lancaster is telling him he has to resign, and March

won't. There you had two great actors at the top of their game, because Lancaster is a great movie actor. I don't think I ever directed anyone who had the same kind of presence on the screen—and off the screen—as Burt. On the screen you couldn't take your eyes off him, and when he entered a room everybody knew it, not because he was overbearing but because they felt his presence.

Right after it, Burt was going to go on and do the third of those pictures that he had to do for UA for $150,000. He said, "How am I going to get along with that guy Arthur Penn?" I said, "Frankly, I don't think you're going to get along with Arthur Penn at all. I know Arthur Penn, and I know you, and to me it's a very bad match." Burt said, "Oh, well, screw it. I'm going to go over there for ten weeks and keep my mouth shut, and do it." The name of the picture was *The Train*.

O'Brien, who was nominated for an Academy Award as Best Supporting Actor, and March.

Opposite page: JF with Fredric March preparing to film the press conference.

THE TRAIN, (United Artists, 1965).

Even more than the others, I should think that The Train *confirmed that you were as much at home with large-scale logistical productions as with intimate dramas like* All Fall Down.

It changed my life in a lot of ways. I was in the last stages of a divorce by that time, being chased around California by private detectives. And the next thing I knew Lancaster was calling me from Paris and saying, "Can you come over and direct this picture?" Penn was out.

It seemed like a perfect time and a great idea to go to Paris, and I did.

It was like *Birdman* all over again. When I landed, Burt and the producer were at de Gaulle to meet me. And they had this script, which was 250 pages long, and unshootable. The producer, Jules Bricken, who eventually left the picture although he kept the producing credit, said, "You're going to love this crew." I said, "Why am I going to love this crew?" He said, "Well, they're all wonderful guys, and we have someone write their names on the back of their shirts."

I said, "Well, I've got news for you. You need a different type of writer. You need a writer who can write a script because there's nothing here that can be made."

It was that kind of atmosphere when we got to the Georges Cinq Hotel. The head of United Artists in Europe, Ilya Lopert, was waiting, and his opening line was, "Let's talk about your co-director."

"What co-director?" I said, or possibly screamed.

"Didn't anybody tell you about this?" Lopert said.

Lancaster started to laugh.

I said, "No, nobody ever told me anything about this. But I'll tell you something, there's never been and never going to be a co-director on any picture of mine."

Lopert said, "But this is a French subsidy picture, and a French director has to have co-credit."

I said, "No way. Forget it."

He said, "You don't understand. The co-director has to do the French version."

I said, "What do you mean, the French version?"

Lopert said, "When you do the English version then he will do the French version."

I said, "Do you mean Burt Lancaster is going to do his lines in French?"

He said, "No, no, no. When the French actors do their lines then they will do the French version. Burt will be dubbed later."

I said, "No, you have it wrong. *They'll* be dubbed later. We're not doing a French version."

"But we have to have the French subsidy," Lopert said.

I said, "You know what you can do with your French subsidy."

"You can't do that," he said.

"I'm going back to the States," I said. It was now four in the morning. I picked up the phone and said, "Get me TWA." As I did that Lopert said, "Is there *anything* that might persuade you to accept this French co-production with a French co-director?"

Four in the morning, but I still felt pretty sharp. Burt and I went off in a corner and consulted. Then I came back and said, "Okay, here's what would persuade me. One, I never meet him. He can never come to the set. He can never direct a foot of film. He spends the entire film at Fouquet's or wherever else he likes. The French version will consist of two close-ups that I will do where somebody says 'Oui' instead of 'Yes.' Then you can say you did a French version and then we'll dub it.

"Two, my name goes above the title as big as Lancaster's: 'John Frankenheimer's *The Train*.' Third, the co-director's name appears in the smallest possible print you can find."

He said, "Okay."

". . .John Frankenheimer has a way with obsession. . ."
—Variety (2/26/65)

The Train, *derived from a true incident, was based on action more than words—what Frankenheimer called a real "movie-movie." In one scene where Lancaster is supposed to kill a German guard, the script had it done with* dialogue. *But when Frankenheimer filmed the scene, he shot it through a window—and you can't hear a word of what is said.*

—Motion Picture Herald (7/22/64)

Frankenheimer and Lancaster discuss script.

"There was a conflict of personalities, a conflict over the type of film being made. I think the director, Arthur Penn, wanted to do one film, the producer and Lancaster wanted to do another. . . I think it was a difference in concept more than anything else."

—John Frankenheimer

I said, "*Next*, I want final cut. Total, utter, final cut."

"All right."

"And, last but far from least, I want a silver Ferrari 250 2+2 with red seats in it outside this hotel by five o'clock tomorrow."

Lopert said, "We can't possibly do that."

I said, "Okay" and picked up the phone again and said, "Get me TWA."

He said, "All right, we'll do it."

They called the next day and apologized. They couldn't get the Ferrari to the hotel before seven o'clock. They were having it driven up from Rome.

And indeed you never met your co-director?

Never met him. Didn't even know what his name was. In the French ads, somewhere near the bottom of the page, was his name.

It must be difficult coming into a picture that was begun by somebody else and has been shooting for two weeks or whatever.

It hadn't been shooting for two weeks. It had been shooting for a week and it was a disaster. We didn't use a frame of the film Arthur Penn shot. It was tough because the French crew had all been hired by Penn. They thought I was instrumental in getting him thrown out, which I had nothing to do with.

But now you had the Ferrari and all you had to do was make the picture.

It was called *The Train* and the train didn't leave the station until page 110. It turned out that Lancaster hadn't wanted to have anything to do with fixing the script. He just wanted to do his job and keep out of the way. He'd shot a couple of days with Arthur Penn and they didn't get along well.

"Frankenheimer perched cameras atop swinging cranes, moving tanks and speeding locomotives. He shoved them beneath the wheels of boxcars and loaded them on helicopters. He once suspended the camera from springs for a difficult overhead panning shot, and had the camera hand-carried through the narrow halls of a hotel.

Once an out-of-control locomotive derailed at too high a speed and chewed its way over three of the five cameras filming the sequence. Yet one small camera, placed strategically at the derailment site, captured the entire feeling of excitement, justifying Frankenheimer's use of multiple cameras."
—Motion Picture Herald (7/22/64)

83

THE TRAIN

Burt was just going to see it through. Then the producer asked him his opinion and Burt, being a very honest guy, told him. The result was the phone call.

I brought over Ned Young, who as I said earlier had done *The Defiant Ones*, and Howard Dimsdale, who'd also been a blacklisted writer, to do rewrites on the script. [Ultimately, Franklin Coen, Frank Davis and Walter Bernstein received screen credit as the writers.]

Some locations had been chosen, but nothing had been shot. We closed down the picture. This was August. I'd go out during the day and shoot the train going through Paris and things like that. There was no dialogue involved in any of that stuff and any one-liners that were needed I could make up on the spot.

When I didn't need him at the camera, Burt would be working with the writers after we had all talked.

We realized that the only location that had been chosen that really worked was this abandoned line near Rouen in a little town called Acquigny. As Burt and I said, "We're in agony on the road to ruin."

None of the other locations that had been picked worked, and we realized we had to stay there. So we devised a way for not having to leave Acquigny. We revised history and said the Resistance changed the name of the stations so the train went in a circle and ended up back where it started. Burt and I worked closely on that.

The writers worked in Paris and came out to Normandy twice a week with pages. Burt and I would go over them and then have them translated into French for the crew.

It was a very tough movie to make because for every take you had to have the train back up for two miles, and then you never knew whether the smoke from the engine would be white or black, and obviously the color of the smoke had to match from shot to shot.

Jeanne Moreau with Lancaster.

To get the long tracking shots of the train in motion, Frankenheimer and his crew devised a jeep on flanged wheels which ran along the tracks ahead of the locomotive.

Frankenheimer blocks opening sequence in film with Paul Scofield and Suzanne Flon.

It was hell! Burt and I kept making it up as we went along, improvising on the spot, depending on the topography. We had the guy go up over the hill and slide down and take the spikes out, but it was never in the script. We just made it. It was old-fashioned off the cuff film-making.

In the end, we never did have a finished script.

When we came to the denouement we really didn't know what to do. We knew there had to be the compulsory scene between Paul Scofield and Burt. The way it was written Scofield came down from the train with a gun and confronts Burt, who has a gun.

It's so many years ago now that it's difficult to remember where Burt began and I ended or I began and Burt ended. But we both came to the conclusion that, because of all of cinema history there would be no suspense because if you saw Paul with a gun and Burt with a gun, the audience would just know that Burt was going to blast hell out of him. If Kirk Douglas were playing the part, it would be a different thing. That might be an interesting shoot-out. I said, "But it's not Kirk, it's a guy who's made his living playing Hamlet."

And Burt said, "Why don't we have him talk himself to death?"

I said, "What do you mean?"

"Smashing up the trains. . . (is) every boy's childhood fantasy."

　　　　　　　　　　　　　　—J.F.

"I went back to a preview of The Train *just to catch those train wrecks again. They're glorious and grinding; the real thing; no miniatures."*

　　　　　　　—Philip K. Scheuer
　　　Los Angeles Times (4/25/65)

85

THE TRAIN

Burt said, "Why don't we give him a speech in which what he's doing in a strange way is asking to be shot."

That's what we did. He made that long monologue, and Burt never said a word. At the end, he just looked at him and shot him, because Scofield was really committing suicide. It worked very well. Then we took those close-ups of the crated art and the slaughtered hostages and what we asked, really, was "What is worth more: human life or a work of art?" We made the point that these Resistance guys didn't know who the hell Renoir was. They'd never heard of these paintings, but the original script had them all Bernard Berensons. They weren't doing it for the paintings, they were doing it out of patriotism. The paintings belonged to France and the Resistance didn't want the Germans to get them. Simple as that. The artistic aspect never came into it, and I think that that's what made the picture real.

It was a nightmarish production all the way, I gather, including not least the fact that the weather was beastly.

Terrible problems with the weather. Look, the Allies couldn't invade Normandy until June, and we were trying to shoot this thing in September and October when the fog comes rolling in from the Channel. We absolutely ran out of weather. I hadn't made the decision to shoot in Normandy. That was all done before I got there. It was crazy, because Normandy is notorious for the fog and we were stuck there. There were days when we couldn't get anything done.

We had to close down the picture in November because it was too cold to shoot in Normandy. We kept going up until Christmas shooting interiors in Paris. Then I stayed over there to edit it, so I knew exactly what I had to get when we resumed.

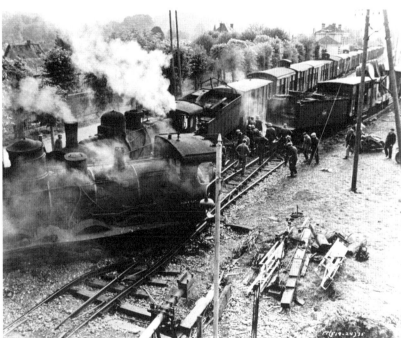

One of the many crashes involving real trains. *Los Angeles Times* critic Scheuer praised their real sound, too.

*"Steam driven trains have often been exciting and photogenic film fodder (*La Roue *of Abel Gance and Buster Keaton's* The General *to name a couple) and it is again true here. . ."*
—Variety (10/2/64)

We invited United Artists to come over and have a look at it. They said, "It seems to us it could use a little more action."

I said, "Well, Burt and I have a great action scene if we can get another six or seven hundred thousand dollars to shoot it. We know exactly what we want to do. We want to have the train delivered to the German colonel and then have it strafed by a Spitfire."

The UA guys said, "You've got it."

The strafing and bombing of the train is the heart of the picture, absolutely unforgettable.

As it turned out, I was almost killed doing that sequence.

We had to do a helicopter shot of the Spitfire strafing the engine first. The topography was that we had a mountain and a tunnel. The train was heading for the tunnel and being strafed by the plane. We needed the helicopter shot right in front of the engine with the plane zooming in at 250 or 300 miles an hour. We had a thousand dynamite caps rigged on each side of the train, so if there was going to be a second take it would have had to be another day.

I'm in the helicopter with the cameraman. We couldn't trust the radio in those days, so I told the cameraman, "Look, if anything happens, you hit me and I'll hit the pilot." The mountain was right there, so I told the helicopter pilot, "If something goes wrong, veer to the left." Then I told the Spitfire pilot, "If you see us veer to the left, you obviously veer to the right." And I told the people on the ground, "If you see the helicopter veer to the left, don't blow the dynamite caps."

We rehearsed very carefully, five times, and the last time we rehearsed an abort, just in case.

We started the shot, the Spitfire was com- ing, the train was moving, the helicopter was moving. Suddenly, just before the shot was supposed to start, the camera operator hit me and I hit the pilot. He panicked. He veered to the *right* instead of to the left. The Spitfire was roaring toward us at 300 miles an hour. I could see the pilot's face and he looked as terrified as as I felt. He missed us by ten feet. If he hadn't we would have all been John Landis statistics. My wife Evans—we'd just been married—was watching on the ground, and she fainted.

But at least the dynamite caps didn't go off prematurely.

But that was only one sequence. The air raid was another colossal operation. I won't ask you to remember all these specifics, but I've just come across a Newsweek *article from the time [April 20, 1964] which said the strafing sequence lasts 50 seconds and involved 140 separate explosions, a ton and a half of TNT and 2,000 gallons of gasoline. Pieces of boxcars went a couple of hundred feet in the air, the locomotive went up in a 1,000 foot cloud of smoke, and the whole thing cost $3,000 a second, although the explosives man, Lee Zavitz, said the whole show would have cost a million dollars in Hollywood.*

Zavitz burned Atlanta for Selznick. He was the best.

We took an old French railroad yard where the company wanted to change the gauge of the rails. We just blew it up for them. The French Army under General de Gaulle's son-in-law put the explosives in place under Zavitz's direction. I'd forgotten how many thousands of pounds of explosives they used. We were in an underground bunker made of huge planks and steel plates when the thing went off. We had something like twelve remote cameras.

One of the accounts said you had a fireball a thousand feet in the air.

Frankenheimer rehearses Lancaster for the showdown scene.

It all went at once. Really spectacular.

Funny, all the problems we had keep coming back to me. I remember we had a stop date on Scofield. He had to leave. So we had two units working with him. I was shooting film eighteen hours a day.

Parenthetically I have to say that Burt Lancaster is the most professional man I've ever known. He expects a tremendous amount from the people he works with, but he gives a tremendous amount. He knows every element of the business. He knows producing; he knows script, camera, acting. Among other things, he's the best stunt man I've ever worked with. He taught me enormous amounts about stunts and action themes. He did most of his own stuff, as you know. He was a great, great athlete.

He helped with every problem we had on the movie. And then, on his one day off, he played golf. When I came back that night from shooting, he was in his room with his head in his hands and steaming towels on his knee. It was swollen like a balloon.

"Frankenheimer's use of locations illustrate once again his eye for telling, pictorial details, the creation of atmosphere, his employment of the weather, and of his cameras which seem to breathe place, time and period. His set-ups never flag in originality. He always goes one step farther than we expect, as in the early sequence in which the bombing raid is to take place at ten o'clock, and the camera finishes its shot by moving up to Lancaster's wristwatch, a 'ten to one' zoom."

—Gerald Pratley

"Frankenheimer cut The Train himself—
literally. Working at night in his Paris hotel with
a Moviola, he spliced the film together with
Scotch tape."

—Dennis Stack
Kansas City Star (8/1/65)

JF working with Scofield under a real train.

Preparing for a tracking shot of Lancaster jumping the wall.

He said, "I stepped in a hole. Look at that knee. I'm never going to be able to walk naturally. The picture's over. This'll have to be operated on."

I said, "Burt, we've gone this far. We can't stop the movie." I mean, we were obsessed. We were producing the movie, writing the movie, we were pushing the French crew beyond anything they thought possible. The weather was giving us hell. But once in a while inspiration strikes. I said, "Why don't we have him shot as he escapes? Then you can play the rest of the picture with a limp." That's what we did. We faked the character being shot in the leg, and Burt played the rest of his scenes with a limp. He had the operation after we finished.

What they'd forgotten to tell me was that I had to edit the film in Paris, so we ended up spending a year in Europe, from the day we got there until the day we left. And in the end, Evans and I went on to live in Europe for eight years.

Given all the production problems, did you imagine that it would be a hit?

We never dreamed the picture would turn out as well as it did. It was a huge turning point in my life. Evans and I got married during the making of *The Train*, as I said. Working there has affected me for the rest of my life.

It was also the first really big action picture I ever did, and I got typed as the man to make that kind of picture for quite awhile. Prior to that I had done mainly intimate type dramas, which is strangely what I'd like to get back to doing. *The Train* was the last of the great action pictures to be shot in black and white.

It was in France that I got seriously interested in a film about motor racing, and that's how *Grand Prix* got started. But in the meantime, there was *Seconds*.

"Lancaster, gymnastic as ever, seems tough and strong enough to stand up to the Nazis, and smart enough to outwit them . . . casting Scofield was a brilliant thought. It is hard to find a major actor for the films who has not been around. Scofield somehow manages that combination of sinister and sympathy we should feel for this paradoxical personality."
—The Hollywood Reporter (2/26/65)

Above: *The final deadly showdown as Scofield realizes he is beaten.*

SECONDS (Paramount, 1966).

Seconds

I've always thought it was Rock Hudson's most interesting performance, although he would never have been my own first choice for the role.

Nor mine. Coming out of *Seven Days in May*, I'd formed a partnership with Eddie Lewis. We liked each other a lot. He had Paramount buy the David Ely book *Seconds* for us. As you probably remember, it's about a middle-aged man who's made some money but who hates his life. He discovers this firm that will arrange his death, put him through plastic surgery and then let him start out in another life.

We agreed that Lewis John Carlino should adapt it, which indeed he did. I'd always thought of the two parts being played by one actor, and the actor that both Lewis and I wanted was Laurence Olivier.

I went to Europe to meet Olivier. What an honor that was; I can't tell you how much I admired the man. When he said he wanted to do *Seconds*, I didn't need an airplane to get home, I was so happy. I told Eddie and I told Paramount, and an executive at Paramount said, "That's nice, but we don't want him. He's not a big enough name."

Unbelievable.

Eddie and I were stunned. We didn't know what to do. We offered it to Glenn Ford, who turned it down. We both thought of Kirk Douglas, but Kirk couldn't do it. I can't remember why. Then I was at a party and met John Foreman, who was Rock Hudson's agent, and he said, "What about Rock?" Hudson was the biggest male star in the country at that point, but I said, "Jesus, I don't think Hudson can act this."

Foreman said, "He's the biggest movie star in the world, the least you can do is meet him." I said, "You're absolutely right. Give it to him to read."

Above: *Frankenheimer on the "hallucination set" he designed himself for the bedroom sequence he wanted to be "almost psyche-delic."*

Opposite page: *Frankenheimer with Salome Jens and Rock Hudson on location in Malibu near the director's own beach house—which was used as Hudson's home.*

91

Francoise Ruggieri, cinematographer James Wong Howe and director Frankenheimer. Howe's magnificent camera work on *Seconds* earned him an Academy Award nomination for Best Black and White Photography.

And I got a call that Hudson wanted to see me. I don't know what I expected; I had mixed feelings. But what I met was a very nice man, very frank, very sharp, very intelligent. He said immediately, "The only way I would be interested in playing this is if I can play the second part, after the guy has had his surgery. That's the only way I could see myself doing it."

I said, "Well, I'd never thought of two actors playing this part."

"That's the only way I could see it," Rock said.

I thought about it, and I agreed. We cast my old friend John Randolph to play the character before the surgery. You make John an inch taller and it becomes very possible. John studied Rock's every movement. Randolph was right-handed but

Rock was left-handed so Randolph become left-handed. He walked like Hudson, he moved like Hudson. We gave him a toupee, because you doubted the Randolph character would have had much hair anyway. We spent a lot of time on the transition.

Then we went in and photographed real operations. The crew members were fainting during the nose operation. Jimmy Wong Howe, the cinematographer, and I were the only ones left standing. And I think we made it believable that John Randolph turned into Rock Hudson.

And Rock, I must say, was a total professional. I got him quite drunk for his big party scene, and he brought that off very well, I thought.

I'm always curious about how much of the

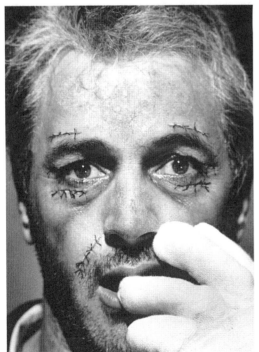

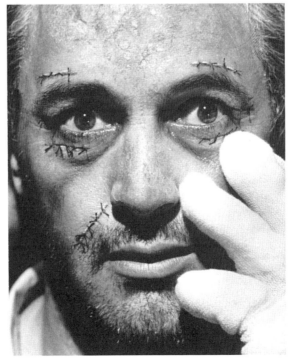

Rock Hudson in his most unusual role— and what many believe was his best performance. Here he is emotionally shaken as he emerges from plastic surgery to begin a second life with its terrifying consequences.

"When we talk about life my philosophy is that you have to live your life the way it is. You can change it but you can't change who you are or what you've done before. And you have to live with that. I think that point was very well brought out in Seconds, *that's what the film was about."*

—*John Frankenheimer*

The grape-stomping scene meant to show Hudson's catharsis was Frankenheimer's idea and was not in the original novel.

"John was conscious of the fact that I had been blacklisted. I had been rejected by Hollywood for 15 years—and what John did was to break that. He stood by what he believed in. So Seconds *broke the ice. . . but what's most important was that I was really excited as an actor. . . I did my part in bits and pieces, but because of John, it was in* huge *bits and pieces. The scene with Will Geer and Jeff Corey was done without anybody on the sound stage except John and James Wong Howe. We did a seven-minute scene without interruption. If I could do that movie again today, I'd be thrilled because of John's technique. I could not have had a better debut in a film."*

—*John Randolph*

". . . as frightening as Frankenstein *was in its heyday."*

—Cosmopolitan (11/66)

original script, Carlino's in this case, survives the editing process.

Two big scenes had to come out. One of them was when he went to visit his married daughter. My wife, Evans, played the daughter and Leonard Nimoy her husband. It was a lovely scene, but it had to come out. It was just too long. And the ending, with Rock remembering the walk with the little girl on his shoulder, was from the sequence of the visit that was cut. The way it turned out, it was a kind of last vision.

Incidentally, that book that Will Geer is carrying around all the time, it was actually his lines.

That nude grape-stomping sequence, by the way, was something they actually did every year up near Santa Barbara. Those people were really all stark naked. We had to build a special vat that hid them a little because the actual vat was too low. By the time we were doing the scene they were all smashed out of their minds. I jumped in because none of the cameramen would get in there with a hand-held camera. I wore a pair of black bathing trunks that lasted for about thirty seconds. One of the women ripped them off. The whole thing was, ah, very stimulating. Trying to keep your eye on the camera with all that going on was very, very difficult.

The irony was that the scene was supposed to be a liberation for Hudson, the return to a natural state and some kind of innocence. But that was still in the days of the Hays Code, and by the time the guys said, "Oh, oh, that's a glimpse of a nipple there," and "Hey, that's a glimpse of male frontal nudity" and "It's just too orgiastic," and made me cut it and cut it and cut it, the result was it *looked* like an orgy. But it wasn't supposed to be and I didn't shoot it that way. The irony is that it was much more innocent in my version than in the one you see after the Code guys got through with it.

"*John Frankenheimer's new film,* Seconds, *is that rarity, a really good shocker, the kind that takes a preposterous premise but then treats it as though it were quite real and entirely normal. Mr. Frankenheimer has already shown, with* The Manchurian Candidate *and* Seven Days in May, *that he is adept at handling such material, but his control is firmer this time. . . I haven't seen a better American film all this year.*"

—Hollis Alpert
Saturday Review (10/20/66)

You could also get a Condemned rating from the Catholic Church, and a major studio wouldn't go out with a Condemned rating on a picture. We had two priests looking over the movie, saying, "You have to cut this, you have to cut that." Under protest we did and it ruined the whole intent of the scene.

We did some very innovative things in *Seconds* and, again, it was in black and white. We needed some hallucinatory stuff, so Jimmy Wong Howe and I had some sets built that were distorted and we photographed them normally. Then we had some other sets that weren't distorted and photographed them with distortion lenses.

There are also some wonderful performances in the film, including John Randolph's and Will Geer's.

There were. But unfortunately it's a flawed movie. The second act never worked. You never really understood why he couldn't make it in the new life. From the time Rock comes on the screen the picture gets into trouble, and it wasn't his fault at all.

What the picture really says is that you are what you are, and you can't set aside all your previous experiences and start over again. It won't work. As an audience you don't know why it hasn't worked for Hudson because it's not clear enough that it won't work for *anybody*. You realize that all the other guys didn't make it, either, and that the idea is a failure. That's what the old man says finally.

The two scenes I told you we had to cut made a terrible difference. The scene where he went back to see his daughter and her husband and their baby ran seven minutes. It really hurt to cut it. We thought the scene where he goes back to see his wife, Florence Reed, would accomplish the same thing, but it didn't.

And the scene near the end where he

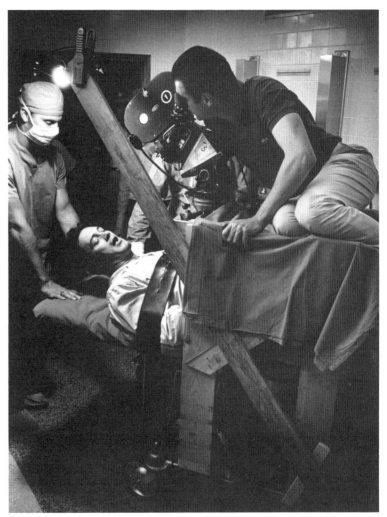

Frankenheimer framing Hudson's horrific last scene.

remembers the image of the child on his shoulder and is reminded of his failure as a father would have driven home the point. But that earlier scene had been cut and the ending lost its force.

I thought the editing was good and the cinematography was extraordinary. But the script didn't work. Paramount lost faith and didn't do much to promote it. They tried to make it a horror movie, and certainly the denouement is horrifying, but the movie just didn't work.

GRAND PRIX (MGM, 1966).

You said you'd begun to think about Grand Prix, *or what became* Grand Prix, *while you were in France doing* The Train.

That's when it began to seem a possibility. I'd always driven very fast. At Williams in the college yearbook when they were handing out "Most Popular" and "Most Likely to Succeed," what I won was "Highway Menace."

Actually, while I was still in college I'd gone down to Pittsfield, Massachusetts, which is just below Williamstown, and competed in a couple of dirt races. I was a great follower of the Sports Car Club of America. But I never had the money to get into it seriously, so I put it out of my mind as you do a lot of things in your life. And as things got going well for me in live television that became all-consuming.

So then in Paris I had the Ferrari, and I got even more interested in racing. I started going to a lot of races in France during *The Train*. When I went to the 24 Hours of LeMans, and a lot of Formula One races and saw those crowds of two hundred, three hundred thousand people, that really triggered it.

When I came back to the United States I went through the Carroll Shelby driving school out in Riverside. I started to compete in G Class Production Races here in California, driving a Triumph Spitfire. My wife went through the Shelby school, too, and we both became good friends with Shelby, who was instrumental in helping us when I did *Grand Prix*.

I called Eddie Lewis, my partner at the time, and said, "Eddie, I've got a great idea for a movie, about Grand Prix racing," and I took him to the Grand Prix race at Watkins Glen, New York. Eddie said, "It's not exactly my cup of tea, but I can see what attracted you to it."

He asked me what we should call it and I didn't know, and Eddie said, "Let's give it the working title of *Grand Prix*. Then the question was whether we would do *Grand Hotel* or *Test Pilot*. By that I mean do we do the story of one man and his rise to the top, with his mechanic or his pal or whoever, Clark Gable and Spencer Tracy. Or *Grand Hotel*, in which you take a group of people and put them in one situation, which in this case would be a season of Grand Prix racing.

We decided to do that. We hired Robert Alan Aurthur, whom I'd worked with in live television days, to do the script. And we had Steve McQueen. That was a done deal. Then fate got in the way. I was doing a favor for a friend, directing a two-day presentation for television for Freddie Fields's wife. There was a meeting with Steve McQueen and I couldn't make it. Eddie Lewis took the meeting for me and he and McQueen hated each other at first sight, and that was it. McQueen wouldn't do the picture.

We offered it to Paul Newman and he turned it down. Then MGM said, "We want a good $400,000 actor in this part." There was only one good $400,000 actor in those days. There were a lot of $500,000 actors and a lot of $450,000 actors and even more $300,000 actors, but only one $400,000 actor and that was James Garner. MGM wanted him because he had done *The Americanization of Emily*.

I tried to point out that Garner is wonderful when he's playing a shit, as in *The Americanization of Emily* and *The Great Escape*. But they wanted him for the leading man, and I said it wouldn't work. I said, "Look, I know an actor's who's perfect. He's actually raced and he's a leading man and he'll be one of the big movie stars of all time." The guy had the same agent as Garner so I couldn't go through him. I went through my friend and former assistant Sydney Pollack. The actor was Robert Redford and what Pollack told him I'll never know, but Redford turned it down, so Garner did it.

Opposite page:
Frankenheimer with director of photography Lionel Lindon.

World champion driver Phil Hill helps director Frankenheimer devise a racing sequence with James Garner—whose character was based on Hill—and Yves Montand.

He drove very, very well. He went through Bob Bondurant's performance driving school. All the actors did. Brian Bedford, the English actor, who was probably the best actor in the whole piece, couldn't drive at all, so we had to use doubles for him with face masks. ·

Yves Montand was perhaps the nicest man, with Rock Hudson, I've ever known, and he was very, very good in the movie. But it was in the nature of the story that he had to die. What happened when I cut the movie was that I gave it to Montand, so the movie became a kind of downer. It wasn't supposed to be that way. It was supposed to be Garner's movie. But Montand was the one you had sympathy for.

The movie was unbelievably difficult to make because we shot everything on real locations during real races. At the beginning we certainly weren't wanted there at all, because all the tracks had had bad experiences with movies before. You go to a place like Spa, in Belgium, where the normal population is 50,000 and on a race weekend it becomes 300,000, and you want to get hotel rooms for a movie company, it's not that easy. But we had a very good production manager in Billy Kaplan. Eddie Lewis didn't come over. I line produced it with Kaplan.

Some of the things we went through with *Grand Prix* were unbelievable. For example, when we did the picture, half of

"Frankenheimer has shrewdly varied the length and importance of the races that figure in the film, and the overplay of running commentary on the various events, not always distinct above the roar of motors, imports a documentary vitality. The director. . . has utilized the mobility of camera via intercutting and frequently dividing his oversized screen into sectional panels for a. . . montage interplay of reactions of the principals—a stream of consciousness commentary—that adroitly prevents the road running from overwhelming the personal drama."

—Variety (12/22/66)

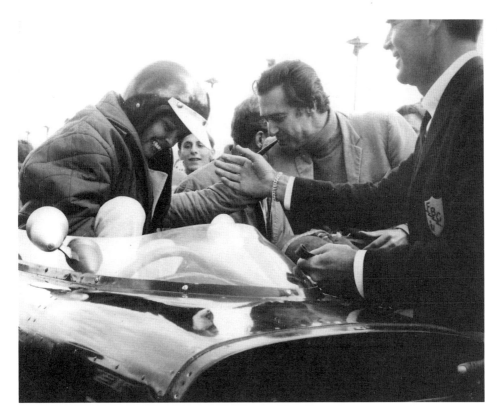

Above left and right: *Director Frankenheimer and James Garner discuss the upcoming scene which depicts the start of a major road race.*

Left: *Evans Evans (Mrs. John Frankenheimer) is helped into one of the many cars used in* Grand Prix.

". . . I hoped (Garner) would be as good as he was in The Americanization of Emily. *He was. Toshiro Mifune is a painstaking actor too. He learned all his English phonetically, but I had to dub him afterwards. It was an excellent dubbing job, in speech and recording. Most people think it was Mifune."*

—John Frankenheimer

Frankenheimer, the cast and some of the crew, relax while the camera is prepared for the next shot. Toshiro Mifune is with James Garner at right.

Monte Carlo was owned by Onassis and half was owned by the Grimaldis, Prince Rainier's family. So when the Grimaldis opened up the road for us, Onassis would close his, and vice versa. Therefore we could only operate on a mile or so of road, then we'd have to stop until the next day.

We had merchants staging strikes. Unbelievable stuff. We were allowed on the track for two hours prior to the Formula One practice, so we closed down all the roads. What nobody anticipated was the massive traffic around Monte Carlo. Guess who was caught in the middle of it and missed the first practice? Colin Chapman, who built the Lotus racers, and his team. Imagine how that went over. "Yer bloody film!" He'd been against it from the beginning anyway. We didn't get much cooperation from Lotus.

Then, at Spa, Belgium, we arrived a week and a half before the race. We were forced to shoot all our cars before the race, because it was all we could do. It rains at Spa every year during the race. Every year. Always. We arrived and of course it was beautiful sunshine. We shot from a helicopter as we'd been scheduled to, and we got some beautiful shots. But I was holding my head in my hands because I knew about the rain. And sure enough on the day of the race it was overcast during the first two laps and then it began to rain.

We'd shot all our stuff in sunshine, so what do you do? The next day—it was dry again, of course—I brought out the second unit and a thousand extras and showered them with fire hoses as they put up umbrellas. We shot for three days with the extras and the rain effect, making the transition. But when we cut the picture together there was this horrible moment when the whole race stopped and people put up those umbrellas. It threw off the rhythm of the picture.

Back in Culver City, looking at that footage, it was three in the morning and I was really in despair about the transition and I got this crazed idea. I went over to the Insert department myself. I put a light on a watch—the same watch I'm wearing—turned on the camera, did a close-up of the watch and then stood above the camera and with an eye dropper dropped about five drops of water on the watch. Then we put a thunder clap over that—BOOM, BOOM, BOOM, BOOM—and that's the way we made the transition in the movie. In *Time's* review, and they loved the movie, they said the most memorable shot in the movie was the watch with the water dropping on it.

But that was later. I was still shooting in August when Robert O'Brien, who was the head of MGM then, came over to see me. He said, "Look, I'm having a lot of trouble

All of the cars in *Grand Prix* were real—no models were used. Nor was there a single process shot in the entire picture. Frankenheimer got the idea for the split screen and multiple images from Frances Thompson's film *To Be Alive* at the New York World's Fair. He was also impressed by Charles Eames' IBM film and discussed the techniques with Eames for use in *Grand Prix*.

with my board of directors. The thing that'll save me is if you have this movie ready for me for Christmas. David Lean did it for me last year on *Zhivago*."

That's a nice little pressure point.

O'Brien said, "You've *got* to do it for me." Well, he was the guy who okayed the picture and I liked him anyway, so I was ready to do it.

We finished shooting the first of October with one and a quarter million feet of film in the can. That's ten or twelve times what you'd expose for a normal film, and close to a hundred times what you'd use in the finished print.

Did you do a rough assemblage as you went along?

No. We had all this film and an editor in California who'd never seen a race. When I got back, they gave us the David Lean

Building at Metro and put four teams of editors on it, which was what I needed.

I lived at the studio for three months and got the picture into theaters without ever having seen the whole thing together. We did the dubbing reel by reel. Maurice Jarre scored it reel by reel. The first time I saw it all together was the day before it opened in New York.

We won the Academy Award for editing and for sound effects. It was a herculean effort.

You were doing some things photographically that were rare at that point.

Lots of use of the split screen with multiple images, and putting 65-mm cameras on cars.

My memories of the film are absolutely visceral.

We put you in the car; we really did.

The Extraordinary Seaman

Movie careers never run smooth. After the triumph of Grand Prix, *you came to* The Extraordinary Seaman.

Yup. After *Grand Prix*, I made this terrible movie called *The Extraordinary Seaman*.

Again, Eddie Lewis and I did it together. We did it for all the wrong reasons. We did it to make some money before we made *The Fixer*. I mean, after the success of *Grand Prix*, if Eddie and I had gone to MGM and said, "Hey, we want to make a movie about the luncheon John and Chuck just had at Adriano's," they'd have said fine. What happened was that a friend of mine, John Cushingham, brought me a very funny script by Philip Rock and Hal Dresner, and we proceeded to ruin it. It was a much better script than the movie I made.

We had a wonderful cast: David Niven, Faye Dunaway, Mickey Rooney and Alan Alda, and a funny script, and we just screwed it up. We didn't make it in Hawaii where we should have made it; we made it in Mexico, and that was horrible. It was the only movie I've made which I would say was a total disaster.

It started out with a funny premise—these four sailors, who are stranded, meet Niven, a British commander on a gunboat stranded on a sandbar. He turns out to be a ghost who is being punished for having gotten drunk before his first battle in the First World War. Funny idea; we just didn't deliver it.

One of the things that happened is that Metro wouldn't let us take our own script clerk. We had to use a Mexican script clerk whose name was Jose. What we didn't know was that the Mexicans do everything without master shots and coverage. In other words, if you have two lines of dialogue and I have two lines of dialogue, they won't shoot the whole scene on you. They'll only shoot your lines on you, and

THE EXTRAORDINARY SEAMAN (MGM, 1968).

Above: *Alan Alda, Mickey Rooney, Manu Tupou, and Jack Carter.*

Opposite page: *The director with Mickey Rooney.*

JF with Evans Evans and producer Eddie Lewis.

my lines on me, and if they need a wide shot they'll shoot one real quick. Boom, and that's it. What they didn't realize is that the way we work is to shoot a master shot, then the whole scene on me and then the whole scene on you. Boom, boom, boom.

One day we were on a miserable location and I came in and Jose was even sadder than usual. I said, "What's the matter, Jose?" He said, "Oh, señor, we are very long." I said, "Really?" He said, "We are already two hours and thirty minutes." I said, "Jesus, it

seems that way, but how could it be so?" And he had all his notes, which seemed to prove he was right.

So I went to David Niven and said, "Good news! We are so long we don't have to shoot this scene, and we don't have to shoot that scene and the other scene. We'll be out of here in two weeks." And we were.

The cutter put the movie together and called me, and I said, "How does it look?" He says, "John, it looks terrific, but they've lost some film." I said, "How do you

"*Director Frankenheimer's forte is melodrama, not infrequently laced with undertones of black comedy. Light comedy, parodying as satire, does not seem to be his particular art and his discomfiture injects the entirety of this comedy, which finds its best comic moments in stock footage of Bess Truman's famous battleship christening. . ."*
—The Hollywood Reporter (1/17/69)

mean?" He said, "Well, we've only got an hour and four minutes. We're missing all this stuff." He mentioned some of the missing stuff, and there was this horrible moment when I had to tell him I hadn't shot it. What happened was that Jose had, let's say, timed your whole close-up and my whole close-up plus the two-shot as three different scenes.

We had a contract to deliver ninety minutes to Metro, so we padded it out with newsreel footage, anything we had, and we gave it the longest titles in the history of the movies.

Metro missed a bet because it was the only movie they had that you could have showed on In-flight between Los Angeles and San Francisco. Somehow Metro didn't see it that way.

I made the film in 1967. They delayed the release until 1968. Meantime I had made *The Fixer*.

My memories of *The Extraordinary Seaman* are memories of David Niven. He was one of the real gents of this business. I was having quite a run there, if you think of it: Paul Scofield, Yves Montand, Rock Hudson and David. Four nicer guys just never lived.

THE FIXER (MGM, 1968).

The Fixer

I think the worst review I ever gave you was on The Fixer.

I remember the really great reviews I get and I remember the really bad ones. I could have almost quoted you word for word on *The Fixer.*

It was so strange, the whole response to that picture. I mean, off of it *Time* did a big takeout on me. I took it down to Arthur Knight's class at USC, the one you teach now, and they gave me a fifteen-minute standing ovation. The *Time* critic, Jay Cocks, was there. I was expecting that I would have to go out and buy a tuxedo for the Academy Awards. The Bernard Malamud novel, the Dalton Trumbo script, how could I miss?

We went to New York for the opening and the first review was Cathleen Carroll in the *Daily News.* Four stars. But Renata Adler was reviewing for the *New York Times* and her review came in—a blast.

Then the next day there was yours in the *Los Angeles Times* and I thought, "Well, that's it; it's all over." To go from a fifteen-minute standing ovation to that was a big, big come-down.

I'd been in that euphoria you can put yourself in. Most of the time you can see the down stuff coming and somehow you're ready for it, but sometimes you put yourself in a mind-set where you don't let yourself see it coming. There were warning signs. Dalton Trumbo didn't like the picture at all and he wrote me a long, long letter as to what was wrong with it. Dirk Bogarde hated the picture.

And, I have to tell you, it was a severely, severely compromised picture. Dalton Trumbo and I made the pants too long. I mean, we made a movie that was simply too long and we had to cut the first part of the movie. Unfortunately, that part was filled with joy and great love and color, the romance with the girl, everything in the life of the guy before he was incarcerated. We had beautiful scenes that all went in the cutting.

It was a mad moment when Eddie Lewis as the producer convinced me that we should cut a lot and start out with the guy's arrival in Kiev. We shouldn't have. I listened to him and he was wrong, but I went along with it. The result was that the movie was so unrelenting I have no desire to see it again. What more can happen to this poor son of a bitch? It's so unrelenting and depressing that I have no great memories of it. And it was a miserable experience making it.

You were working in 1968 Hungary.

Yes, and it was a terrible place to be in 1968 as you can imagine. I hated it like I never hated any other place I've ever been.

Alan Bates was divine, but Dirk Bogarde was mean; he makes life difficult for all the other actors. We did not end up friends.

On the other hand, I'll tell you a couple of funny things that happened.

When we made the deal with the Hungarians they said, "We'll supply all the below the line elements, but you must use some Hungarian actors." I said, "Well, that's going to be difficult unless you have Hungarian actors who speak English. Do you?"

They said, "No we don't but we have great actors." I forgot about it but when we were ready to start shooting they said they wouldn't supply anything because we hadn't cast any Hungarian actors. Dalton Trumbo was with us and I said, "What'll we do?"

He said, "I'll write in this part of a police chief, and we'll cast this great-looking guy." His name was Zoltan, as I remember; we'd been introduced to him. "And we'll give him one line," Dalton said. "'You're under arrest.' You can shoot that in close-up and we'll dub it later." Sounded good to me.

Opposite page: *The director with script writer Dalton Trumbo.*

"I feel better about The Fixer *than anything I've ever done in my life."*

—JF (1969)

The scene was at a cave where they took Yakov after he was arrested and where the body of a child was supposedly discovered. They were going to confront him with it.

The thing was that the mouth of the cave was, let's say, here on Mulholland Drive, but the interior was in Palos Verdes. The two locations were that far apart.

Eddie Lewis had come over for two days because some Metro people were coming to see how we were doing. Eddie said, "We've got to shoot this scene in one day because of the Metro people." I said it was impossible. He said, "We've just got to do it."

So early in the morning I have everybody at the mouth of the cave: Tom Bell playing a kind of Rasputin character, Georgia Brown, Alan Bates, Ian Holm, Dirk Bogarde and, of course, Zoltan the police chief. He's about third in line entering the cave. We shoot it in a hurry. We're done by eleven and we get to the interior of the cave early in the afternoon.

It's a real cave, and you had to go down 300 steps to the actual place we're shooting. Terrible. All the equipment has to be schlepped down; it took hours. Finally we do a rehearsal and I say to the A.D., "Where's Zoltan?" The Hungarians had a meeting; they were always having meetings. Then the spokesman came to me and said, "Zoltan has no lines in this scene." I pointed out that this was a continuation of the earlier scene and he had to be in it.

He said it was impossible: Zoltan was performing in the theater that night. By this time, I had lost it. It seemed like the sixty-fifth or sixty-ninth day of the movie because we were so far over schedule because of their screw-ups. I said, "I don't give a damn where he is. Go buy out the theater and get him here." Another meeting. Still impossible. Zoltan is doing Chekhov for visiting Russian dignitaries. I put my head in my hands, and the spokesman said, "But don't worry, we will get you Zoltan's twin brother."

"The Fixer *was something that had the same theme, really, as* Birdman of Alcatraz—*which is the dignity of man, the fact that man is capable of many, many things.*"
—*John Frankenheimer*

You're kidding!"

That's what I said: "You've got to be kidding." But an hour and a half later down the steps, flanked by two enormous guys who looked as if they had to be secret police, comes Zoltan with a terrified look on his face. Except it isn't Zoltan, it's his twin brother, who is a physics professor at the university.

They had burst into his house and grabbed him from the dinner table. He obviously thought he was going to be killed, because here in the cave were all these people in Russian army uniforms, and even I was wearing my huge Air Force parka with military insignia on it. If I ever have to direct a scene with a man facing a firing squad, I hope he'll look like Zoltan's brother. He was perfect.

Through the translator I said, "Tell him everything's okay. All he has to do is put on the costume and walk past the camera."

We do a first take and when he passes the camera he looks at me as if I still might fire at him. I said, "Cut! Tell him not to look at me." After eight takes, I said, "Give me a Russian uniform." I put it on and stood opposite the camera. If you look carefully you'll see me there in the background. And Zoltan's brother looked at me and not the camera and we finally got the shot.

There was another scene, which did not end up in the movie, in which Yakov has to cross the river and sell his horse. And there was supposed to be a river man's shack. We were shooting ten miles out of Budapest, which really did look like the Russian steppes, which it was supposed to be.

By this time whatever could go wrong was going wrong, so I was double-checking everything. I had them put up the boatman's shack in the studio a week before we shot, just to be sure it was right.

I get to the location. The French cameraman, Marcel Grignon, knew what the shot

Above: Frankenheimer consulting with Trumbo.

Below: The director instructing the crew. Filmed entirely in Budapest on location and at the Mafilm Studio, *The Fixer* was the first American film to be shot entirely in a communist country.

Right: *Hugh Griffith and Elizabeth Hartman.*

Middle: *Soldiers arrest "The Fixer" (Alan Bates) as Ian Holm looks on. Dirk Bogarde is at right.*

Bottom right: *Alan Bates and Dirk Bogarde.*

Below: *Frankenheimer checks camera angles.*

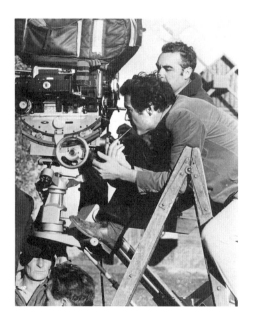

was to be. But the camera isn't set up. I ask why, and Grignon says the boatman's shack isn't ready. I went to the Hungarian A.D. and I said, "Where's the goddam boatman's shack?" He said, "There it is," and there it was, on the ground, in five pieces. I said, "Well, get somebody to nail it together.

"That's problem," he says in a heavy accent. "No nails."

I said, "I'm going to kill you." I felt that close to it. I said, "Get in one of the cars and go into town and buy some nails. I'll pay for them."

"We cannot buy nails," he said. "Must requisition nails from government. Two days."

Nothing to be done, it really took two days?

There was just no way around it. We had to pack up and go back into the studio that afternoon and shoot something else. The frustrations were incredible.

To give you another example. The beginning of the picture took place in the Jewish village, the *shtetl*. We found an old village about thirty miles outside Budapest that looked perfect.

I said, "I love it, but there are power lines and television antennas. Obviously I can't shoot them."

They said, "Oh, no; do not worry." They always said do not worry. "We take down the power lines and the antennas."

I said, "But what about the people who live there? They're not going to like it."

They said, "Do not worry. Leave it to us."

I don't have to tell you what happened. We arrived for the shoot and I found the cameraman sitting there totally dejected. I said, "What is it?" And he said, "Look." And the television antennas were there, and the power lines were up. I went to the Hungarians and said, "You said you would take down the antennas and the wires."

"We didn't have any fades or mixes in The Fixer. *Everything was just straight cuts."*

—JF

Producer Eddie Lewis and Dirk Bogarde with Frankenheimer.

They said, "But what about the people who live there?"

It must be particularly awful to go through the physical exhaustion and all the exasperations, and then be as unhappy with the end result as you became.

It's not good. That's why I flinched when you mentioned the movie. You couldn't beat the system over there; you simply couldn't beat it. All Trumbo and I could do at night was go over the script, and remember how good the book was and plow ahead. And we made the movie too long and we paid for it dearly.

And Trumbo turned on me savagely. He'd been involved in every day of the shooting and he knew all the problems we'd had. But after I showed him the rough cut, he wrote me that five-page letter I told you about, which was one of the most scathing I ever received, telling me all the things that were wrong with the movie that were obvious to both of us. He'd been there.

He was a wonderful writer, and the blacklist hurt him badly. I guess it left him extremely defensive.

Interlude with Bobby

After The Fixer, *I know there was time out for your remarkable association with Bobby Kennedy, right up to that fateful night at the Ambassador Hotel.*

I'd gotten to know Pierre Salinger, Jack Kennedy's press secretary, from the days of *Manchurian Candidate* and *Seven Days in May.* Kennedy wanted to get that picture made, *Seven Days.* So when we asked permission to shoot outside the White House, Salinger came to me and said, "On the weekend you want to shoot, Kennedy will go to Hyannisport."

We were given a tour through all the parts of the White House we wanted to duplicate. We had a big briefing on the Secret Service and what they did and how they functioned. I was invited to a Kennedy press conference to see how he handled all of that. I never saw such charisma in a man as when I watched Kennedy in those press conferences.

When I was doing television in 1960, I was asked to do some stuff for John Kennedy. I was very a-political then, wrapped up in my career and going through a divorce. I didn't feel like it and I didn't do it. It was that simple. After November 1963, of course, I felt terribly guilty that I hadn't done it.

So when Bobby announced his candidacy, the first thing I did was call Pierre Salinger, who happened to be in Los Angeles. I said, "Pierre, I really want to help this time; I'll do anything you ask." Pierre said, "There's a gathering at Sportsmen's Lodge tonight. Come on over and meet the candidate." I did, and Senator Kennedy and I got on very well very quickly.

Pierre said, "Look, he has to go to Gary, Indiana, tomorrow and do a debate with some high school students and then give a speech later. Would you come over and film it?" So I did it. Anyone could have done it. I guess I even somewhat resented being demoted to cameraman. Then I had to tape the speech, and I asked him if he wanted to rehearse it. He said, "No; let's just do it." So I put a camera on him and we did it, and he walked over afterward and said, "How was it?" I said, "Senator, it was terrible. You don't sound convincing at all to me. Put it this way, if I saw this speech I certainly wouldn't vote for you."

Wow!

He looked at me in a way that made clear people didn't usually talk to him like that. Then he said, "All right, what can you do to improve it?"

I said, "The first thing I'd do is work with you for half an hour and we'll see what we can do." He turned to an aide and told him to cancel an apppointment so we could have a half-hour. And I worked with him and the speech came off pretty well. To make a long story short, I spent 102 days with Bobby. I did all the television, all the ads, and needless to say donated all my time. We became very good friends.

He was coming to California and I invited Bobby and Ethel to stay at our house in Malibu. They had two or three of the kids with them. We had a wonderful day at the beach and he went surfing. About noon he said to me, "I really don't want to go into Los Angeles tonight; do think we could get the press out here?" This was the day of the California Democratic presidential primary. I said I thought we could arrange that, and Salinger agreed, so I rented five televison sets and put them all over the house.

Then at six Salinger called and told Bobby the networks wouldn't come out to the house and Bobby had to be on a network telecast at eight. He'd beaten Humphrey fifty-five to one in South Dakota. He asked me if I could get him to the Ambassador and I said, no problem.

113

During the day, playing in the surf with his kids, he dove for one of them who'd gone under for a minute and he got a small cut on his forehead. I said, "You can't go on television looking like that." So I borrowed some of my wife's makeup and put it over the spot.

I was going to take the Ferrari, which is two-place, but he said his political adviser, Fred Dutton, had to go in, so we took the '65 Rolls I'd given Evans. I screamed up Malibu Canyon and down the freeway. You know I drive fast anyway. I said, "We're going to get arrested!" He said, "I'll pay for it" and we ran red lights and we got to the Ambassador at five minutes to eight. He went in and did the telecast. Salinger had made arrangements to open a disco called The Factory, which was usually closed on Tuesday, for a victory party. But Gene McCarthy kept holding off his concession speech and finally it was almost eleven. Bobby said, "I don't want to go to a party. What I really want to do is go back to Malibu with Ethel and you and Evans." I said, "Let's just do it."

Finally McCarthy conceded and Bobby said, "I want you standing next to me on the podium." I said, "Bobby, I don't think it looks good for you to have a Hollywood director standing next to you. It's not the image." He said, "You're right." And the man who stood next to him was shot, too. That would've been me.

Bobby said, "When I say, 'Let's win it in Chicago,' go and get the car. I'll come right out."

I was standing there in an archway, feeling like someone in *The Manchurian Candidate*. I can see Bobby's face on a big television monitor in the ballroom and I can see his back for real. As I stood there a figure went by me and it was as if there was electricity coming out of his body. I've never felt anything like it before or since. Of course it was Sirhan Sirhan.

When Bobby said, "Let's win it in Chicago," I left and got the Rolls and brought it to the entrance. The next thing I knew there were policemen banging on the car and saying, "Move it!" I said, "This is Senator Kennedy's car." They shouted, "Move it," then a black woman ran out of the hotel shouting, "Kennedy's been shot!" The cops started hitting the car with their batons. It had to be repainted later. I drove off and turned on the radio and got a CBS flash which said, "Senator Robert Kennedy, his brother-in-law Steven Smith and movie director John Frankenheimer have been shot." The other guy was six three. It's really disorienting because you know *you* haven't been shot and all you do know is that something horrible had happened.

Another of those times when everybody knows exactly where they were and what they were doing and how they heard what had happened.

I'd stopped smoking two months before, but I remember stopping at a convenience store and buying two packs of cigarettes. I drove home with Evans at about twenty miles an hour. We were in shock. We knew by then it was all true, but we didn't know where he'd been taken, and all his clothes and stuff were at our house. When we got to the house it was like something out of an Antonioni movie. We had all these rented television sets and we turned them all on and everywhere we looked there were more pictures of the tragedy.

There's a bizarre footnote to all this. I'd been working on a documentary to run the night before the California primary, but it was delayed because Dick Goodwin of Bobby's staff and I kept having arguments on how to do it. We finally finished it at three o'clock Sunday morning. Dick said,

"Jeez, it's got to be at ten television stations today." I said, "How do you intend to do that?" He said, we'll charter ten Lear jets and send it out with them, and he made some calls and arranged it. He asked if I'd drive him to LAX with the stuff, so we got in the Ferrari and half way there he said, "Oh, God, I forgot my credit cards. Can we put it on yours?"

In those days there wasn't a limit on Diner's Club, so I charged $32,500 worth of Lear jets on my Diner's card. Two days later, Bobby was shot and everything went to hell.

Three months later I was directing second unit on *The Gypsy Moths* in Kansas and an A.D. came up and said there was an emergency call, and it did sound urgent. A man said, "Is this John Frankenheimer?" I said it was. He said, "I'm John Frankenheimer, too, but I'm a lawyer with Loeb and Loeb. Don't take offense, but do you by any chance have a Diner's Club bill for $32,500?"

I said, "My God, I'd forgotten all about it." He said he'd gotten the bill by mistake, thought his friends were pulling a joke on him and tore it up, then another letter, then a registered letter. "And now," he said, "there are sheriff's deputies here to arrest me. Please talk to them."

I called Ted Kennedy and asked him to pay it. He said I should pay it as a tribute to Bobby's memory. I said I'd donated 102 days of my time to Bobby and that was all I could afford, since my father hadn't cornered the whiskey market. The Kennedys paid it.

THE GYPSY MOTHS (MGM, 1969).

The Gypsy Moths

The Gypsy Moths *in 1969 came next. An aviation picture must have been interesting to you because of your Air Force background.*

I loved that movie, because I think it takes a piece of Americana and shows it the way it is, or was. I really think we captured the Midwest in that movie. And it was an extraordinary cast: Gene Hackman, Lancaster, Deborah Kerr, William Windom. Scott Wilson was very good as the young guy, and Sheree North was wonderful. Deborah Kerr was magnificent to work with and I thought magnificent in the movie. William Hanley wrote the script, from a novel by James Drought.

But what I remember most out of that movie, I suppose, is Hackman. I kept wanting to augment his part. What a terrific actor he is. I think maybe the two finest movie actors I ever worked with were Fredric March and Hackman. I'd work with Hackman on anything he wanted to do, I really would.

I never met Drought. He was a rather eccentric guy who lived in Connecticut and published his own books. The book was brought to Eddie Lewis and me by two producers, Hal Landers and Bobby Roberts. They had nothing to do with the movie except for bringing the property to us.

Was Hackman flying then? I know that later he had his own planes.

I don't know; don't think so. The picture might have started his interest in flying. At that point Gene was not yet a star. He wasn't getting the kind of money that meant you could afford planes.

Every picture presents its own kind of challenge, and I should think the parachuting was the challenge in Gypsy Moths.

Well, it was—that, and making the story work. I don't think we ever recovered from

Burt Lancaster and Deborah Kerr.

the fact that our leading actor went out of the movie half an hour before it was over. I don't think the audience cared enough about the young boy, Scott Wilson, to make it work.

But the parachuting really was a challenge. We did an awful lot of jumps and I used a lot of the same techniques I'd used on *Grand Prix*: the jumper's point of view, shooting from the ground, shooting from the air, shooting from all over the place.

With long lenses on their cameras the operators couldn't find the jumpers quickly enough; they were going crazy. We had to rig the cameras with gun sights beside the lens so they could spot the jumper in a hurry and then put their eye to the lens.

Because I'd driven cars during *Grand Prix*, the jumpers wanted me to jump, too. I said, "So I feel panicked the first ten times, then what?" They said, "Then you go on feeling panicked." I said, "Not for me, I have a problem with heights anyway."

I did go up in the plane, one of high-

Opposite page: *Gene Hackman, Burt Lancaster and Scott Wilson, "The Gypsy Moths"— a trio of barnstorming skydivers who have come to defy death in Wilson's old home town.*

"John Frankenheimer likes and believes in actors and he's very perceptive. If I'm cast, I always feel I can bring something of my own to a part. Not every director agrees or sees it this way but Frankenheimer is not rigid, not iron-bound by his own idea of a scene. That made working in The Gypsy Moths *a gratifying experience."*

—Gene Hackman

Top: The "moths," Wilson, Hackman and Lancaster landed before a magistrate after one of their publicity stunts.
Top right: *Hackman and Bonnie Bedelia.*
Above: *Sheree North with Hackman.*

winged Howard monoplanes they used for parachute-jumping. It was very strange. I'd watch the guys bail out one by one, and then I'd be standing there at the open door. Thank you, not for me.

But don't misunderstand: it was a delightful movie to make. The trouble with the movie came after it was made.

We began with the management for whom we made the movie: Robert O'Brien at the top, with Bob Weitman as head of production. They'd commissioned the movies. Then there was a management change at Metro and in came a man named Bo Polk, who'd been in the flour business in Minneapolis, with General Mills or Pillsbury or somebody.

And didn't last a year at the studio, as I remember.

He lasted just long enough to screw up *Gypsy Moths* totally.

Did they recut it?

"What John Frankenheimer did for sports car racing in Grand Prix *he has now done for sky-diving in* The Gypsy Moths. *That is to say, he has made as subjective as possible the experience of the parachutist as he dives from a plane thousands of feet in the air and then* descends *sometimes at the rate of 200 miles per hour. . . such a strong sense of participation is aroused in the movie goer many in the audience close their eyes to shut out the dizzying feeling."*

—Motion Picture Daily (8/27/64)

The director testing the rigging.

They did recut it. It's the only picture I've had recut. They didn't do a serious recutting job. They just did enough to louse up one section of the movie, which is the morning after the Burt Lancaster-Deborah Kerr affair. It was recut clumsily. Certain things were trimmed to make it palatable to the Radio City Music Hall, where they had decided to open it. It was a disastrous idea; *The Gypsy Moths* is just not a picture for the Music Hall, especially without any publicity.

Then Polk was out and James Aubrey came in. He was the *coup de grâce*. The week before the movie opened, Aubrey gave a long interview to *Time* in which he said, "The obvious trouble with our company is that we have a movie coming out in which Burt Lancaster and Deborah Kerr are making love. Who cares about that? Who wants to see that?" He must have missed *From Here to Eternity.*

Bo Polk had booked the film into the Music Hall, and Aubrey held on to the booking. But he cut the advertising budget down to nothing. The cutting had been ordered by Bo Polk, to go from what you might today call a hard R to a soft R, although the new ratings weren't in effect yet. Then they just didn't back it at all, but to this day it's one of my favorite movies.

I WALK THE LINE (Columbia, 1970).

You followed The Gypsy Moths *with* I Walk the Line, *with Gregory Peck. I looked up my review of it from October 1970 and I see I called it "vivid and well-acted." Script by Alvin Sargent from the novel* An Exile *by Madison Jones. I see I also wrote that "we never get to care deeply about Peck. We're interested by him but his fall from grace isn't pitched high enough to make him a truly tragic figure." And I added that his "pre-existing heroic image makes it difficult for him to appear convincingly flawed."*

I always get nervous looking back at reviews, but did I have it right?

I'm afraid so. It was a movie I wanted Hackman for. But Eddie Lewis and I were under contract to Columbia and Columbia had two other released pictures with Peck, and they insisted we use him. And of course it killed the movie. Gregory Peck has been very good in certain movies and he's a very good actor, but having him play a Tennessee sheriff just shot credulity all to hell.

It really did go against his image, didn't it.

It did. The audience just wouldn't accept him in that part. And the sadness was that we had a bunch of very good actors in the movie: Tuesday Weld as the bootlegger's daughter Peck falls for, Ralph Meeker as the deputy, Estelle Parsons. I cast my wife's grandfather, who was eighty-two years old, to play Peck's father. His name was J.C. Evans, and the part called for him to be seventy years old. He told my wife, "If John wants me to play this old man, they're going to have to make me up to look old." He was quite wonderful. Will Geer dubbed his part eventually.

Peck aside, what are your feelings about the film now?

I think it was an interesting movie. It captured a certain part of the country very, very well. And I think we captured those mountain people very well, with their family loyalties and their inbreeding and their own kind of morality. They didn't think making moonshine was immoral, they just knew it was illegal.

You shot it in Tennessee.

In Cookville, Tennessee, and at the studio.

Opposite page: *The director conferring with Gregory Peck (top) and Tuesday Weld (bottom).*

Below: *Frankenheimer tells Weld where to stab Peck with a meat hook.*

THE HORSEMEN (Columbia, 1971).

The Horsemen

As I remember, The Horsemen *opened while I was at the Cannes Festival in 1971, and I didn't get to review it, but I have lively memories of a very unusual film in terms of theme and locale.*

The Horsemen was a novel by Joseph Kessel, and Dalton Trumbo wrote the script. As you know, it's set in Afghanistan and it's about a national game of theirs called *buzkashi*, which is said to have been invented by Genghis Khan to get his troops in the proper fighting spirit for battle. It's a very, very violent game. The body of a headless calf or sheep is stuffed with sand. It weighs something like 200 pounds. The idea is that the horsemen try to pick it up and carry it around a pole which is five miles from the winning circle. The horseman who dumps the carcass in the circle wins. I think polo developed out of this game. Originally the carcass was the body of a prisoner of war. The game has been civilized to some extent, anyway. But it's still the most violent game I ever watched. Only two years before we were filming, the government outlawed the use of knives in the game because too many players were getting killed. It's really, really tough.

The only actor Eddie Lewis and I even considered to play the hero was Omar Sharif, who incidentally is a lovely man. Then there was the question of who would play his father. We decided to cast Jack Palance. It took an immense makeup job to age him, but he also had to play the man at a younger age in a flashback.

The part of the slave girl was very difficult to cast, and I've always felt that Leigh Taylor-Young, who did it, never received the credit she deserved.

For the rest of it we used English actors. And we actually went to Afghanistan to shoot it, and it's the most beautiful country I've ever seen. During the shooting, the government offered me a gorgeous mountaintop site and all I had to do was promise to build a house on it. I really did think about it, but quickly realized that it was still a wilderness and you could only get to it by helicopter. Just as well, it would probably have been taken over by a Russian general. But you could see why the Russians never beat them. Nobody could ever beat them. They're a strong sturdy people. And the country is divided into sections that are each like a different country, with its own language or dialect.

It must have been a terrifically difficult film to shoot.

It was a fascinating experience, let me tell you. Obviously we had to shoot *buzkashi* games and Eddie Lewis had made a deal with the Afghan government to supply the four best teams in the country for the movie. I wanted to check out some of the players beforehand, but they were all off competing in the provinces so I couldn't meet them until the first day we were going to shoot.

I'd gone location scouting and picked the first location, which was a *buzkashi* stadium about ten miles out of Kabul on a really long dirt road. We had to drive through the Khyber Pass, one of those places you've been reading about forever, and now you're there.

I wanted a crowd for the game but we had only a small budget for extras, so I thought I'd have a raffle to get crowds into the stands. I'd done that on *Grand Prix*. The government said it wouldn't work in Afghanistan. But we decided to give away a Volkswagen Bug. We put it on a trailer and hauled it through the streets with a loudspeaker explaining what we were doing. What I hadn't realized was that the per capita income in those days was about $60 a year, and a car was way beyond almost anybody's dreams.

Opposite page: *From left, Omar Sharif, Habib, Jack Palance and the director. Habib was one of the greatest of all* buzkashi *players and served as an advisor, as well as one of the more prominent players in the games filmed by JF.*

"The documentary-type presentation of the people and customs of remote Afghanistan is excellent in The Horsemen. . . *And there are some fine character creations from the 'name' stars. . ."*

—Dallas Morning News (7/2/71)

Horsemen pull on the headless calf. Omar Sharif, who did most of his own riding, is the horseman at left. Habib is next to him.

It was June and it was already hot and I was living in a terrible house which was the best the American embassy had been able to find for me. The only alternative was the government hotel. I wanted to start at five in the morning because the sun rose very early. At four-thirty the driver came. He had eyes like silver dollars and he spoke no English, but he said, "*Buzkashi* everybody." I didn't know what he meant until we hit the road. It was clogged with horses, trucks, wagons, walkers. It was six before we got to the stadium and I still couldn't get near it. Three hundred thousand people came out for the raffle, and we only needed 5,000.

They broke down our tents, they broke everything. We couldn't shoot, of course. We had to call out the Army to get things under control. It took two days.

Now we went out again, and there were 100,000 people there. The soldiers escorted me through the crowd to meet the *buzkashi* players, who were waiting for me. Chuck, you've never seen anything like them. They must have averaged 250 pounds, but some were 280 and 300 pounds. All muscle, sitting on their horses. Bearded Tartars and Mongols. Their costumes were unbelievable, and they were sitting there looking at me.

"Physical courage and stamina interest John Frankenheimer in the same way a moth takes to a light bulb—an attraction that occasionally produces an intense experience as well as singed wings. It's easy to see what prompted him to tackle Horsemen as a project, just as it was clear what motivated him to make The

Gypsy Moths and The Fixer. What went wrong earlier goes wrong again, but the sense that Frankenheimer will once again make a very good if not great picture is also present."
—The Hollywood Reporter (6/28/71)

125

THE HORSEMEN

I found they didn't all speak the same language. Half of them spoke Pashtu, the others something else. There weren't two good translators available either. One was good with English, the other with French. So I said everything twice, once in English, once in French. But I didn't know what to say, because it occurred to me that none of these people had the vaguest idea what making a movie entailed. All that expensive Panavision equipment meant nothing to them. And now we had 100,000 people starting to chant at the players.

The players whip each other. That's their offensive weapon, and they are lethal. We'd had some fake ones made and handed them out. I explained the first shot I wanted. The player picks up a calf, somebody whips him and he rides away. I set up the camera and found that the players were laughing among themselves and making fun of the phony whips. We rolled the camera and these guys fooled around like mincing little children.

I asked their leader what the problem was. "Why won't you do this for real?" Through the translator he said, "We don't want to hurt ourselves on frivolous child's play. This not a game. We play the game."

I tried something else and we wasted about three hours and I said, "My God, this movie isn't going to work." The crowd was getting very restless. Someone came over and said, "What are you going to do?" I said, "I don't know, but I do know what we're going to do until we get things figured out. We'll play a real game this afternoon, and the movie company will donate a hundred dollars to the winner."

Now it was time to pass out the lottery tickets. The French assistant director said he'd do it. I said, "I think we ought to let one of the Afghans do it," but he insisted. He said, "I'll just have someone drive me around in the Jeep and I'll hand them out." That's what he did, except that people

Omar Sharif with the director.

started piling on the Jeep and grabbing the lottery tickets. Somebody stole his watch and broke his wrist. We had to take him to the hospital. That gives you an idea of the atmosphere.

We finally got the tickets distributed. The winner was a tailor, who couldn't drive. We brought him out to the VW and he fainted dead away.

So now the game starts. The only thing I can relate it to is the scrum in rugby, where everybody is in a heap and then one of the players emerges with the ball, or in this game, the calf. Well, I'd picked a player to be Sharif's double and I'd put him in Omar's costume, which was a black jacket. I thought I'd picked very well, because the guy who emerged with the calf was Omar's double. The cameras are on him and suddenly three players hit him. Thirty seconds into what is going to be an hour game and he goes flying off his horse and breaks both legs. The ambulance picked him up while

About the filming of the buzkashi *match, film critic Roger Ebert said, "There hasn't been a sustained action sequence on this scale since the chariot race in* Ben-Hur.*"*

the game was still on. So I filmed an hour with no double.

Through the interpreter, I say, "You must come back tomorrow in the same costume, on the same horse." The next day they arrive in different costumes, on different horses. The script girl had taken Polaroids of many of the players in their costumes the day before. I walked up to one of the players with his Polaroid and said, "Tell him he has to be in this costume." The player picked me up by the shirt and showed the other players the picture. They all wanted a picture. I saw my chance. I said, "Tell him he doesn't get a picture unless he changes into the costume from yesterday." He ran off and got into the right costume in a big hurry. One of the players thought we weren't going to take his picture and he started crying. In the end we had to shoot pictures of every one every day. We were rapidly running out of Polaroid film. We called every Columbia branch in the world to send us film, and that was a chore in itself because you could only call out after six in the afternoon for about an hour and a half. Columbia must have thought we were shooting the whole film on Polaroid.

The crises never stopped. We had to shoot on the steppes in the north, right next to Russia on the northern border at Kunduz. We had our own helicopter and pilot, who was French, and we were scouting locations. I said, "Look, Pierre, we've got to be very careful because we're so near the border." He said, "I know where I am." Then we saw a black spot in the distance but it wasn't in the distance very long. It went vr-o-o-o-m past us and you didn't have to be an expert to know it was a MIG. The MIG pilot said, "Helicopter, what are you doing?" I said, "Pierre, answer him because if he hears my American accent, he'll shoot us down." Pierre said, "I have an American accent." I said, "Answer him." He said, in English but with a heavy

accent, "We're French and we are looking for a location for a movie." He said, "Fly due south, immediately." He escorted us to the border and another MIG showed up on our other wing. Very close, very scary.

At least they asked questions first.

That obviously saved us.

I wanted to shoot a convoy of nomads. But the women could not be photographed because of their religion. It occurred to me that my wife Evans, with dark makeup, would look right and she would get to ride a camel. I wanted her to carry a small animal so I negotiated for a small Afghan goat. I paid a dollar. I don't know if you know the animal, but they're beautiful, with long brown and white hair.

We went on to Spain to shoot inserts and we took the goat with us. We wanted to take him home but we couldn't import him because of the fear about hoof-and-mouth disease. So we gave him to the man who was handling the horses on the film, and had a big ranch. We went back a year later and asked how Bahmian was; that was what we'd named him. The man said, "He has a hundred wives and he services all of them." He died only a little while ago and I think he must have had the greatest life in the whole history of goats.

We chose twelve of the best players to go to Spain for the shooting. But they'd never flown and had apparently only seen planes at high altitudes and they didn't want to fly. One of them asked me, "Why can we not ride our horses to Spain?" I told them it was quite a long way, and we finally persuaded them to fly.

How long were you involved with The Horsemen *altogether?*

A year and a half. And I'm still bitter about the fate of the picture. When we set

A one-legged Sharif.

out to make *The Horsemen*, it was agreed by Columbia Pictures and by Edward Lewis and me that it was to be a roadshow picture. In those days that meant reserved seats, a running time of three hours or a bit more, plus an intermission. A major event, a great big movie and budgeted as such.

One day in Spain I was shooting an immense convoy of trucks, Afghan trucks all colorfully painted, with Sharif going along on his horse with his broken leg. I had a couple of thousand extras and truck after truck.

And that was the day the powers that be from Columbia came to the location to see me. They stood around in their dark suits and said, "We've decided at Columbia we don't want any more road-show movies. We're going to release this one just like any other, and what we want is a movie that

Above: "Sharif . . . maintains his composure, and Palance (left) seems more restrained than usual. . ."
—Variety (6/23/71)

"The Horsemen is very good in a way that we are not used to taking seriously anymore, with the result that it is receiving many very shallow and patronizing reviews. . . With its almost Biblical language. . . and its frankly adventurous story, the film might easily have been just another laughable Tartar horse opera. . . Instead, director John Frankenheimer relishes the land and the men who live there, celebrating without irony or false emotion their lives of nomadic violence and reckless courage."
—David Elliott
Chicago News (8/2/71)

runs two hours and not three and a quarter. There are going to have to be some cuts."

That's a terrible jolt.

I said, "You're not talking about cuts. You're talking about a total restructuring of the film." Dalton Trumbo's script was damned good, and the whole idea had been to move from the great scope of the action into a very personal story.

They said, "What would the cuts affect?" I said, "Well, in the first place we can have as long a lunch as we like because what we're shooting today will not be in the movie. We'll just let everyone go home. What we've planned for tomorrow won't be in the movie. We've already shot a lot of stuff that won't be in the movie. We've already *paid* for a lot of stuff that won't be in the movie. Are you sure you can't reconsider?" They couldn't reconsider. So I finished the film in Spain in the summer of 1970.

Eddie Lewis said, "You like Paris. Why don't you cut the film there." I was in a funk about the picture and I still hadn't got over the death of Bobby Kennedy two years before. Paris seemed like a great idea, so Evans and I got an apartment. I edited, scored and dubbed the movie in France and took it back to the United States. The head of publicity at Columbia, Bob Ferguson, loved the movie. But he wasn't speaking to the head of distribution, Norm Jackter.

We had a terrific preview on Queens Boulevard in Forest Hills, on Long Island. Jackter was there and he said, "I don't know why we made this movie. I don't know who'll want to see it. I don't know where we'll play it." And I knew he was going to dump it, after a year and a half of very hard work. I said, "But look how it just played." He said, "An unsophisticated

audience. Nobody is going to come and see the movie."

I went on a publicity tour for the film and in Minneapolis I realized that fourteen other films were opening the same day. I said, "This can't be," and I walked off the tour. The picture was mostly ignored in the United States but it was a big hit in France, and I won the French Academy Award.

It's got to be heartbreaking.

It was, and that was two in a row with Columbia. We were under contract to do another film with them, *The Devil Drives*, the story of the explorer Sir Richard Burton. I had a play or pay deal. Before I realized that they really didn't want to make the picture, I did a long location tour of India, the one place where for a reasonable price you could have made a movie the way that one should have been made. I spent two months there and when I tumbled that the film wasn't going to get made, I prolonged the location search and then went back to Paris, where I continued to be paid for not making a movie.

It was a curious time, all my friends among the Grand Prix drivers were being killed in their cars. The same afternoon edition of one of the Paris newspapers reported the death during practice of Jochen Rindt at the age of twenty-eight and of the great chef Michel Simon at ninety-two. At which point I said, "That did it." I sold that Ferrari and enrolled at the Cordon Bleu. I studied cooking for four months and worked at different restaurants. We stayed in Paris nearly four years that time, and during that period I was presented a novel, *Impossible Object*, by Nicholas Mosley, and it became another bizarre adventure.

The Impossible Object

Yes, Nicholas Mosley. He's a very well-regarded novelist. Joe Losey filmed one of his novels, Accident, *and I thought it was one of Losey's best. Mosley's father was the notorious Sir Oswald Mosley, who led the British Union of Fascists before World War II, the Black Shirts I think they were called. He was, as they say, detained when the war broke out. But Nicholas has survived his father's reputation.*

That's him. Well, I liked the book a lot and we found the money to make it. It was a French-Italian-English co-production. We recruited a great cast—Alan Bates, Dominique Sanda, Lea Massari, and my wife Evans was in it. Michel Legrand did the music. Bates is a married writer who has an affair with Sanda, or possibly imagines he does. It was a clever script, mostly by Mosley himself with some additional work by two other writers. The producer was Robert Bradford, a naturalized American born in Germany and married to the novelist, who wasn't very well known then, Barbara Taylor Bradford. He was head of the syndicate that had put up all the money.

We made the movie and he said, "You've made one of the greatest movies ever made." I said, "Bob, we have it, but don't get carried away. Just get a distribution deal for America."

The fact, which we didn't know, was that Bradford had gone bankrupt and had had to borrow the money to complete the film from Alexander Salkind, who later made the *Superman* movies.

Chuck, I have a feeling that it was really kind of a movie version of the musical in that film of Mel Brooks's, *The Producers*. I began to think he'd sold about 300 percent of the movie and if it had ever come out and been a success he'd have had to go to jail. Anyway, what happened was that he never got a distribution deal for America.

This was 1972. The movie was in bankruptcy. The Atlanta Film Festival was com-

THE IMPOSSIBLE OBJECT (Valoria, 1973).

ing up. So I stole a print of *Impossible Object* and entered it in the festival. The judges included Roger Ebert, Cathleen Carroll of the *New York Daily News* and some others. Fox was backing the festival strongly because they had *Harry and Tonto*, the Paul Mazursky film with Art Carney.

Anyway, we won first prize, hands down. But we had no distributor and it became a small scandal: *Where* is the movie? Well, it has shown up on television as *The Story of a Love Story* and it is, or has been, available on cassette. End of sad story.

Above: *The director's wife (Evans Evans) plays the actor's (Alan Bates) wife.*

Opposite Page: *Director Frankenheimer with the crew on location in Morocco.*

THE ICEMAN COMETH (AFT, 1973).

The Iceman Cometh

I should think that in any capsule summary of your career the next film, The Iceman Cometh, *is going to rank high. Images from it come into my mind as if I'd seen it yesterday.*

Eddie Lewis called me in Paris and said that Ely Landau wanted me to direct *The Iceman Cometh* for that special series of his, American Film Theater. And I thought, No, I wouldn't be interested. Evans and I wanted to stay in Paris and we were about to buy an apartment on the Rue du Bac in the Seventh Arrondissement.

Then I remembered I'd seen an adaptation of another literary classic by a director who had really screwed it up, a novel by James Joyce.

Would that be Ulysses?

Ulysses. Yeah, Joe Strick's, and I thought it didn't work at all. My ego kind of got in there and I said, "If I don't do this someone else will and they're liable to screw it up. You better do this."

I didn't remember the play and I couldn't find a copy of it in English in Paris, but I read it in French and it was beautiful. I called Eddie back and I said, "I'll do it with one of three people: Marlon Brando, Gene Hackman or Lee Marvin." I made one provision: I wouldn't do it with Jason Robards. I'd worked with Jason. He's a wonderful actor and a friend of mine, but Jason had done it so often on stage that the idea of directing him in *The Iceman Cometh* was very unexciting.

I went to see Brando, who was in Paris. He was a friend of Dominique Sanda, with whom I'd just worked. He said, "I'd love to do this but I could never remember all those lines. I'd just never get them down." I never got to check out Hackman's availability because in the meantime Lee Marvin called and said he really wanted to do it.

So Marvin signed on, and we got Freddie March to come out of retirement to do Harry Hope.

Landau wanted to open it up. He wanted to have shots out in the street, when Harry Hope goes out of the bar. I said, "Ely, you can't do that. The moment you open this thing up you destroy the whole theme and spirit of the play, because the whole point is not what they see, it's what they *think* they see. You can't impose that kind of reality on O'Neill; you'll ruin the play."

With the possible exception of this new movie I'm doing for HBO, which is called *Against the Wall* and is about the Attica prison riot, *Iceman* was the best ensemble cast I've worked with, where there was real love between those actors, who worked so well together. There was such caring on everybody's part that people would come in on days when they weren't working to watch the other actors work. We shot the whole thing in continuity, so Lee Marvin was there a week before he ever actually got in front of the camera. He'd rehearsed and rehearsed a lot, but once shooting began, he was still there every day, watching.

March was obviously a big influence on the ensemble.

March was very sick and couldn't come out for any of the rehearsals. We hired a very good actor, not just a lookalike, to read Harry Hope during the rehearsals. I got Ed Lauter, who is indeed a very good actor.

Freddie finally came to the rehearsal hall for the last day of rehearsal. We did a run-through and it was like a bolt of lightning. He knew every line and he was mesmerizing, which I think he was in that part. He was an inspiration, but all those actors were: Robert Ryan, Freddie, Lee, Brad Dillman; Jeff Bridges was wonderful, Moses Gunn, George Voscovek, my wife Evans. Robert Ryan and I had worked together on "The

Opposite Page: *Fredric March (left) came out of retirement to do* Iceman. *He is pictured here with Lee Marvin. When March died, his family ran* The Iceman Cometh *instead of having a funeral. His wife said that was the way he would like to be remembered.*

"The Iceman Cometh is a success indeed. It is not merely a worthy production of a great play; it also possesses moments of its own greatness. . . The movie belongs most to Robert Ryan, and it is an eloquent memorial to his talent."
—Jay Cocks
Time Magazine

"Fredric March's performance is, quite simply, perfect."
—Dan Sullivan
Los Angeles Times

Lee Marvin with John Frankenheimer.

Robert Ryan with the director.

Marvin, Bradford Dillman, Ryan, and Jeff Bridges as Frankenheimer directs a key scene.

"John Frankenheimer's filming of The Iceman Cometh *has been a resounding personal triumph."*
—Charles Champlin
Los Angeles Times

When Frankenheimer saw the original set for Harry Hope's bar—which he wanted to have an absolutely confined feeling—he had it reduced by four feet.

"John Frankenheimer directed fluently and unobtrusively without destroying the conventions of the play."

—Pauline Kael
The New Yorker

"The director has provoked an astonishingly good performance from Lee Marvin."

—Boxoffice

"What truly matters is that this powerful O'Neill drama, running almost four hours, has been faithfully recorded for posterity with a first-rate cast. Now the play can never die."

—Cosmopolitan

135

THE ICEMAN COMETH

Snows of Kilimanjaro" on *Buick Playhouse.*

I'd hired Thomas Quinn Curtiss of the *International Herald-Tribune* to do the adaptation. I think he'd known O'Neill. We worked on the script in Paris. We shot the film on a sound stage at Fox and every day the actors would come up to me with the original text of the play and say, "Look, you know what I say here explains why I do thus and so. But it's been cut." So we ended up doing pretty much the original play text.

We'd rehearsed for three weeks and shot it in thirty-five days. I'd sent the cinematographer, Ralph Woolsey, book after book of the Dutch masters. I'd spent hours in the Louvre looking at the originals. That's the look I wanted and that's what we got. Woolsey did a wonderful job.

Landau's idea was very interesting: to film those great plays and have theaters show them on Monday and Tuesday nights, which are traditionally the slowest nights of the week. He had a ticket arrangement with American Express, as I remember.

Ely Landau was very well meaning, but, God, he screwed up in the financial arrangements with American Express. The distribution of the film was a disgrace. Like all of Ely's stuff, the ideas were marvelous and the execution was terrible. There was some sort of computer foul-up so American Express couldn't fulfill the ticket orders. I think the project went into bankruptcy and the rights went here and there, but so far as I know Paramount has them now.

Still, it was just about the best creative experience I ever had. *Grand Prix* was the most fun I ever had, but *The Iceman Cometh* was the best creative experience.

He was wonderful in Cat Ballou, *but I think* Iceman Cometh *was Lee Marvin's finest hour, don't you?*

Marvin and Frankenheimer.

Yes it was. But he was awfully good for me in something else, which you probably never saw. It was on television, *Producer's Showcase,* called "The American," about Ira Hayes, the Indian who was in the group that raised the flag on Iwo Jima. Merle Miller wrote the script.

I also did a *Climax* with Marvin, called "Bail Out at 43,000," with Charlton Heston, Richard Boone and Nancy Davis—Mrs. Ronald Reagan. It's a young Lee Marvin and he was great, such a great actor. Then he lost his stride and they trashed him. But he was a talent.

When he died, it seemed to me another case where there ought to have been more roles, more great things to remember.

99 AND 44/100 PERCENT DEAD (20th Century-Fox, 1974).

While we were shooting *Iceman Cometh* at Fox, Joe Wizan came to me with a script by Robert Dillon called *99 and 44/100 Per Cent*, a kind of black comedy about gangsters.

At that time, Evans and I were living in a rented house in the Malibu Colony. We owned a house in Malibu but it was rented to Norton Simon. We'd realized that after our years in France we were tired of being foreigners. We are Americans and this was where we wanted to live. We loved Malibu and we decided we were going to buy the house we were renting. So it seemed entirely propitious when Wizan came along with the script for *99*.

We made a development deal with Fox and I had a meeting with Gordon Stulberg, who was then the head of the studio. He said, "We'll make this movie but the only person I can see for the lead is Richard Harris." Gordon had made *A Man Called Horse* with Harris.

Well, when you realize you have a go movie instead of just a development deal, you're tempted to say, "Hey, that's great," and I did. But taking Richard Harris to play an American gangster—a role that should've been played by Robert Mitchum—was just not the greatest choice ever made.

We also had Eddie O'Brien, Bradford Dillman, Chuck Connors and Ann Turkel, who was married to Richard or about to be. Ralph Woolsey was the photographer again and Henry Mancini did a good score. Richard and I had our share of problems, but we came out of it friends.

But the movie was a failure. You look at it and it's just not good work on my part. I shouldn't do that kind of satire, but I thought the writer, Robert Dillon, was one of the most imaginative people I'd ever met.

Edmond O'Brien and Richard Harris.

Chuck Connors and Kathrine Baumann.

THE FRENCH CONNECTION II (20th Century-Fox, 1974).

French Connection II

And Robert Dillon was a co-author on French Connection II.

For several reasons, not the least of which was that I spoke French, Fox asked me to direct *French Connection II*, which they wanted to shoot in France. They had a title and they had Gene Hackman and no script. I'd worked with Hackman and Hackman liked me. I told Dillon, "Fox has agreed that you and I could do this movie. But they've got no story." This was even before we actually shot *99*. Dillon ran *French Connection I* and he called me after the screening and said, "I've got it, we'll make Popeye Doyle the junkie." And that was the whole basis for the script.

He wrote a script which is pretty much the structure we shot. It was rewritten by Alex Jacobs, an English writer who was very good with action, and finally by Pete Hamill. All the talk about baseball in the cold turkey sequence was by Hamill. It was all written, not improvised. Hackman added tremendous life to it, and threw in a few things of his own.

There is very little directing with Hackman. You just try to set the stage for him. I always try to challenge Hackman to do more, and to give him everything I think he's going to need. For instance I had them build real cells, not just scenery cells. They tried to talk me out of it as being too expensive and unnecessary, but I said, "We're working with an actor who is *very* strong and he needs this stuff and will make it work for us."

I remembered working with Burt Lancaster, another very strong actor, in *Birdman*. They'd built scenery cells for that one. And as the character he went into a rage and hit a wall and knocked it down. If you've seen it happen once, you don't want to see it happen again. So we built real cells, with iron doors. There's a scene in which Hackman is screaming and ripping at the door

and yelling, "I want a hamburger," and if it had been scenery we wouldn't have had a set left, because he was really incensed.

There was another scene in which he was doing a monologue about baseball and Mickey Mantle. I'd ordered some cold chicken and an apple or an orange, I forget which, and I told Gene, "I thought maybe you could use this in the scene." And he said, "Yeah," and broke off a chicken leg and said, "This is the bat, and this—the orange or whatever—is the ball." And we set it up that way.

With Hackman, I tried to shoot everything with two cameras because he's so brilliant you don't want to waste anything on a long shot, because he does it just a little bit differently every time. So I had both the close-up camera and the long-shot camera on him in that scene. And we'd have had it perfectly on take one except that one of the cameras broke down. So we rested about five minutes, and he did take two and that's what you see in the movie.

The other thing about Gene in that movie is that we were able to steal scenes. There's a scene outside a restaurant where he has an argument with the French detective, played by Bernard Fresson. My problem with doing scenes like that with extras is that they never behave correctly. If somebody's having an argument on the street and two guys are really yelling at each other, people watch, but extras overdo it, like they're trying to get their own faces on camera. You tell them not to look, and they don't look at all, and you have to tell them to look but be natural. It's a mess.

So for that scene, I knew the restaurant we were going to use, and more or less where they'd be, so about ten in the morning we backed up two vans into the parking places. There were black drapes over the windows. Hackman and Fresson rehearsed the scene by themselves about a block and a half away. I got into one of the vans and the

Opposite page:
*The director with his star,
Gene Hackman.*

The director showing the policeman how he wants him to point out the man Popeye Doyle (Gene Hackman, right) is seeking.

"Popeye is a colorful and interesting. . . character, and when the Marseilles drug people kidnap him, forcibly create a heroin habit in him, and then release him, you have a very special kind of jeopardy that the film and Mr. Hackman exploit most effectively. The perverse intensity and anguish in these sequences recall some of Mr. Frankenheimer's best work in The Manchurian Candidate *and* Seconds.*"*

—Vincent Canby
The New York Times (5/19/75)

two guys came down the street like any two tourists. They took their positions for the cameras and then they walked away again. If the positions hadn't been right I'd have had to get out of the van and say something, but I didn't. They came back again and did the scene, and the reactions of the people passing by are real.

It makes a difference, and I think audiences feel the difference even if they don't think about it.

I did that time and time again in the movie. All the stuff of Hackman walking around Marseilles is hidden camera stuff. By the end of the shooting, we really knew we were on to something.

There's a scene in a bar when Hackman goes in and orders a whiskey. Gene said, "Who do you have for the bartender?" I said it hadn't been cast yet. He said, "Why don't you get a guy who doesn't speak any English." So we did, a fine French actor, but who didn't speak any English, so neither of them has any idea what the other is saying. They improvised the scene and it's what you see on the screen.

Gene said, "Do you think it's okay for Popeye to make a pass at some girl?" I said, "Why not?" I found two good-looking girls and put them at a table. I said, "Both of you want to be actresses?" They did, and I told them, "Okay, then whatever happens in this scene, you've got to stay in character. Just remember, that when this person approaches you, if he does, he's *not* Gene Hackman. He's an American, a coarse American. He's absolutely typical of what you think an American is." It worked out very well.

I remember your telling me once that you got help on the picture from some very unexpected sources.

Yeah, and we needed it. The weakness the French have is with their production people. The crews are great, but the production managers and people like that aren't great. So Fox sent over a line producer named Bob Rosen, who rapidly became my best friend and inseparable associate on films. We've done nine films together and this was our first.

The problem was we couldn't get any permits. The production people were totally incapable of operating in Marseilles. We invented the chase with the streetcar and told the French. They said, "Impossible. You can't do that in Marseilles; they won't let you." We wanted to tie up the harbor and needless to say we were told that was out of the question as well.

Popeye meets his French counterpart (Bernard Fresson, left).

Then one day a guy came to the location. Rosen didn't have any French and the guy didn't want to talk through the interpreters, so I came over and he said, "I understand you have problems with the police." I said, "Terrible problems." He said, "A car will pick you up at this intersection at five minutes past seven this evening. And if the meeting goes correctly, there won't be any more problems."

Sure enough, at five past seven a black Citroen picked up Rosen and me and whipped us very fast to the very top of Marseilles—a beautiful villa overlooking the whole city and the port. The gates opened and once we were inside the villa we knew just where we were, so to speak, because the guys who were there were just unmistakably what they were.

They were really tough guys from the Union Corse. Then from another room came a very elegant woman who looked to be about eighty years old. She said, "Gentlemen, we understand you have been having a lot of problems." We said that was

Above: *Esteemed Hollywood pioneer director King Vidor (left) inspects one of the handheld cameras used in* French Connection II.

"(Frankenheimer) retreated to the early days of the cinema, and sat the unit photographers in a wheelchair to simulate a crude dolly for traveling shots. Different from French Connection I. . . *the sequel. . . emerges as more of a character study of Hackman. . . 'I had to go a lot further with the character', explained* Frankenheimer. 'It gave Gene Hackman a chance to go above and beyond what he did in the first movie. Otherwise, it would have been a ripoff and that is the one thing I didn't want to do.'"*

—Patrick McGilligan
Boston Globe (5/14/75)

true. She said, "Hmm. Look, you tell me what you need, and just as long as you don't do this movie too closely to what we do, you'll have all of our cooperation."

I wonder if they'd got hold of the script somehow.

As a matter of fact, she said, "We've read your script and we'd like you to change it." The method we'd invented for smuggling in the drugs was fairly close to what they actually did. She came up with the idea of bringing it in on the leads of the ship, which are right on the keel at the bottom of the hull, which was ingenious. We would never have thought of it.

"Would that work for you?" she said. I said it would be fabulous. She said, "Good. Anything else?" Rosen said, "We need a laboratory." She said, "You just tell us where you want it and we'll take care of it." We said, "What about equipment and stuff like that?" She said, "Don't worry about equipment."

And immediately we started to get the permits we needed. The French production guys couldn't understand how we got those permits. We got permission to close off the whole harbor on a Sunday. We caused a traffic jam that went all the way to the Spanish border. Suddenly we had a laboratory. The set designer said he'd never seen anything like it. The cops looked at it and said, "But this is a real laboratory."

The lady was as good as her word. She was—

Corsican.

How do you suppose they got a copy of the script?

Maybe from someone in our crew. Don't know, but it was the luckiest thing that ever happened to us.

The fire scenes at the end are really spectacular, and done years ahead of Backdraft.

We had a great Hollywood special effects guy, Logan Frazee. We got a lot of Popeye Doyle behavior out of Frazee. He was really the American abroad, not knowing a word of French and trying to work with the French special effects people through an interpreter. He said, "You got bullet hits," and they went, "BA BA BA BA BA!" He said, "Wait a minute! You guys don't have any good bullet hits, do you, or you wouldn't be doing all this bullshit." And they didn't. But by the end of the movie they loved him and gave him a party. He's the best special effects man I ever worked with.

Fernando Rey made a wonderful villain.

Lovely guy, but I'll tell you something that'll make you laugh. We were obviously locked into Fernando Rey because of Billy Friedkin and the first picture. But Rey's speech was so bad he had to be dubbed by a French actor, in both the first picture and ours. His Spanish accent was just too heavy, so there you are.

The picture looks so authentic throughout that you think of it as an all-location film, but in fact some of it was designed.

It sure was, and the production designer, Jacques Saulnier, was very very good. He built that police station in the studio, and the jail. I've done three movies that required extensive uses of prisons, *Birdman*, *The Fixer* and *French Connection II*. *Birdman* and *French Connection II* were by far the most impressive, and in both cases they were built. So there you are. We used a real prison in *The Fixer* and it was so cramped we had to compromise the camera positions and the lighting so badly you got

"One of the best of the thriller films. Hackman not only repeats his award-winning role but improves upon it."

—Hollis Alpert
Saturday Review

"Claude Renoir's superb cinematography makes one feel and smell the waterfront and back alley environment. . . Frankenheimer's direction keeps all personal and production elements in total perspective and balance."

—Daily Variety (5/14/75)

Frankenheimer, Hackman, and Fresson.

the impression that it was a set. I always use that example whenever someone says there's nothing like a real location. Bullshit.

The whole backdrop outside the window of the police station was one of the best things I've ever seen. It was forced perspective and it was three dimensional. He built all those other rooftops. He built the whole Marseilles skyline. It was fabulous.

The picture has a terrific look.

It really does. It was my second picture with Claude Renoir and he's the best cameraman I ever worked with. He was fast, he was a great man to be with, he had great ideas about the script, and he saved

my butt time and time again on that movie and on every movie we did after that. I'll give you an example.

The dry dock sequence was very tough to shoot, very tough to light. The cameraman had to light up half of Marseilles in the background so that you could understand where we were. Otherwise you'd have had no sense of the city at all.

We'd shoot in one direction and then turn around and shoot in the other direction, but to change all the lights for the second direction was a monstrous job. What I tried to do was decide at the beginning of the night on one direction, and then hope not to have to change that night.

But one night there was nothing I could

do. It was summer and the nights were fairly short. We had to change, and it had been a particularly tense night, a lot of action, a lot of rough stuff. It was about a two-hour job to change the lights. About forty-five minutes after I'd given the order to change, I realized in horror that I'd forgotten a key shot in the other direction.

I went to Claude and said, "This is a disaster," and I explained what had happened. I said, "How long will it take you to relight it?" He said, "How long will it take you to get the actor here?" I said, "What do you mean?" Claude said, "I just wanted to protect us against something like that. I kept the lighting. I'm just adding more lighting over here. Bring the actor in and we'll shoot it."

I mean, it just saved me, and he did it on all the movies we worked on. That's what you're always looking for in a cameraman: someone who's a collaborator, who's on the same wave length you're on. I've had it the other way around, with the cameraman really trying to screw me up.

I'd wanted desperately to work with Renoir, who'd done all these beautiful, gentle French movies. But at the beginning I told him, "Claude, I'm not sure you can do this. Because of the way the first film was shot, we're going to have to do most of this one handheld or with long lenses. It's got to look jagged and raw. You better look at the first picture." He did, and he said, "I don't have a problem with this. A lighting cameraman is a lighting cameraman."

The whole crew was a joy to work with. A lot of them I'd used on *The Horsemen* and *The Impossible Object*. Man for man, I don't remember working with a better crew.

The use of language in the film was interesting.

We used no subtitles in the picture. We used the French language as another enemy

Popeye Doyle (Hackman) chases a suspect into a burning building.

of Popeye Doyle. He felt totally left out, totally isolated, like a fish out of water amidst this language of which he understood not a word. We used French continually, but we never had a plot point in French that the audience had to understand. We wanted the non-French speaking audience to be as polarized as Doyle, to be as frustrated as Doyle.

It was a terribly difficult film to dub into French. I'm not sure it made any sense. I've never seen it. I don't see how it could make any sense, because he's always saying, "What? What did you say?" And it's a pity to have somebody dub Hackman in French because you lose so much if you lose his voice.

I remember writing that it wasn't simply a sequel, it had a life of its own. And it was a success, wasn't it?

Yes, it was a success. In fact, it got me *Black Sunday*, which was the next movie.

BLACK SUNDAY (Paramount, 1976).

Director John Frankenheimer monitors the crash of the Goodyear blimp (reflected in the camera viewer) into the football stadium.

Bob Evans, the head of Paramount then, and Dick Sylbert who was vice-president in charge of production at the studio both saw *French Connection II* and that was it. I had wanted to do *Black Sunday* very much. I'd been at a party at Irving Lazar's and he asked me if I'd read a book called *Black Sunday*, which he had just sold to Paramount. He gave me the book and I loved it and I told him so. He said, "Okay, I'll call Barry Diller and we'll work on it." I called my own agent, Jeff Berg, and asked him if he'd read the book. He said, "Yeah, and it's a piece of shit." I said, "Well, it may be a piece of shit to you, but I want to do it."

I left ICM for a lot of reasons, and I'll never forget that Sue Mengers reached me at the Beverly Hills Hotel and said, "If you leave this agency and go with Irving Lazar we will do everything we can to see that you never work again."

Well, that was right kindly of her.

It was a real enough threat. I told Lazar I couldn't go with him. He said, "I've worked very hard for you. I got you that movie. I expect some kind of reward. I'll accept a present. I've always wanted a Volkswagen Rabbit in grey." So I bought him a Volkswagen Rabbit in grey. I finally left ICM again six months ago and went with William Morris.

But Lazar did get to Diller.

Yes, and the deal was done. But there was a problem early on. Ernest Lehman had been hired to do the script even before I was hired and it wasn't finished when I came aboard. Evans kept saying, "It's coming, it's coming." I said, "We're beginning to have a problem with the date, because we've *got* to shoot the Super Bowl."

Well, the script finally came in and it was virtually the same length as the novel, 292 pages long as I remember. I told Evans it

was unusable. He said, "We'll just cut it." I said, "You can't just cut it. You have to restructure it. You have to take whole elements out." That's when I brought in Bob Rosen to help me. We had this window of time because of having to do the Super Bowl, but we couldn't budget the film because the script ran 292 pages.

So we hired Kenneth Ross, who'd written *Day of the Jackal*. He and Rosen and Evans and I went over the structure we wanted. We worked night and day with three teams of secretaries and in three weeks Ross had a budgetable script. The story went from beginning to end and it was a budgetable size. We came up with a budget of seven and a half million—no, eight million dollars.

Barry Diller said, "I'll only do this film for seven million, not a penny more." I remember the day very well. We went back to Evans's office and Sue Mengers was there. Mengers said, "It's very simple. Lie. Say you'll do it for seven million and, whoops, it went over half a million." Bob Rosen said, and I'll never forget it, "I can't be dishonest, can't make a movie that way. I won't sign a budget that low. It's my responsibility and I won't lie to Paramount."

Instead Bob went down to Florida and figured out a way to do it for their price. If I directed a film for United Way down there, and Robert Shaw narrated it—he was just coming off *Jaws* and he was the first one we hired—the United Way people in Miami would provide us with a half-million dollars worth of extras to sit in the stands.

So that solved the budget problem. But we had another problem and it was huge. Huge! We needed a blimp, of course, and at that time there was only one in America, the Goodyear blimp. And how do you sell Goodyear on using their blimp if they know it's going to carry a bomb into the Super Bowl?

"John Frankenheimer's film of Black Sunday *is an intelligent and meticulous depiction of an act of outlandish terrorism. . . Strong scripting and performances elevate Robert Evans' handsome production far above the crass exploitation level. . ."*

—Daily Variety (3/25/77)

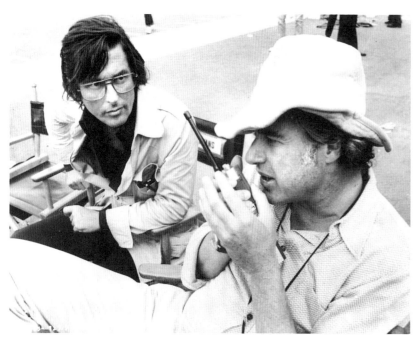

Producer Robert Evans with the director.

Lead actor Robert Shaw and Frankenheimer discuss scene in stadium just before blimp crash.

Rosen said, "Somewhere in the world there has to be another blimp." And Bob found a guy in Germany, a former Luftwaffe pilot who had a blimp. His name was Willenkomper. We went to Germany to see him about his blimp. There were pictures on his walls of P-47s, P-38s and B-17s he'd shot down. He really was Dr. Strangelove.

We said, "How do we go about getting the blimp into the stadium?" He said, "No problem. We fly it in." We said, "Jesus, you can't fly it in; you'll kill everybody." He said, "Oh, we may hurt a few people, but it'll look wonderful."

A grand sense of humor.

I'm not sure he was kidding. Anyway, we knew we didn't have a chance with his blimp. So now we wonder how we can persuade Goodyear Tire and Rubber Company to use their blimp. Because if we don't have a blimp we can't make a movie. It was that simple, but we didn't tell Paramount that.

From the time of *Grand Prix*, I'd actually had a very good relationship with Goodyear, because we'd made a tie-in with them and I'd done everything I said I'd do. Bob Lane, their vice-president in charge of publicity, had become a friend. So Rosen and I went to Akron to see him.

He said, "Are you guys really trying to tell me that we should give you this blimp, knowing that it's going to carry a bomb into the stadium. What kind of an image is that for us?"

Rosen said, "Look, we know where we can get a blimp, and everybody's going to think it's the Goodyear blimp because it's the only one they know. We don't even have to paint Goodyear on it; we'll paint something that's almost Goodyear, so close nobody'll notice that it's not Goodyear." He said, "John Alonzo will shoot it backlit, so it's all black and menacing." Bob and I had rehearsed this, and I added, "The other thing is that if we don't get your blimp, I'm going to have to have that other blimp come into the stadium, and run the risk of those propellers chewing people up."

Talk about arm-twisting!

You could see him go. "Ah, jeez, you are?" he said. I said, "It could really be messy." But then we said, "But with you guys collaborating—because everybody thinks it's Goodyear anyway—you have certain script approvals, and we won't do anything that brings discredit on Goodyear." Lane said, "But what about the pilot? He works for us." I said, "We thought about that. We'll make it a free-lance organization that supplies pilots, so that the pilot is working for someone else." "Now look," he said, "if we say okay to this we can't have this thing chewing up people."

So we got the blimp. That was one of the great, great sales moments of all time.

You had an interesting cast.

We'd all agreed on Robert Shaw, and as I said he was the first actor we hired. Bruce Dern I'd always wanted to work with and he seemed a natural for Landers. The role of the terrorist girl was really a tough one. Bob Evans was doing *Marathon Man* with Marthe Keller and she seemed right for it.

So now we shoot. We made up a lot of things as we went along. For example, we were walking through that part of Miami Beach where a lot of old Jewish people live in hotels and sit outside in the sunshine. We needed a really good action sequence and I remembered the chase scene through the streets in *French Connection II.* So Rosen and I looked at each other and said, "This is what we're going to do." We'd have the chase go right by those hotels, with the old people watching. As usual, the production

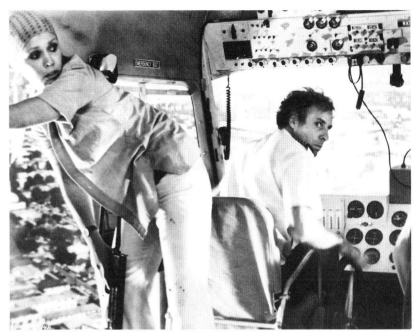

Marthe Keller and Bruce Dern ("at his unhinged best").

Fritz Weaver and Shaw.

people said it couldn't be done, that we didn't have extras and so on. We did it anyway.

We didn't want anybody to have a heart attack, so I got on a loudspeaker and I said, "Look, we're doing a movie. You'll hear sounds like a gun going off. It's not a gun, it's a toy."

So now we shot Bekim Fehmiu running through the street, and the guns went off and the people looked at each other, that's all. That's exactly what they would've done if it had been real, I'm sure, and it was great. We shot it in two days, and then we shot Bekim on the beach and that was about four days. It became one of the best chase scenes I've done.

All of it building toward the really, really big show in the Orange Bowl stadium.

What we had to have was one day with a huge crowd reacting to the blimp. In pre-production we had photographed a game between the Miami Dolphins and the Baltimore Colts. It had taken place at one eastern time and it wasn't influenced by television, so the blimp wasn't needed and Goodyear gave it to us to use.

We used that game as a back-up, because there was always a chance that if the weather was terrible at the Super Bowl and there was a lot of wind, the blimp wouldn't fly. And if the blimp wouldn't fly we had no picture. So we had to make our own Super Bowl with this Dolphins-Colts game, and during that game we'd actually been able to fly the blimp right up next to that light stand. But what we lacked were the big wide shots of the crowd reacting.

We had elements of the blimp to drag through the crowd, like the cabin. We had a piece of the tail. We had the nose piece that we put on cranes and dragged through the crowd. Now we needed twenty to thirty thousand people reacting to the blimp coming in.

So we staged this huge promotion on a Sunday, our last Sunday in Miami. We had five camera crews, all on triple time. The press gave us tremendous publicity. We were going to have stunt men doing races, stunt men on fire, stunt men vs. Dolphins players in track events, cast members throwing footballs in a contest with the Dolphins' quarterback. And we were going to give away lots of prizes, including a $5,000 prize and an appearance in the film. The day was going to cost about $200,000.

When we arrived early in the morning, it was dark and overcast. But by nine-fifteen I had some of the best shots in the movie of people reacting. I had a great assistant director on *Black Sunday*, Jerry Ziesmer, who was just incredible with crowds. He'd stand in the center of the field with the public address system and whip them up to do anything we wanted.

Then at nine-thirty it started to rain like you can't believe, like it can only rain in Florida. I was sitting in my trailer with my head in my hands. It had been raining for an hour and a half. Bob Rosen came in and said the weather report was that it wasn't going to let up all day. He said, "We're going to have to pull the plug. If we do we won't have to feed the people or give away the prizes and we can cut the day short for the crew." We also had thirty football players in Steelers and Cowboys uniforms, which the NFL had really charged us a fortune for. I asked him what it was going to cost to do it again another day. He said a third of a million dollars. I said, "You really think we've got to pull the plug?" He said he did.

I got Jerry Ziesmer on the walkie-talkie and told him to get on the PA and announce that we were calling it off. He said, "Are you sure you want to do it?" I said I was and he said okay.

Twenty minutes go by and it's still raining to beat hell, but I don't hear an

The director talks to stunt coordinator Everette Creach and explains how he wants the stuntmen football players to react as the blimp crashes (below).

Frankenheimer used ten cameras to cover the Super Bowl game. On the final day of shooting the climax, he had four camera crews working on triple time. . . and when the real blimp approached the light stand it was only twenty-five yards away.

announcement and nobody is leaving. Suddenly I look out the window of my trailer and I see blue sky. I go outside. It's beautiful. I run back inside and get Jerry on the phone. I screamed, "Did you make the announcement yet?" He said, "I'm about to." I said, "DON'T!"

What happened was that Jerry started toward the middle of the field toward the microphone and it was raining so hard he couldn't get there, so he started back to the elevator to the press box. He ran into his girlfriend, Linda, and invited her to come with him to the press box. They were mad for each other and, what can I tell you, she delayed him. And she thereby saved us a third of a million dollars. She got the part in the picture. She got the five thousand dollars. It's my favorite movie story of all time.

I remember that I gave Black Sunday *a Sunday review, very positive. But I also* remember that it was a disappointment at the box office.

We had an exhibitors' screening and I've never had such fantastic reactions. They stood up and screamed with applause. We got a letter from Sumner Redstone, a major exhibitor back East, saying that *Black Sunday* was going to be bigger than *Jaws*, one of the biggest pictures ever made, and on and on. Bob Evans and I had been around the movie business long enough to take that kind of thing with a grain of salt, but the enthusiasm was *so* great that it was hard to ignore it. It made the disappointment later that much harder to take.

That screening was in November and we'd had to show the film without reel fourteen, which was the special effects after the blimp comes into the stadium. The special effects weren't ready. If they had been, and it's an old, sad story now, the life of *Black Sunday* would have been completely different. As it was we had to wait until May for the special effects because they screwed them up three or four times.

In the meantime the movie *Two Minute Warning* came out. It was not the same at all but it took place in a football stadium, and it certainly took some of the lustre and the novelty off *Black Sunday*. But what was also true, I'm afraid, was that our picture came at the end of a cycle of disaster movies, and I think that for the moment the audience had had their fill of them, but even the exhibitors hadn't realized that when they saw the film in November.

Off that earlier excitement, I had about two million dollars worth of new commitments. And the film didn't do badly, it just didn't do what everybody thought it was going to do.

It was the start of a bad time for me, and I think Bob Evans would agree it was the start of a bad time for him as well.

Then you were involved with a project with Dino De Laurentiis.

As I told you, I came out of that exhibitor screening of *Black Sunday* with two million dollars in firm commitments, including a play or pay deal with Dino to do *The Brink's Job*, as it was finally called, for $600,000. It became clear after a while that Dino and I wanted to do two different movies. He wanted *Big Deal on Madonna Street* and I wanted to do a really serious look at what happens to men after a huge heist, and who cracks first. I wanted to do a study of those guys after the robbery. Dino didn't want that.

We hired George V. Higgins to rewrite the script. As you know, Higgins is a specialist in New England dialogue and he wrote a brilliant script, but when it was translated into Italian for Dino, it wasn't funny. He kept saying, "No gagas, no gagas." Again, looking for *Big Deal on Madonna Street*. He said, "This is not a-funny." I said, "Dino, it *is* funny." If he'd had *Divorce Italian Style* translated into English, that wouldn't have been funny either.

I guess it became clear to both of us that we were on divergent paths and the movie wouldn't get made. But I had a play or pay contract—you get paid even if the picture doesn't get made, as you know—and I was damned if I was going to quit.

So it came time for a showdown meeting with Dino. I brought George Higgins and Bob Rosen along and we sat in Dino's huge office on Canon Drive. He had a desk the size of the island of Sicily. It was the biggest desk I ever saw. You sat a bit lower than he did and he was backlit. It was very dramatic.

He said, "I have ideas about the movie and I want you listen. Now, Scene 62." I turned to Scene 62. He said, "This is what I do," and some of the things he said were brilliant, things I hadn't thought of. For the first time I saw that he wanted to make the kind of movie I wanted to make. I said, "Dino this is really great."

He said, "And-a next Scene 131." Again, brilliant notes. I was overwhelmed, as was Higgins, as was Bob Rosen. I said, "This changes everything." He said, "Scene 202." My script ended at Scene 183. I said, "Scene what?" He said, "Scene 202." I said, "I don't have it." He said, "You must-a have." So I walked around and looked at his script. Sure enough, Scene 202. He was reading from an entirely different version of the script. Scene 131 had nothing to do with my script and neither did Scene 62. His ideas for Scene 62 were wrong for *his* Scene 62, and the ones for Scene 131 were wrong for *his* Scene 131, no matter that they made sense for mine.

So we were still in disagreement and we couldn't get around it. He ended up paying me a lot for not doing the picture, and he was very honorable.

[*The Brink's Job* was eventually made in 1978, directed by William Friedkin.]

You're obviously in great shape, and you're playing a lot of tennis again.

I started playing tournaments when I was twelve or thirteen and I played tennis relentlessly until I was twenty-two. Television kept me busy as hell but I still played some tennis until I was twenty-eight. By then I was in a miserable marriage with a deeply disturbed woman and I only wanted to get out of the house.

Then I met Evans and I stopped playing altogether to concentrate on being with her. After a while it became easier to have a drink after work than to be out on the tennis court. Symbolically I threw the racket away.

So when I had a physical at age fifty-seven, the doctor said what do you do for exercise, and the answer was not very much.

John Frankenheimer, circa 1980.

". . . When you've been blasted critically or the public doesn't respond to the movie, you really start to think, 'What did I do wrong?' and 'Have I lost it? Is it there still?'. . . The only thing you can do is try to put the thing in perspective. . .

. . .This is a very, very serious business we're in because we're dealing from our guts. We're dealing in our feelings, with putting the very things that make us human beings up there on the screen. . . So when you get killed for something, it's not just criticizing the way you write an insurance policy. . . They're getting to the very innermost part of your soul. . . Up to now I've been resilient enough to come back. It's taken a lot of work."

—JF (1991)

Well, my cholesterol was out of sight and my blood pressure wasn't worth talking about, and I'd better start getting some exercise or else. Walk, run, swim or ride my bicycle at least a half-hour a day. All of them bored the shit out of me. The bicycle was the least offensive, and I'd ride up and down Old Malibu Road, past the tennis club, where I'd hear the plunk of the ball. The funny thing was, I'd never really thought I'd played tennis for myself, but mostly to please my father. But now I called Tim Barry, a pro I ran into on a private court, and asked him to give me a lesson. I had to borrow a racket.

The muscle memory came back and to my surprise I could actually return the shots. I went back to him a couple of days later, and I couldn't hit a thing and I was sore all over. But I liked it. A half-hour and I was totally winded. I started seeing him three times a week, and I figured, "If this is good, why don't I find a second pro and play with him two days a week," which is what I did.

Then I hired Harold Hecht, Jr., the son of one of my old producers. He'd competed on the pro tour for four years, and I played with him every day. I've been at it nearly six years now, and the morning Hecht and I beat Tim Barry and another pro in a doubles match was the best tennis I've played since college.

I don't know why I tell you all this.

Maybe it has something to do with being a perfectionist.

Aha, you're remembering that incident about being a perfectionist I told you about.

You just mentioned it quickly, in passing.

I was at a support group meeting in London and I was feeling very, very depressed. And there was an old Irishman named Brian at the meeting. He said, "Johnny, you look depressed." I said, "Well, I am, Brian; I'm very depressed."

He asked me why and I said, "Well, things just aren't going my way and I'm a perfectionist. Yeah, that's what I am, a perfectionist."

Brian looked at me and said, "Well, what are you perfect at?"

That kind of line puts everything in perspective. I laughed like hell, and felt much better. It brought me completely out of my depression.

PROPHECY (Paramount, 1979).

Michael Eisner, who by then was head of Paramount, said he wanted me to do a monster movie. He thought it would be fabulous for a director with a style like mine to do a monster movie. So Bob Rosen and I hired David Seltzer, who'd just come off *The Omen*, to do a script. He came up with an idea, which looked good on paper.

Intended to be an ecological warning, I think, about some huge mutant creatures caused by mercury poisoning.

That was the idea. Ironically, it turned out to be a profitable movie. Every couple of years I find a check in the mail from my participation in *Prophecy*. But honestly I don't think it's a well-made movie. I was going through a very bad personal time.

I hadn't realized it, but I was getting a drinking problem. My generation was brought up to drink. Three martini lunches and all that. But there was alcoholism in my family, the half-Irish side of my family. My father was a practicing alcoholic. I never got drunk. I could drink more than anybody. But what happened after *Black Sunday* came out and didn't do what everyone thought it was going to do was that I just went over the edge. I had never drunk when I worked. I only drank when I was alone, but I realized later that I was dependent on alcohol, and alcohol began to color my decisions, like the decision to do *Prophecy*, which I should never have done. I caught myself in time, got into the Program and haven't had a drink for nearly twelve years. But *Black Sunday* was the start of a black time for me.

Compounding the problem with *Prophecy* was that Eisner and I totally disagreed about the cut. I cut an R version of the movie. Paramount insisted we cut it to PG. I've never really gotten over that clash. I told Eisner he was ruining the movie and I refused to do the cut. He sent in his then-assistant Don Simpson and told him to cut the movie. Rather than having that happen, I ended up doing it myself, but under duress.

It didn't work as a PG. It wasn't scary. The R version I think was. The big problem with the movie was that the audience was way ahead of us. They knew from the beginning what was going on. Halfway through, our hero says, with incredulity, "There's a monster out there." The audience broke out laughing, wondering why it took this dimwit so long to figure it out.

Did you actually shoot in Maine?

No. In Vancouver and at the studio. I thought Talia Shire was good. I thought Richard Dysart and Robert Foxworth and Armand Assante were all good.

I just don't think I was good. And you saw too much of the monster. It didn't work. It looked like something you'd like, not something you'd be terribly afraid of.

I was at a preview screening at, I think, the Chinese, and it was a raucous crowd, making catcalls that seemed to have nothing to do with what was on the screen.

There was a claque of Rick Baker fans in the audience the first two nights. They thought he should have done the monster. It was actually done by Thomas H. Burman. Tom Burman.

I looked up my review the other day and I'm afraid I was unkind. I said there was a moment when "horror" looked like Smokey the Bear posing for 'September Morn.' I also said that when mutation horror misses, it evokes Godzilla rather than some Godawful ecological truth.

The experience—not the review—drove me into a black, black period. That claque

Above: *Talia Shire and Robert Foxworth.*

Above right: *Foxworth, Shire, Victoria Racimo and Armand Assante.*

Right: *Foxworth injects adrenalin into a nearly-dead infant creature as Shire watches.*

"As monsters go, the ones in Prophecy are less fun and far less mysterious than Godzilla."
—Vincent Canby
The New York Times (6/15/79)

The director (right) prepares the cast for a key scene. From left, Assante, Shire, Tom McFadden, Racimo, and Foxworth.

really ruined the movie in Los Angeles but, as I said, it made money overall.

My agent, Jeff Berg, came to me with a book by Denne Peticlerc and Peter Bart. Lorimar, via Merv Adelson, who was head of Lorimar, wanted to do it as a movie. They offered me a lot of money on a play-or-pay deal. The catch was that the deal was pegged on the budget and the script.

It was about Cuba and an aristocratic family which was against Castro. Two sons ended up on opposite sides of the conflict. It was a very good script and a good book, but in the end Lorimar didn't want to do it. They said the budget was too high and used that as the leverage to cut me out of the deal. So I was out of a Paramount contract and out of a Lorimar contract.

After that unpleasantness, I went off to Japan to do a movie called *The Challenge* for CBS Theatrical Films.

THE CHALLENGE (Embassy, 1982).

Above: *The director (right) explores possibilities of a scene with Toshiro Mifune, with whom he had worked fifteen years earlier on* GRAND PRIX.

The Challenge

It was a pretty good movie, a kind of modern day samurai film. The script centered around two ancient samurai swords with mythical properties attached to them. It's also about the culture clash between Japan and America. A lot of martial arts in it, a long look at what it takes to be a samurai today. Donald March was running CBS Theatrical Films then, and he was the one who wanted to do it. Had a script by Richard Maxwell and John Sayles. Scott Glenn and Toshiro Mifune were the stars, and they were both very good in my estimation. Glenn was coming off a Bob Evans picture, *Urban Cowboy*, I think. He seemed right for a down and out who is set up by a semi-Mafia Japanese group.

Ivan Moffat, who'd been a big help to Bob Rosen and me on *Black Sunday*, came over to Japan to help us with some big script problems on this one.

But as happens time and time again in this town, there were management changes, and the new management wanted nothing to do with whatever the previous management had done. Donald March went out and Mike Levy and Joe Wizan came in. Joe said, "If we'd come aboard a week earlier you wouldn't be shooting." Too late they got on the bandwagon and liked it, but by then it really was too late. The studio never got behind the picture. It's another of those Sam Goldwynisms: "If people don't want to see a movie, you can't stop them." If the studio bosses don't like a movie, there's not a damned thing you can do.

There was a terrific mix-up at CBS over who was going to distribute the movie and the movie never got the kind of release it deserved. It got some good reviews. Mifune, as I say, was wonderful, which is no surprise to anyone.

Mike Levy did love the movie, but then they threw him out. Gabe Sumner was in there but nobody quite knew what to do. They finally made a distribution deal with Embassy. Shooting in Japan was a very strange experience. We shot primarily with a Japanese crew, and I really didn't understand the Japanese very well. I wish I'd known then what I know now. Which is mostly that it's really impossible for them to say No. You'd say, "I'd like a shot of Chuck that starts on his left eye, close up, then I'd like to dolly out through the window and around the tennis player and then go back to Chuck's right eye." They'd say, "Hai, hai" and go off and have a meeting. And after the meeting you'd ask, "How long will this shot take," and there's another conference and they come back and say, "Two years."

You'd ask for a shot and they'd disappear and nothing would happen and then you'd realize they didn't have the faintest idea how to do the shot. Very few of them spoke English and I wasn't getting anything done with our interpreter, who was a woman.

Then an American who'd lived there for years said, "The reason you aren't getting anything done is that she's not translating what you're saying. In Japan, there's no way a woman can talk to the men the way you're talking to them. 'Do this, do that.' She has to put everything a whole other way." That made sense to me.

Then we found a really tough-minded Chinese woman who was trilingual, English, Chinese, Japanese. She came aboard and things started to get done.

The casting took longer than for any movie I've ever done, because just to get an actor for a two-line appearance involved a meeting with the actor and his agents that was as formal as a tea ceremony.

I needed an actor to play Mifune's brother, and we found a man who was evidently the Japanese Clint Eastwood, named Atsuo Nakamura. He spoke good English. I kept enlarging his part. I brought him back to CBS on Radford in Studio City to loop some lines. He had a long scene

161

Above: *Frankenheimer finds the best way to frame Scott Glenn (above right) for a scene in which Glenn proves his loyalty to Samurai master (Mifune) by experiencing "live burial" as a self-imposed test of endurance.*

Right: *Frankenheimer (in light jacket) rehearses a fight scene between Glenn and Atsuo Nakamura. Glenn's double is standing left of director; at right is stunt coordinator Steven Sagall.*

"A final shootout scene combines the best of old-fashioned swashbuckling sword play with a good deal of both Bondian and Star Wars flashing of all kinds of deadly modern paraphernalia. . . Scott Glenn . . . may well prove to be just the star material Frankenheimer thinks."
—Daily Variety (1/28/82)

Scott Glenn, Toshiro Mifune and Donna Kei Benz, who plays Mifune's daughter.

with Scott Glenn and he was going back to Japan the next day. I said to my assistant, "I've been involved with this script for so long that I can't *hear* it anymore. Go get the guard at the gate, get somebody, to come in and watch this scene so we'll get an idea what they understand and don't understand."

He brought in a very nice black guard from the gate. He watched the scene and I said, "What do you think?" He said, "That's a real good scene but let me ask you a question: what language is the one guy speaking?" He didn't understand a word

Nakamura said. I'd been in Japan so long he sounded like Olivier to me. We had to loop him completely with an American actor. But it can happen.

What happened to me was that my claim that I never drank while I worked went out the window because on *The Challenge* I drank while I worked. And when I came back from that movie in 1981 I knew my life couldn't go on the way it was going. So I checked myself into a detox program at St. John's Hospital and when I came out I got into a support group and I've been okay ever since.

THE RAINMAKER (HBO Theatre, 1982).

The Rainmaker and Others

You did an Elmore Leonard novel in here someplace.

That was a bit later. Meantime I went back to television and did something for HBO. I directed *The Rainmaker*, with Tuesday Weld, who'd done *I Walk the Line* for me, and Tommy Lee Jones. It was a very pleasant experience all round. I did it on tape. Wanted to see if I could still handle that. I have a tape of it, but it was never put out commercially on cassette.

There were other projects in this period that were never made.

I got involved in another racing picture. This one had a father-son story that would culminate at the 24 Hours of Le Mans. I spent ten months on that project, working on scripts, making trips to Europe to line up the race tracks. I had everything ready to go, and Ned Tanen was going to produce it at Universal. Then Tanen left Universal and there I was again with a new management. I had a first meeting with the new head of production, Bob Rehme, who has since gone on and on. But when I pulled into the parking lot and saw a Lincoln Town Car in his space I knew I had no chance.

Bob said to me, "Look, I really don't have any interest in automobile racing at all, and I don't think I really want to do this movie." So there we were with eight to ten months' work out the window.

After *The Challenge*, I'd also gotten involved with Michael Phillips, the producer, and his then wife Liv Feret on a property called *Wilderness*, a novel by Robert Parker, to which Richard Dreyfuss was committed. Phillips was going to raise money privately for this and I had every reason to believe he was going to bring it off. He was very up front with me.

But we could never solve the script. It's not a Spenser novel, this one. It's about a very urban city guy and his wife who make friends with a character who seems like Burt

Reynolds in *Deliverance*. The wife gets very attached to him. Then they go on a camping trip and they're set upon by gangsters, for reasons I don't remember. The Reynolds-type character is incapacitated and the husband, the wimp from the city, has to become the Reynolds character in order for all of them to survive. He has to do all these things, and he does, and perseveres. It's quite a good story.

Dreyfuss is still involved with it. We had a lot of talented people involved, including David Freeman and the guy who wrote the remake of *No Way Out*, Bob Garland. But we never solved the script and we never made it. Michael was very nice to me, very honest with me, and he honored his commitments. I helped Michael try to raise the money and, again, it was a project I was involved with for six or seven months, and again it came to naught.

Opposite page: *Tuesday Weld and Tommy Lee Jones star in Frankenheimer's first television production in more than twenty years.*

THE HOLCROFT COVENANT (Universal, 1985).

Above: *Director Frankenheimer poses with Producer Edie Landau, Michael Caine and seated to the left, Victoria Tennant.*

I went over to the festival at Avorriaz, where I was honored, but things were shaky and I was getting a bit discouraged. Then while I was there I got a call from my agent at the time, Peter Rawley, saying that Edie and Ely Landau wanted me to make *The Holcroft Covenant* with James Caan. I'd been a great fan of the Robert Ludlum books. Read them all. I love thrillers, that kind of book, and *The Holcroft Covenant* had been one of my favorite Ludlums. I also liked Ely Landau. He was a charming charlatan. I knew him during my time in live television and I worked with him on *The Iceman Cometh* here in Los Angeles. Then just at the time I was reading the script, Ely had a bad stroke and his wife took over the project. She'd had no experience producing and the active producer became a guy named Mort Abrahams, whom I'd worked with long ago in New York when I was an assistant director and he was a producer.

I told them I thought the script had a lot of problems and I suggested they get hold of John Hopkins, an English writer I'd worked with.

I think he created the terrific English police series, "Z Cars."

That's him. You had to have an English writer because it's an English story. My contention was that there are very few English writers who can also write the American idiom and American dialogue. He's married to Shirley Knight, the American actress. His kids were brought up in America. He lives here so he has more knowledge than most of the American idiom. So John came out.

Concurrently they arranged a first meeting for me with Caan, the star of the picture, who'd okayed me as the director. We had a long meeting, and Caan was talking about a movie that I didn't really see in the

material. He said he was doing the movie because it was a love story. But a love story it's not; it's a thriller. Yes, he falls in love but it's not much of a love story. I didn't understand Caan that day and I'm sure he didn't understand me. But you tend to tell yourself that those meetings go better than they actually do, because you want the thing to succeed.

It became painfully obvious that Hopkins's script didn't work. I got the Landaus to hire my friend George Axelrod to fix it and George came over to Europe, where I was scouting locations. George improved it greatly, but we hadn't totally finished it when we had to start shooting. We had a firm start date that was insisted on by Caan's people. Caan arrived, and the first thing he said was that he wasn't starting without a finished script.

We pointed out to Caan that we hadn't liked the start date, but we'd hired a crew and put them all on payroll and were committed to the starting date that his people had demanded.

I flew from London to Germany on a Saturday because we were going to start shooting on a Monday. Caan said he would follow the next day. He said he was going to meet with Axelrod first. He wasn't feeling well but he said he'd be there.

On the Sunday morning I was standing at my hotel window, looking at Lake Constance and watching the crew lay out this complicated dolly shot, in which Caan was supposed to get off this lake boat and walk along the quay being stalked by two men who are going to kill him, except that the two men don't know there is another killer behind them who is going to kill them to save Caan. It was going to be our first shot, long and complicated.

Now the phone rings and it's George Axelrod to tell me, (A), that Caan had not kept the meeting with him, and (B), that instead of taking the plane to Munich Caan

"There's a dark flush about The Holcroft Covenant. . . *a kind of mad, sleek glitter that sucks you right back to memories of the classic paranoid political thriller* The Manchurian Candidate. . . *lunatic events roll by with a* crispness that suggests acid etching a nightmare on glass."

—Michael Wilmington
Los Angeles Times (10/18/85)

Above: *Victoria Tennant with her two leading men, Michael Caine (top) and Anthony Andrews (bottom).*

had had the hotel book him on the Concorde to New York. This was the day before shooting was going to begin.

So I was the person who had to call Edie Landau in California and tell her that her star was not only not reporting for work but would be only a local phone call away the next day.

She and Abrahams said, "You have to shoot anyway."

I said, "Shoot what? The film is called *The Holcroft Covenant* and we don't have Holcroft."

They said, "You have to shoot something for insurance purposes. Use a double for Holcroft."

I said, "Well, it would be nice to know who'll be playing Holcroft, Mickey Rooney or Wilt Chamberlain."

They said, "Oh, that's right. Well, isn't there anything else you could shoot?"

I said, "We can shoot the assassins." They said, "Great!" These three guys were stunt men and I told them, "Fellas, you're never going to get this much attention again as long as you live. We'll get dolly shots of you, Steadicam shots of you; you're going to get so much coverage you can use it as a career reel." And that's indeed what we did.

Meantime, we're trying to solve our star problem. This was an Eady Plan picture, which means that you have to have a major percentage of English people in both the cast and the crew. It was a tricky situation because it wasn't clear whether Caan had just walked off the movie or had walked off the movie for cause, complaining that there hadn't been a finished script. If it went to arbitration and we lost, there'd be no money left to hire another non-English person.

But the gods smiled. Michael Caine was just coming off a movie and he was available. I'd always wanted to work with him, and he accepted. Michael Caine playing a role written for Jimmy Caan required certain changes in the script. But Michael was just a dream. He made everything a pleasure.

And I worked with a woman I'd been in love with since age eighteen, Lilli Palmer. I was in college and I saw her on stage in *Bell, Book and Candle*. I hated Rex Harrison for

"When you say that film is a director's medium. . . I can't really go along with it. I think you have to fight for everything you get and I think that there is no great director who can make a great film out of a lousy script."
—J.F.

marrying her. Harrison moved better than any man I ever saw. In the second act of *Bell, Book and Candle*, Harrison took his evening cape and with a flick of his wrist wraps it around him and walks out. I was playing in *The Importance of Being Earnest* at Williams, totally miscast, phony English accent and all. I was so knocked out by Harrison that I had the costume people get me a cape and I practiced endlessly in front of a mirror to get that flick of the wrist just the way Harrison did it.

Opening night and my adrenaline was going like mad and I flicked the cape around me, and it kept going around my neck. I was choking, and to this day I've never gotten laughs like I got. People thought it was part of the play. I was a triumph. I told Harrison about it years later.

Anyway, Lilli Palmer played Caine's mother and at seventy-three or seventy-four she was divine. I took her to dinner at the Connaught Hotel in London with some corporate executives I knew who were as infatuated with her as I was. She was wearing a backless gown and when she walked in, everything in the dining room froze. No one could stop looking at her. She died about a year later, of I think mysterious causes.

She was also a wonderful writer, novelist, memoirist. I'm sorry I never met her.

The post-mortem on the movie was another of those black farces that seem to attract themselves to me from time to time. I think it was a bit of *The Producers* syndrome again. I think if the picture had ever turned out to be a hit they would have had to account for a lot of money that somehow or other went down the tube. The head of EMI, which financed the film, resigned about eight months after the film was released in 1985. One item that made the papers was that his personal expense account for the year was almost two million dollars. This was during the time we were making our film.

But that news was a bit later. We ran the movie for Universal which was going to distribute it and Marvin Antonowsky, the head of marketing, and all his people loved it. They said, "This movie is going to do very well and we want to spend a lot on prints and ads. What we need is back-up to the theatrical release." In other words they wanted the ancillary rights—television, including cable. Universal had this lousy deal with EMI, in which Universal had to distribute everything EMI made, under the terms of some sort of buy-out deal, I think. And EMI said, "We're keeping the ancillaries," and Universal said, "Screw you."

Universal put it in sixty theaters or whatever their minimum contractual requirement was and played it a week and then abandoned it. EMI released it on video cassettes and that was that. It killed me, because the picture never had a chance.

The more ironic because it got some nice reviews.

Some very good reviews. Michael Wilmington called it my best work since *Manchurian Candidate*. But that and seventy-five cents got me a trip on the New York subway.

We had to cut the picture in England because of the Eady Plan requirements, but my wife and I liked England a lot so we just stayed on.

I was involved with Frederick Forsyth on *The Fourth Protocol*. Again I got George Axelrod the job of writing the script, although in the end Forsyth got solo credit. During the time I was involved in the movie they never did raise the money and I moved on. Eventually Rank financed the film and it was directed by an English director, John Mackenzie.

52 PICK-UP (Cannon, 1986).

As I said, I'm a fan of crime fiction, mysteries, thrillers, whatever. And while I was in England I read Elmore Leonard's *52 Pick-Up*. I called my agent and asked him to find out if the movie rights were owned. I said, "If they aren't, I'd really like to get them because I think it's a great book and I could make a terrific movie out of it."

He called me back and said they were owned by Menachem Golan and his partner Yoram Globus at Cannon. I said, "Oh God, that's awful." He said, "No, they've started a whole new policy in which they're going to make classy movies. They're hiring a lot of good people and they're going to up the budgets. They want to be a major and be competitive with the other majors."

I said, "Call them and see if they want me to direct the picture." He called back and said they did and that the terms were acceptable. So we went back to Los Angeles and I met with Henry Weinstein who was producing. I knew Henry from before, because he'd replaced Selznick on *Tender Is the Night* as I told you. He'd been very apologetic about the fact that I'd been forced off the picture and he'd been nice to me over the years since.

Henry suggested a Los Angeles playwright named John Steppling to do the script. Steppling did do the script but whenever he deviated from the Elmore Leonard book, it didn't work. Meantime Roy Scheider called me and said he loved Leonard's stuff and the character in *52 Pick-Up* particularly and he'd like to play him. Menachem agreed to hire him and as soon as Roy came aboard he and I got together with Leonard and the three of us collaborated on making the script a dramatization of the novel, which is essentially what we shot.

From the beginning, Weinstein and the production people had said, "We're going to make the picture in Pittsburgh." I said, "But it's set in Detroit." They said, "You can't shoot in Detroit. Detroit has Team-ster problems and no crews; you have to bring them in from Chicago. And we can get great deals in Pittsburgh." They began to sound like the Pittsburgh Chamber of Commerce.

Well, I wanted to make the picture so I went to Pittsburgh and looked at locations and I must say Pittsburgh was great. I always thought of it as coal mines, steel plants and smoke. But it was just the opposite and I came back very enthused. Meanwhile we'd hired Ann-Margret to play Roy's wife.

We got the budget, nine million dollars, and I took it to Menachem. He said, "It's a million dollars too high. I won't pay a penny more than eight million dollars." I knew he meant it, because he told me exactly what he was going to pay Roy Scheider for the picture. It was a million dollars, and not a million dollars and one cent. Roy was asking a million and a half. I went to Roy and said, "I don't know what your agent's telling you, but I'm telling you he likes you, he thinks you're perfect for the part and he wants to work with you. But he's not going to pay a penny more, not if you have Jeff Berg and Mike Ovitz negotiating together for you. That's the way he does business." So Roy agreed to do it. And I knew Menachem was just as firm about the budget.

I went to him and said, "Menachem, why are we making this picture in Pittsburgh?" If he'd said something like the city had given him a deal on five more movies, I wouldn't have known what to say, or how to make the movie at his price. But what he said was, "I don't know why we're making the movie in Pittsburgh. I thought *you* wanted to make the movie in Pittsburgh." I said, "Ever since I've been on the picture I've been told it was a done deal." He said, "Not so." So I said, "We could make the movie here in Los Angeles for a million dollars less. The crews are here, no airline

Opposite page:
Frankenheimer with Roy Scheider.

Above: *The cast gathers for a first reading of the script. From left around the table: Doug McClure, Lonny Chapman, John Glover, Ann-Margret, Vanity, JF, Kelly Preston, Roy Scheider, Clarence Williams III and Robert Trebor.*

tickets, no hotels. We'll save it on expenses." He said, "Fine," and that was it.

Menachem was wonderful to me. He left me completely alone as long as I stayed on budget, which I did. I'll give you an example. The Scheider character learns that the girl he's had an affair with has been killed by three guys. There's a video tape of it. He's got to decide to go out and kill those guys. It was a crucial decision for him to make, and the audience has got to understand what's going on inside him, how it's driving him crazy and now he's got to do it.

I didn't know how to show all that. Then I thought that one way it might work was if he was driving almost in a daze and got

stopped at a railroad crossing by a long freight. The red lights are flashing in his face, the bell is ringing, the sound of the train is grating on his brain and it's all like a nightmare. So I wrote it all into the script. But the production people called my people and said, "No train. It would cost $20,000, and it's not in the budget."

Never being one to take no for an answer lightly I called and asked to see Menachem, who by then was directing Stallone in that arm-wrestling picture, *Over the Top*.

I explained the situation and he said, "I love the movie up to now from what I've seen, and if you have to have the train, okay. But if there's a way to make the thing work

"[Frankenheimer] elicits performances that are so frighteningly real you believe everything. . ."

—Michael Dare
L. A. Weekly

"It's fast-paced, lurid, exploitative and loaded with marvelous energy. John Frankenheimer. . . hasn't done anything this darkly entertaining since Black Sunday."

—Janet Maslin
The New York Times

173
52 PICK-UP

without the train, I'd really appreciate it. Think about it. If there's no other way, I'll okay the train."

Well, you feel like you want to help someone who says it like that. I thought about it, and in the end I accomplished the same thing with an automobile accident in the rain, with much the same kind of feeling. And we did it for a lot less money, needless to say.

We finished the picture and it ran about an hour and fifty-five minutes. I arranged to screen it at 7:30 on a Tuesday night for Menachem and Yoram and their key executives. I went in there with fear in my heart, because I'd heard all the stories about how they re-cut pictures, butchered them. And I didn't have final cut.

It was a very long hour and fifty-five minutes. Then the lights came up and everybody was quiet, and Menachem and Yoram talked to each other for a few minutes. Menachem said, "It's really very, very good. It's too long, but it's very good. If you'll meet me at eight-thirty in the morning in the cutting room, I'll give you some ideas for cuts and changes."

Chuck, I didn't sleep that night. I thought, "My God, what am I going to do? How can I fight? What are my rights?" I walked into the cutting room feeling as if the bomb was about to go off. Throwing out stuff I liked in the movie was going to be warfare.

Menachem was there when I got there. He was early. He said, "Look, I have to tell you something before we start. This is your movie. You have final cut on this movie. Anything I say is strictly a suggestion. You use what you want and throw out what you don't want. I think it's a little long, but if you want it to go out this way, it's going out this way."

I almost cried, because it was so opposite from everything I'd expected to happen. And we spent the morning together. He had

Roy Scheider and Ann-Margret.

John Glover and Clarence Williams III.

Frankenheimer told film critic Kirk Honeycutt that he wanted to give 52 Pick-Up *the look and feel of an old black-and-white movie. Honeycutt—who, in 1982, called the film "one of the best thrillers of the 1980s"—pointed out that "the decor and costumes and everything, even the cat, is black and white."*

Ann-Margret as a wife who finds her political career thwarted by her husband's scandal.

Vanity and Kelly Preston as key characters in a world of vice.

ten or twelve ideas and half of them were terrific. They're in the movie. And he came up with about five minutes of good cuts.

Then it stopped being good. Yoram and his distribution guy had no idea how to distribute movies. That was part of their downfall. Yoram said, "We're spending two million dollars on the distribution of the picture." I said, "It's not enough, you can't get this picture out there for two million dollars." He said, "That's all we're going to spend." I said, "But you love the movie." He said, "That's all we got." I said, "Nobody knows this picture exists. It's a secret. You've got to get out and promote it." But it was never done. Cannon never previewed films for critics. I made them do that. In fact I made a terrific mistake. I knew Sheila Benson at the *Times* and I arranged a special screening for her. I guess the scenario was that she didn't like the movie and didn't want to give me a bad review, so she assigned the review to another *Times* critic, who was not a regular film critic and who gave me the worst review I've ever had in my life.

I mean you've never read anything like it. I got raves from everyone else, including Janet Maslin in *The New York Times*. Roy Scheider called from New York very ebullient and said, "Great review in *The New York Times*." I said, "Wait'll you read *The Los Angeles Times*."

Menachem took double truck ads quoting all the great reviews and saying *52 Pick-Up* was the best reviewed film Cannon had ever had.

But they still didn't know how to market the picture and never really spent any money publicizing the picture. The story was really *Fatal Attraction*, you know. The people who saw it loved it, but not enough people saw it. It was a big hit on video cassette, but it never took off at the box office. It's a very good movie, and it should have been a hit, could have been a hit.

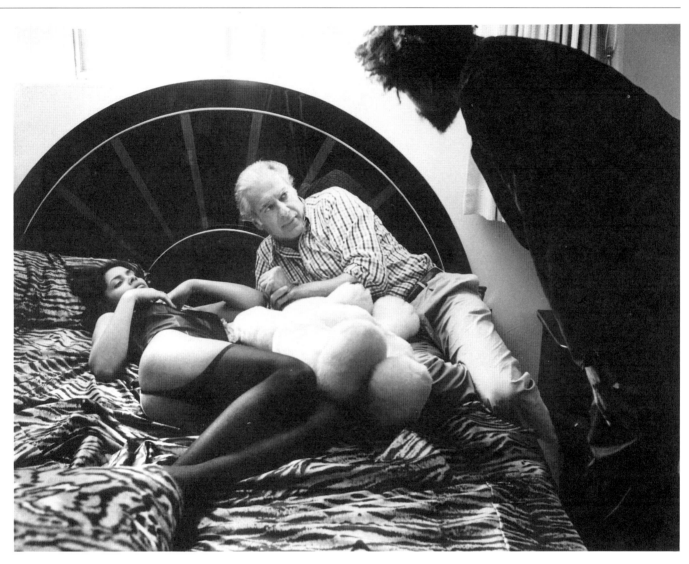

It's maddening, isn't it. You make the picture, but ultimately you lose control. You're at the mercy of the studio, whichever it is.

Yeah, you have to win the battle twice. You've got to get the picture made, and then you've got to get the studio behind it to promote it. Paramount really got behind the two pictures I made there, *Black Sunday* and *Prophecy*. They gave them everything they had. Frank Mancuso got

Above: *The director in recumbent rehearsal with Vanity and Clarence Williams III. "John. . . wanted to do a film," Roy Scheider said, "that was faithful to Elmore Leonard's writing, and his writing is definitely R-rated."*

Prophecy into the theaters a week before Memorial Day weekend and it did huge business.

DEAD-BANG (Warner Bros., 1988).

Upper right: *Don Johnson and Penelope Ann Miller.*

Right: *Tim Reid with Johnson.*

Below right: *Johnson with Michael Jeter.*

"There's a lot of action, and director Frankenheimer zips through it with aplomb. The film is loaded with swift Steadicam and crane moves, not to mention multiple dissolves that encapsulate necessary chunks of exposition. The film also makes exceptional use of little-used L.A. locations."

—Hollywood Reporter
(3/28/89)

The next project wasn't calculated to raise your spirits either, I'm afraid. The horror stories about Dead-Bang *got wide circulation around the industry.*

It was a project I'd developed at Paramount, about a cop named Jerry Beck. I had a script done by Robert Foster, but when Ned Tanen finally read it, he didn't want to make it and gave it back to me in turn-around.

I got a producer named Steve Roth involved and he took it to Bernie Brillstein, who was running Lorimar. Roth was a friend of Jeff Berg's and had an office at ICM which is how he came to my attention. Brillstein liked it and offered to finance it if we could get one of a group of actors. Don Johnson of "Miami Vice" fame was at the top of the list. They really wanted to make the picture with him. So Roth and I went to Miami and got him, for three and a half million. Johnson was play or pay from the moment they signed him. I didn't get play or pay until a week before we started shooting, so I had no leverage with Johnson at all. Bob Rosen came aboard as executive producer so that lent a note of sanity to the production. But it was a horrendous experience, maybe the worst I've ever had.

A friend of mine was on the picture and had his own stories about the arrogance of the star.

The production designer, Ken Adam, got to the edge of a nervous breakdown. It was terrible. In the middle of shooting, Lorimar was sold to Warner Bros., so there was nobody to support us at all. I finally got Roth removed from the picture because there were huge problems with him. He was always trying to create artificial problems so that he could appear to fix them.

Johnson refused to work with the actors we'd hired. Connie Selleca would've been perfect. She's a beautiful girl with a New York accent, exactly what we needed. She was a character who could have stood up to the Johnson character. But she was fired and paid off. The only actress Johnson would accept was Penelope Ann Miller, a good actress but wrong for the part. She's talented but quite average looking.

But there was no way to stop Johnson. Warners sent helicopters for him every time we had an argument. They weren't interested in our movie, they were interested in Johnson, so whatever he wanted he got.

He had contractual rights to make the script he had accepted, so he would never allow us to make cuts. Rosen and I pointed out to him that if we shot the script as it was the picture would last three hours. Finally, when it was too late, he let us make some cuts. His key scenes, the scenes that established the character, became extraneous. Instead of being worked into the fiber of the script, they became cut-able, and of course after the previews they were cut.

At that point the Warners people were quite honorable. Bob Daly and Terry Semel. They looked at the movie and wanted Johnson's key scene with Penelope Ann Miller cut because it slowed down the movie. It was too long, but Johnson hadn't let us cut it. When it was cut, the movie became a straight action picture. The studio decided not to screen the movie for the critics, which I didn't know because I was already up in Calgary shooting my next movie. I said, "The critics will kill us."

They said, "We don't want to spoil the opening weekend because we think Don Johnson is a movie star.

I don't have to tell you we did get killed because the critics saw the film as something Warners didn't believe in and was dumping. It did no business, and Don Johnson was proved not to be a movie star.

THE FOURTH WAR (Cannon Releasing, 1989).

Above: *Director John Frankenheimer consults with his longtime friend and producer Robert L. (Bob) Rosen on location in the bitter cold of Calgary, Canada, doubling for West Germany.*

"Tightly directed by Frankenheimer with an eye for comic relief as well as maintaining tension, Fourth War *holds the fascination of eyeball-to-eyeball conflict."*

—Daily Variety (3/14/90)

The Fourth War

You must have been up in Calgary shooting The Fourth War.

I was. Wolf Schmidt, who owns Kodiak Film, had come to me with a script called *The Fourth War*, about these two warriors who are still fighting the Cold War and running the risk of making it a hot war again.

Roy Scheider said he would commit to it if I would direct it. I liked the idea and I wanted to work with Roy again so I agreed to do it. Again Bob Rosen was the line producer. We went to Calgary because we knew we couldn't shoot it in West Germany where it took place. They didn't have any snow when we wanted to shoot. We had the script rewritten by Ken Ross, who did *Day of the Jackal* and also worked on *Black Sunday* with us.

Aside from the fact we were working in absolute bitter cold it really went well. Scheider was a joy after Don Johnson. We had some problems because we weren't sure some things would work. But I have to say I loved doing the film.

Schmidt made a distribution deal with Cannon which I was bitterly opposed to. But what determined the fate of the picture was that we made a movie about the Cold War and by the time it came out there was no Cold War. We made a picture about a frontier that didn't really exist as we showed it. It became a historical picture, and the reviews were mixed. I know you didn't much like it.

Yet there are images that stay with me: particularly that field of snow that was the no man's land between the two sides.

Yes, but it left something to be desired. Not great material.

Top: *Jurgen Prochnow warns Roy Scheider not to cross his border as Lara Harris looks on.* Middle: *Tim Reid disagrees with his combative commander Scheider.* Bottom: *Scheider is warned to curb his aggression by Harry Dean Stanton.*

YEAR OF THE GUN (Triumph Releasing, 1991).

Above: *Sharon Stone as a nervy American photojournalist in Italy. After working with her in* Year of the Gun, *Frankenheimer said, "I would like Sharon to play in every movie I ever do."*

For a lot of reasons, personal and professional, I'd been feeling very low when the producer Ed Pressman came to me with the idea of doing *Year of the Gun*.

He had the money, he had the script and he had a time he wanted to do the movie. It was to be done in Italy, and all the way around it seemed a stroke of fortune for me.

We had trouble casting the movie. Several actors we wanted turned us down. We ended up with Andrew McCarthy. I insisted on having Sharon Stone in the picture. I'd met her during the casting of *Dead-Bang* but Steve Roth, the producer, didn't want her because he thought she looked like somebody else. I was still trying to keep peace with Roth at that point so I didn't push it like I should have. In retrospect it's just as well, because it would never have worked with Sharon and Don Johnson.

It's ironic that we had the script rewritten after we cast the lead. If Jay Presson Allen had been hired to rewrite before we cast the lead, we would have gotten an actor much higher up on the list. What happens, especially when you have independent financing, is that the financial people give you a list of people they'll accept. A script by Jay Presson Allen would have attracted some other actors, I'm sure.

I'm not here to take shots at Andrew McCarthy. He's a nice guy and I was happy to have him. But he was just not strong enough for the role.

We went to Rome and of course the dollar was falling against the lira. Pressman's money was not in lira and we couldn't buy the lira so the budget kept getting cut and cut and cut.

Due to Pressman's way of financing we did not have a strong domestic release. We had Triumph, which is the releasing arm of Columbia, and Columbia was going through some terrific changes, which didn't help.

Andrew McCarthy and Valeria Golino.

"Director John Frankenheimer (Black Sunday) can still make suspense scenes crackle. . . Frankenheimer and cinematographer Blasco Giurato do a standout job with the taut, hysterical action scenes. . ."
—Daily Variety (9/12/91)

We got some very good reviews, wonderful reviews, but it was just not a success. I like Pressman and we still get along well.

181

The extended family in a 1991 photo: from left, Bud and Kristi Frankenheimer Davis, John and Evans, George and Elise Frankenheimer Riggs. JF's grandson Dylan is standing in front of his mother.

I think it's harder and harder for a director like me to keep functioning in the Hollywood we live in today because most of the executives who make decisions don't really know what a director does.

Also, the quality of the people around the director—the cameramen, art directors, editors, special effects people—has gotten very high, so that somebody who really doesn't know very much about directing a movie can walk in and walk out of it okay. When I was a younger guy doing this you had to know everything. You were out there all by yourself. It was you who determined the camera angle, the lens, everything. Today it's not that way at all. The director sets the scene, but the cameraman decides how to shoot it. Pictures are remade in the editing and everybody gets in on the act. Then there is the question of the double battle, as we were saying before. You battle to get the picture made and then you have to win the second battle of getting the studio behind it.

Even if they're behind it you have these terrible test screenings. You are really in the hands of the test audience. If the test results aren't good, chances are the studio will change its mind about spending money to promote the picture.

In the case of *Dead-Bang*, the test screenings said we ought to cut the scene that was crucial to Don Johnson's character. Warners didn't say you *have* to do this, but there was a hint that the picture would open on In-flight if I didn't.

So the business about final cut is fine and you have to fight for it. But basically they always have the last say, because they determine how much they're going to spend to promote the picture.

It's a business where you can get very lucky, Chuck. But I think that more than ever the odds are against doing something really good.

In the old days when you had a Jack Warner or a Harry Cohn, it was different. Even in my time I've had Arthur Krim and Max Youngstein at UA, Leo Jaffe at Columbia, Bob O'Brien and Bob Weitman at MGM. They were powerful and they wanted to make money as everybody does today. But they also wanted to make something that they could be proud of. Think of Zanuck and *Gentlemen's Agreement*, Warner and *Johnny Belinda*, Warner and *Who's Afraid of Virginia Woolf*.

I think it's possible to do good work. I think you have to persevere. You can't let down. You have to be positive. To be a movie director you *have* to be positive. If you thought about what could go wrong before you got to the set, you'd never get there.

It's a question film makers are always asked, I suppose, but it's interesting to know if you were indeed influenced by the work of particular directors.

When all's said and done, the director who influenced me most was Carol Reed. I'm still looking for a film of his that's almost impossible to find: *The Key*, with William Holden, Sophia Loren and Trevor Howard.

I remember it vaguely. World War II. Carl Foreman wrote it from a novel by Jan de Hartog.

That's right. I keep waiting for it to be shown on one of the movie channels. I have a satellite dish and every week I look at the movie schedules.

Then there are the rest of the directors. Sure, I've been influenced by Orson Welles and his use of the camera. I use a lot of depth of focus and wide-angle lenses. Hitchcock certainly. You'll remember I borrowed from him on *Manchurian Candidate*. George Stevens certainly. You look

"I have no great secrets or revelations as to how I make a film. I just know that making films is the most important thing in my life."

—JF (1977)

". . . directing a film is placing the camera, choosing the lens and editing the footage— not just being able to take good meetings."

—JF (1991)

at "Winter Dreams" and the set is almost a rip-off of *A Place in the Sun*. William Wyler, certainly. And that's about it.

You like the great craftsmen. Those men are all architects of the cinema. There's nothing slapped together, nothing haphazard.

That's right. There's almost nobody today, perhaps with the exception of Scorsese, who I really think fits in that category.

I've just finished a very good book on Carol Reed: *The Films of Carol Reed*. Alexander Korda was his guardian angel. Korda had a tremendous influence on Reed, and Reed was an influence on me.

David Lean would've fit in that category of great craftsmen.

David Lean definitely, but sadly he's no longer with us. I think I might have told you about the most exciting night of my life, or did I?

I was very close to William Wyler. We were very good friends. Every time I screened a film for him I'd do it in a projection room where we could turn the sound up very loud. He'd lost a lot of his hearing in the war. He paid me one of the greatest compliments I've ever received. He said, "You place the camera better than anybody I've ever seen." Coming from him, that was pretty damned good.

We had dinner quite often and one day he called me at Paramount while I was working on *Black Sunday* and asked me if I was busy for dinner that night. Well, I was, but the way I felt about Willie Wyler, when he asked about dinner you weren't busy. I told him I could be free and I said, "What's going on?"

He said, "A friend of mine called me on short notice and he's coming out. He loves your work and wants to meet you, and I think you'd enjoy meeting him."

My wife and I got to his beach house at seven-thirty and Willie opened the door. A man got up from a chair and all I could see at first was that he was tall and quite thin, had gray hair and was wearing a safari jacket. He turned and it was David Lean. And he and Willie and I talked until five-thirty in the morning.

If anybody says, "What was the best night of your life?" It wasn't with a beautiful girl; it wasn't here, wasn't there, it was the night with those two men. And what I learned was that these great directors had the same problems I did. Lean couldn't stop talking about his problems with Robert Mitchum. Wyler couldn't stop talking about his problems with one actor and another. Lean was talking about how Sam Spiegel paid off the wrong people and the Moroccan Army was shooting real bullets at them during *Lawrence of Arabia*.

You've worked with a number of good producers. That's important because it has seemed to me that producers who really know their stuff are an endangered species in the industry.

Producers have been very important to me. Marty Manulis, Fred Coe, John Houseman, Eddie Lewis, Bob Rosen, Bob Evans and, not least, Harold Hecht, who was a man of taste even if we had our arguments. The three I worked with most, Manulis, Rosen and Lewis, are all still alive. It took three producers to replace Manulis when he left *Playhouse 90*—Coe, Houseman and Herbert Brodkin. The producer I was closest to was Eddie Lewis; we were real partners.

What I always tried to do on a project was have my own producer in there. Bob Rosen is the case in point. With the men I'm talking about, there was no such thing as a line producer below them. Those are guys who produced their own movies. I mean, that's what a producer *does*.

Eddie and I had a kind of final parting of the ways when he wanted me to direct *Executive Action*, which was Dalton Trumbo's take on the Kennedy assassination, based on a story by Donald Freed and Mark Lane.

I said, "I can't do it. I can't do that to the Kennedys."

Eddie had raised the money for it, and it finally had a good cast—Burt Lancaster, Robert Ryan, Will Geer. David Miller directed it. But I couldn't go along with it.

Eddie and I did a lot of pictures together, including *Seven Days in May* and *Grand Prix*. At least eight.

CURRENT MOVIES

I was going over the list of the ten top movies at the box office last week. I realized that there were maybe only two of them that I could've directed. There's no way I could have directed *Mo' Better Blues*, obviously. There's no way I could've directed *Boomerang*. There is sure as hell no way I could've directed *Honey, I Blew Up the Kid* or whatever that was, and a couple of others in there. Of the two I could have directed, I would definitely have screwed up one of them. I mean, it would have been a different movie and it probably wouldn't have ended up in the top ten but it would've been a much better movie. That's *A League of Their Own*. I wouldn't have dared to do that soft, sentimental mood Penny Marshall did. It would've been a hard, tough movie.

Tom Hanks playing a tough baseball manager? You never believe it for a moment. Geena Davis is simply extraordinary; she can do anything. But aside from Geena Davis you don't believe one moment of the movie, which is why the audience likes it. It's such an unreal, sentimental story that the audience can say,

"*Yeah*." The audience I saw it with loved it. I felt like a creature from another planet.

STUDIOS

It's in the nature of the industry now for directors not *to be under long-term contracts to studios. How do you feel about that?*

I was certainly under contract to CBS for a long time in television. Four and a half, five years, and I liked that. I was under contract to Paramount for a couple of years after I did *Black Sunday*. I found that to be okay. I was also under contract to Columbia with Eddie Lewis for a while. We did *The Horsemen* and *I Walk the Line* under that contract. Before that I was under contract at MGM, from about 1967 to 1969. Most of the time the contracts were specific projects approved in advance. At Paramount it was different, a more open contract. The problem there was the management kept changing, David Picker, Barry Diller, Michael Eisner.

Actually, I liked having one place as a kind of home. I don't have that at the moment, but I would like to have it again. In the great days the studios had an incentive to spend lots and lots of money promoting the careers of their stars, including their directors. Today you don't have that. The system controlled costs, it also controlled behavior. If you got temperamental, they could always dock your salary, put you on suspension, and of course they did.

TALES FROM THE CRYPT: "Maniac At Large" aired August 19, 1992 on HBO.

Tales From The Crypt

John, the episode of Tales From the Crypt *you directed in 1992 was really the beginning of your return to television, where you'd started your career. How did it come about?*

My agent said he'd had a call from Gil Adler, who was the working producer of the series, asking if I would consider doing it, a half-hour episode to be shot in four days. The agent said the show was prestigious and it might be fun. That's agent talk: shooting a half-hour in four days isn't likely to be fun.

I had two reasons for wanting to do it. *The Year of the Gun* had just come out and made no money. Nothing was happening. But I'd never done TV on film before and I was curious about the technique.

But I still wasn't sure. I complained to an old friend that the pay was only scale, there was no budget and I didn't think I could do it. I was going to call and tell them I wouldn't. My friend, a very wise man, said, "Sure, call 'em and tell 'em no, and then sit by the phone waiting for it to ring again, while you dream about the good old days." I picked up the phone and said I'd take the job.

I met the young cameraman, John Leonetti, and confessed my anxiety. He said, "You shoot it the way you want to shoot it, and I'll figure how to light it." So we designed some complicated shots, and that was the beginning of our relationship. [Leonetti next shot *Against the Wall* with Frankenheimer.]

It was about some killings in a library and the librarian turns out to be the serial killer. Great cast: Blythe Danner, Salome Jens, with whom I'd worked before, of course, a young rock star named Adam Ant and Clarence Williams, with whom I was to work again in *Against the Wall*. It was stylishly shot, I must say, and it was hugely successful.

It was the first time I'd used digital editing. I had a good time doing the show, and the whole experience turned out to be very pleasant and very positive. So when HBO called and wanted me to do *Against the Wall* on a 30-day shooting schedule, I knew I had a fighting chance of bringing it off, and I did.

Above: Blythe Danner.

"I don't know how you can say you don't *have to be a street fighter if you're a director. I remember one night at a party at Bob Evans' when a lot of us were standing around and Arthur Penn said, 'You know what we all have in common? It's the ability to get up off the mat and start again.' And it's true; we've all had to."*
    —JF

Opposite page:
Adam Ant (left) and Clarence Williams III.

AGAINST THE WALL (HBO, March 26, 1994).

As we speak you've come full circle to a major television operation, except that television itself is vastly different from your pioneering days.

Four networks and possibly a fifth in the making, dozens of channels thanks to cable, and movies for cable television that I find quite remarkable. I could even make a case that the kind of daring we associate with the days of live television survives, insofar as it survives at all, in the movies made for cable, for HBO and Turner in particular.

It'll never be the same as it was in live television, of course. Today you can hardly hire an actor for the budget we had in those days for a whole ninety-minute show. But in another sense it may be that we have the best of both worlds. You have all the technical resources of theatrical films, which we didn't have in live television, plus there is at least occasionally the kind of creative freedom in terms of content, the story material, that was so wonderful in live television, as we've discussed. The budgets are lower, and you work on a killing schedule, but in television we always did. And what we achieved on *Against the Wall*, given the budget we had, is I think remarkable if I do say so myself.

Having seen it, I couldn't agree more. It's a real indictment of the conditions that led to the Attica prison riot. There's extraordinary action but a very human story as well, which was the mix of so many of your films.

I'm very proud of *Against the Wall*, which is what HBO is calling it. Originally they wanted to call it "Line of Fire," which I told them wouldn't work because of the Clint Eastwood film. I liked "Overkill" or "Order to Fire," but I like *Against the Wall*.

You've said the HBO experience was a good one, and I gather you had a very supportive production executive.

He's a young guy named Hutch Parker, and he's been terrifically supportive. He was sensitive about his age; he was only twenty-eight when we started working together. He said, "I know I'm young—" I said, "Not by my standards! When I was your age I'd already directed 140 live television shows and I'd won the Emmy a couple of times. No, I don't think you're young." I think that kind of put him at his ease.

If you have the wrong guy at HBO it can be a murderous place. It's been a graveyard for quite a few directors. What they tend to do is deliberately underbudget the pictures, to put the director in conflict with the production company. Then they kind of use that to their advantage. We didn't let that happen. I just kept telling them, "You can't make this picture with the figure you're trying to make it with." When they told me early on that I was over budget, I explained to them that they weren't over budget, they were over some figure they had arbitrarily picked out of a glass bowl, or whatever. The figure had nothing to do with reality.

They had *Against the Wall* arbitrarily budgeted at $5.1 million. By a miracle it only cost $5.8 million.

So I used that argument and they loved the footage they were seeing, so they said, "We-l-l-l," and I really didn't have too many problems with them.

It's not like working for a major—thankfully. You don't have those restrictions in subject matter and you're not trying to pander to this huge, huge, huge audience. But since it's not a major, they want to get a dime's worth out of every nickel, sometimes to such an extent that they save money and waste money at the same time.

Sometimes they hire inferior people. For example, from the beginning I wanted the editor I now have, Lee Percy, but they wouldn't pay his salary. So I had to take someone I considered a terrible com-

"In a perfectly pitched performance, Samuel L. Jackson portrays Jamaal, a lifer. Jackson read 'Eyes On The Prize,' read books, and drew on personal experience. . . (He) has performed in penal institutes and shot movies behind prison walls. Those experiences heightened his sensitivity to the eerie power of a locked door."

—Nancy Randle
Chicago Tribune (3/20/94)

Opposite page: *The director sets the scene for Samuel L. Jackson.*

"John Frankenheimer has triumphantly returned to the medium that catapulted his career 40 years ago with a simmering, seething retelling of the 1971 Attica rebellion."
—Daily Variety (3/25/94)

From left, a novice prison guard (Kyle MacLachlan) and a Muslim leader inmate (Jackson) are caught up in the chaos of rebellion.

promise. The guy worked on the movie for three and a half weeks and when I looked at what he'd done, I fired him on the spot. So I ended up with Lee Percy anyway.

Bob Cooper, the senior vice-president, is a good man. He's tough, very tough, but you always know where you stand with him. If he likes what you're doing, he leaves you alone and let's you do it. I had a very good experience with him.

But, going back to the movie for a minute. What I had to do was make a very big picture on a small budget, with a thirty-one day shooting schedule. When I thought about the scope of the movie, I had a discussion with the cameraman, a young guy named John Leonetti. I said, "This has

to look like a documentary!" I just didn't want anyone coming away from the picture and saying, "My God, this is brilliantly composed." No way. I wanted people to look at this movie and say, "My God, it looks like a newsreel!"

We made a very big decision to shoot this picture in natural light, which is what we did. We used no lights on any of the daytime shots—including some of those inside the prison. In the cells we used one or two little lights, but most of the light is from the windows. We used a bluish kind of light in the prison. We obviously lit the bar scenes because we chose to go for warm tones.

Was the bar a set or a location?

It was a location. We didn't have any sets at all. We dressed the locations, of course.

Was the bar in Tennessee?

It was all in Tennessee.

The prison is one hell of a place. Tell me about it.

It's a Tennessee state prison, built in 1884. I'd seen a prison in Ohio that was fabulous. It was the right color, which is that reddish brick, but Ohio isn't a right-to-work state and Tennessee is. We could only afford to shoot in Tennessee. Simple as that. We'd gone to Tennessee and seen that prison and in most ways it was terrific. But it was also immense and pure white. The yard just stretched on and on. You couldn't have filled it with Steven Spielberg's next project, or with his budget. At first I thought there was no way this location was going to work.

Then I thought it over, and I discussed with my art director, Michael Hanan, what we could do to make the place work. I

"If this was a major studio feature, we'd have $15 or $20 million to work with. But they'd also want to put Eddie Murphy and Tom Cruise in there. There's nothing wrong with those guys. They're both wonderful actors, but I'd prefer to have the actors I have now. This is the best cast I think I've ever worked with, all the way down the line." —JF

said, "The first thing we've got to do is paint the whole place, the whole thing." Then we had to build a wall, within the yard. The guard wall with the guys on top was built. The rest of the stuff existed in the prison. So then we shot the movie.

Who plays the prison superintendent, the bald guy?

Carmine Argenziano. I think he's a brilliant actor, but I've cut him out of two movies before this. I cut him out of *Dead-Bang*. He had a great scene with Don Johnson at the beginning of the picture, but the scene had to go because we were too long. I cut him out of *52-Pickup*. He had a tremendous scene at Joe Allen's with Roy Scheider, which also had to go because of length. So this time I was determined to put him in a part which could not be cut out.

I think it's the best-cast picture I've ever done. You could argue that *Seven Days in May* was, but certainly *Against the Wall* is one of the three best-cast films I've ever done, the other two being *Seven Days* and *The Iceman Cometh*.

It's fascinating that your protagonist is Kyle MacLachlan, but there's absolutely no spillover from his role in Twin Peaks. *You never even think of him here in that connection. Did the possibility ever worry you?*

No. I knew what he had to do in this. We talked it over, and he did it. He was terribly conscientious, and we worked well together. Never a moment of disagreement.

Did you rehearse?

Yes, that's what saved us. I rehearsed everything, all the yard stuff, everything. All blocked out before we ever started to shoot. I couldn't have *done* the movie without

JF directing Steadicam operator David Crone in an extended exterior shot of the prison yard.

rehearsing. I just could not have gone in there and planned those scenes from scratch with the whole crew standing there. I had two weeks of rehearsal. So the actors knew pretty well what they had to do, and I think they were also able to modulate their performances quite well thanks to the rehearsal.

The other thing that's important to say is that the writer, Ron Hutchinson, was with me the entire time—during the rehearsals, during the shooting, every day. It was really a terrific collaboration, more like the stage than a movie, more like live TV used to be. He reshaped a lot of the script as we went along.

You said that as the actors emerged, their parts were enlarged substantially.

For example, the young black actor who wore his hat backwards, Steve Harris, and Clarence Williams.

"I guess people will see different things in the film. I hope somehow that it makes an impression about man's inhumanity to man."

—Michael Smith

Michael Smith (left) is the real prison guard whose story is the basis for the drama. He stands here with MacLachlan, who portrays him in the film.

Harry Dean Stanton plays Smith's father, who had worked at the prison for 25 years. Anne Heche is Smith's newlywed wife.

"When they filmed a couple of violent scenes, it was so close to what actually happened, it gave me the same sensation that it did 20 years ago."

—Michael Smith

The Harris part is really poised between madness and a terrible, savage sanity.

He has that very important moment in the prison yard when he says that they're never going to get out of there. He was the only one who knew; he and the warden. They both knew it wouldn't happen. The counterpoint I like is Frederic Forrest as the crazed lieutenant on the prison side and Clarence Williams on the prisoners' side of it. They balance each other out. What it really comes down to is the material; it's the script that makes the difference always.

What was the source? Was there a book?

No, it was the young guy, Michael Smith, the new guard. His story, more or less, was the takeoff point for the script. Irwin Meyer, who is one of the executive producers, found the guy and initiated the project. He did the initial interviews with Smith and hired Ron Hutchinson. I came in after they had their first draft. I changed a lot of stuff, but nevertheless I came aboard after the project was initiated.

Now I'm hoping to do another project for HBO, on Robert Kennedy, and I'm initiating that. Ron Hutchinson will be the writer again, and Jonathan Axelrod, who is the executive producer of *Against the Wall*, will be the executive producer on that one, too. I'll produce and direct the Kennedy project.

And HBO is hot for the project.

Bob Cooper at HBO is a great man and was a great admirer of Robert Kennedy, and he wants to do it. As long as he stays the head man, it'll get done.

I was horribly offended by the way they treated Bobby Kennedy in the movie *Hoffa*. And for a whole generation of young people those movies, like *JFK* and *Hoffa*, are history. I want to set the record straight.

"Intensely involving and socially trenchant, HBO's Against The Wall is the rare TV movie that contains the force and complexity of a quality feature film."

—Los Angeles Times (3/26/94)

"Since I directed Against The Wall, I've been offered more (feature) projects than I have in ten years."

—JF

193

AGAINST THE WALL

One tends to romanticize or intensify relationships that are suddenly halted. I don't know how my relationship with Bobby Kennedy would have played itself out, had he lived. No one's ever going to know that. We were very close. I wasn't looking to be ambassador to Ireland or whatever the hell else. We crammed a whole lot of stuff into a hundred days.

I hope the movie goes forward; I agree with you that Bobby has been misrepresented.

I could make a lot more money by going out and doing one of these studio pictures. I really could. And I'm not saying that there aren't some great studio pictures being made. The ones that are being offered to me would mean a lot more money than the HBO stuff. But it's not a question of money right now in my life. It's a question of doing stuff I can believe in. *Against the Wall* and the Robert Kennedy thing both qualify as things I really believe in.

As I watched Against the Wall, *I thought about how much it seemed to be your picture, how much it reflected the kind of things you have always done so well. I remember your picking the camera angles and shots in the live TV days. The low angle shots of the guards and the inmates on the prison stairs were dramatic without being self-consciously arty and pretentious. You were right, very documentary-like indeed. The pictures you've done have been stories of substance. It makes all the difference in the world.*

It really makes a lot of difference. What it means is that I can have lunch with Charles Champlin and not have to apologize for the material. "Well, I did the best I could"— Bullshit! That's not good enough.

I'm just curious. How many extras did you have? It looked like a lot. Two hundred?

That's the most I ever had. In the long shot, when Clarence Williams is walking across the yard, what you didn't see was all the extras running around the camera to line up again. That's all one shot, as you know. There weren't many days when I had 200. It looked like more.

Thirty-nine people were killed in the riot, Chuck. That's a lot of people. The interesting thing is that the firing in the actual riot lasted ten minutes. We do it for a minute and a half. Michael Smith said you've just never heard anything like it.

Was Smith himself around as an advisor on the project?

He was around for a good deal of it.

Is the sequence of events in the movie pretty much the way it was in reality?

Exactly the way it was. We shot it with two cameras mainly. There's an awful lot of Steadicam work in there. The other camera was usually hand-held, too, by John Leonetti, who is so good it doesn't look hand held. One of the HBO people saw the film and said, "I'm so glad there isn't a lot of hand-held camera stuff in here." I laughed my head off.

As far as the editing of the picture goes, there's not one shot that isn't in the movie. No scenes are cut. We had it timed down to a cut that was about three minutes longer than the final cut. I'm very proud of that. I'm very proud of *Against the Wall*.

On September 11, 1994, John Frankenheimer won the Emmy for "Outstanding Individual Achievement in Directing for a Miniseries or Special" for Against The Wall.

"I think that people want to see heroes. I feel that there is a return, if you will, to more simplistic values like good and bad. At the same time, I want to tell interesting stories that have a point of view. My point of view. I believe that there is nothing that a man can't do. . . I mean, I believe in the indomitability of the human spirit. . . I believe that a good story is the most important thing. . . and my one hope is never to bore an audience. I suppose my point of view is the person who hangs in there, and despite all kinds of odds, does something rather well, whatever it may be."

—J.F.

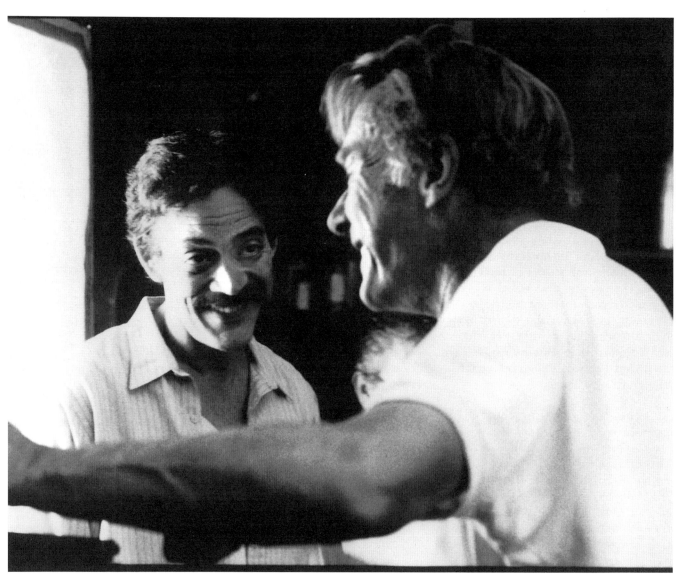

THE BURNING SEASON (HBO, September 17, 1994).

The story was intense, the schedule grueling, but photographer Jim McHugh managed to catch Raul Julia (left) and JF in a light moment.

The Burning Season

HBO had a very interesting project called *The Burning Season*, about Chico Mendes, who was murdered because of his campaign to preserve the rain forests. It was developed by David Puttnam, who produced it. Warner Bros. backed out because of the cost, but HBO picked it up. There's been a lot of interest in the industry because it's not only an important environmental story, it's also a great drama. You have to admire HBO a lot for taking it on, and I'm really excited about it.

We can get spoiled by the kind of money you can get out here. But I can live quite nicely on what HBO pays me. I think that what's really important is that *Against the Wall* reminded me of why I got into the business in the first place, and now *The Burning Season* are further reminders.

You shot The Burning Season *in the Spring of 1994. Where exactly was your location?*

It was on the east coast of Mexico, about a hundred miles south of Vera Cruz in a place called Catemaco.

Is there rain forest there?

Yes. There's jungle, there's accessible forest, and there are towns that you really believe are Xapuri in Brazil. Sonia Braga, who comes from Brazil, of course, thought she was *in* Brazil. There's terrific countryside, there are rivers. There was everything we needed to make the movie.

Had David Puttnam done some scouting when he was going to make the film at Warners?

Puttnam was going to make the movie in Costa Rica. They'd built the sets in Costa Rica, spent $2 million in fact. I think we should probably have made the film there.

The guy who scouted the Mexican locations for HBO was an in-house producer and he made a lot of mistakes. He believed everything the Mexicans told him and they're the greatest rip-off artists of all time. They lied, and he believed them and it ended up costing HBO a lot of money. The Mexican crews are very bad. We'd have been better off taking a full complement of technicians. As it was, we had a core of technicians from here, fourteen or fifteen, who were really incredible.

I also found tremendous anti-Americanism among the Mexicans. It's the last place I'd recommend anyone going to make a movie. But we went. The heat was awful, the food was inedible, but one goes on.

Who finally did the script?

Ron Hutchinson, who had done *Against the Wall.* William Mastrosimone had started it at Warners, then William Nicholson, who wrote *Shadowlands*, and then Michael Tolkin, whom Warners also brought in. Ron and I took the Warners script, and Hutch Parker, the HBO executive, and Puttnam, and the four of us put it in the form we wanted to make.

And you had Sonia Braga in the cast...

And Raul Julia as Chico; and Eddie [Edward James] Olmos; a wonderful actor named Tomas Milian, a Cuban who is a big star in Italian movies; and very good actors like Luis Guzman; Tony Perez from here; Tony Plana from here; Carmine Argenziano, my old friend from *Against the Wall* and times past; Jose Perez from New York. An interesting footnote about Jose is that the last time we worked together he was the blind kid who got murdered in *The Young Savages.* He was twenty, playing seventeen, in 1960.

"Admirers of the vintage films of John Frankenheimer. . . will rejoice at the presence of the master hand in HBO's The Burning Season. *Finely textured, beautifully and inexorably paced, the new vidpic joins the earlier master-works in its exploration of the remarkable heroism of unremarkable men. . . Raul Julia (gives) a riveting performance, perhaps his best work to date. . ."*

—Variety (9/12/94)

"Raul Julia brings presence and passion to his portrayal of Chico Mendes. . ." *TV Guide.*

We had a very interesting girl named Kamala Lopez-Dawson, who's playing Chico's wife. We had Nigel Havers. He plays the British documentary film maker who was so important in those lives.

Was there a source text?

They bought a couple of books, and one of them was *The Burning Season,* by Andrew Revkin. That's what we're calling the film, with a kind of subtitle that will say "The Life and Times of Chico Mendes."

It must have been a rough film to do.

It was exciting because the script was terrific and the actors were great. We had very little preparation time so we couldn't rehearse much. So a lot of it was kind of discovering it as we were going, and taking the time to do the scenes. And that was the big thing—taking the time on the HBO schedule, which I did. I felt focused and think I worked well with the actors.

I thought the art director, Michael Hanan, who'd also done *Against the Wall,* did a brilliant job, as again did the young cameraman, John Leonetti, from *Against the Wall.* This time I had a wonderful assistant director, an American. I had a great special effects man, Cliff Wenger, who was able to create a lot of fires without really destroying a lot of stuff. We were able to cut down a few trees, which they wanted cut down.

I did a personal movie in which there are some huge things. What I was interested in was not making some *noble* movie, Chuck. I wanted to make a movie that was passionate, that was a political thriller, that was a love story, that was a rite of passage, that was the story of a man who was betrayed and who died for his ideals.

I wanted to make *The Birdman of Alcatraz* outside of Alcatraz. It's the first time I've ever said that, but that's what I wanted to make.

You seem to have a very good sense of Chico.

I read everything around, everything that's been written about him, and saw all the documentary footage. You just have to spend time down in that kind of place where I was and you can understand a lot about that guy. And one of the things I can do as a director, thank God, is put myself into a situation. I can't live it, but I can imagine it.

Chico was just a guy who was trying to do his job as head of the rubber-tappers, whom they seized upon to make some kind of a national symbol as the guy who's saving the rain forest. He said, "I'm not saving this

Above: The director working with Julia and many of the extras in setting up a blockade scene. *Below left:* Edward James Olmos, Sonia Braga and Julia. *Below right:* Olmos, as Mendes' mentor, Wilson Pinheiro, reflects with JF on the meaning of the scene being prepared.

"Frankenheimer is the best director I've ever worked with, period. He's not playing any kind of weird passive-aggressive games. He just screams at everybody. . . He's a classic story-teller and that's all you need. Because this is a classic story."

—Esai Morales

(Morales played Jair, a union rubber-tapper who urges the pacifistic Mendes to fight against the ranchers of the rain forest.)

rain forest. You people who are trying to save this rain forest, you're against progress. We love progress. All I'm trying to do is not keep my members poor."

One of the things I've tried to do in this movie is really to play the various levels in all these things. There are a lot of different people with a lot of different agendas that come together dramatically on screen in the same scene. There are a lot of layers to this movie, I hope.

I used as a kind of visual theme in this movie, fire. So I'm thrilled they're calling it *The Burning Season*. There's a lot of fire in this movie, a lot of destruction, just burning, burning, burning.

I used the Steadicam extensively in the film as I did in *Against the Wall*, and two cameras on a lot of stuff. I really used the same visual approach as in *Against the Wall*; fluid, hard-edged, reality-based images.

An interesting problem came up. Presumably you have everyone speaking fluent Portuguese. In *Gorky Park* I thought the idea of having everyone speak with English accents was terrific. Then they put in Joanna Pacula who blew everybody's cover because she's Polish.

I tried to be consistent with the accents, with just a slight lilt to the voice. I hope it's going to be effective.

All the newspapers, all the written material is in Portuguese. There are certain songs the rubber-tappers sing, and they sound better in Portuguese. The hymns do, too.

There's a story you won't believe, except you will. The prop man got a young guy who was hanging around to translate the documents we see on screen into Portuguese. Somehow there's always a guy like him hanging around, a perennial student. He knew Portuguese and Spanish. And we were about to do a scene in which you see one of the documents. Luckily for me, luckily for all of us, Raul Julia knows some Portuguese. He took a look and said, "You know what this document is?" I said, "Well, sure." He said, "It's pornography." This guy had translated everything into pornographic stuff. By then he was long gone and we never saw him again. But it could have been really bad. If we'd shown it in Brazil or Portugal I think we'd all have been out of the movie business.

From left: President of HBO Worldwide Pictures Robert Cooper, Sonia Braga, Executive producer David Puttnam, Edward James Olmos and producer-director John Frankenheimer at the Los Angeles Premiere of *The Burning Season*, September 12, 1994. The night before Frankenheimer had won an Emmy for *Against The Wall*.

Raul Julia, who had wanted to play Chico Mendes ever since he read about his assassination in 1988, prepared for his role by watching documentary footage of Mendes. He also was inspired by a book filled with Mendes' own words. Julia, who died on October 24, 1994, would be honored posthumously by winning a Golden Globe Award and a Screen Actors Guild Award for Best Actor in a Miniseries or Telefilm.

Always a delicate question, but it must have cost a lot as movies for cable television go.

Warner Bros. had $10 million invested in it, for the scripts and the sets and all. Then they decided they didn't want to make it. They figured it would cost $20 million at least, and they didn't want to spend it. So what they did was give it to HBO, taking the foreign distribution rights for their $10 million investment. We made it for around $9 million. It was a killing schedule, but we did it.

It's an exciting time for you, isn't it?

It's good, and I can appreciate it, which is nice. When I was younger I took everything for granted. I take nothing for granted now. Some nice things are happening, and it's nice to be able to enjoy them. And now I'm not worried that it's not enough. The thing I've been able to stop doing is judging myself against other people's accomplishments. That's something that took me a long time to learn. Now I'm happy doing what *I'm* doing, and that's enough.

Golden Globe Award recipients for *The Burning Season* celebrate after the ceremonies. From left, Raul Julia's widow, Merel, accepted the Best Actor award for her late husband; producer-director John Frankenheimer collected one for Outstanding Miniseries or Telefilm; Mrs. Edward James Olmos, Mrs. Frankenheimer and Edward James Olmos—Best Supporting Actor.

ANDERSONVILLE (Turner Pictures, 1995).

How did Andersonville *originate?*

I got a call from Ethel Winant, with whom I'd worked in live TV. She was the associate producer and casting director on *Playhouse 90*. We'd done 50 or 60 shows together and I'd kept in touch with her through the years. We'd also worked together on *All Fall Down*. She was John Houseman's associate.

She called me just before *Against the Wall* was broadcast. She said she'd seen a screening of it and how wonderful it was, and would I direct this script that she and David Rintels were doing for Turner. Before they could offer it to me, Allen Sabinson of Turner wanted to see *Against the Wall*. I said I wanted to read *Andersonville* first. They sent it over and I thought it was interesting, interesting enough to let Sabinson see *Against the Wall*. He loved it.

There was a question of timing. I said, "I'm talking about doing a movie for HBO [*The Burning Season*], so I couldn't do your movie until the fall. But if you'll postpone it until then, I'll do it," and they did.

It's a four-hour movie and I'd never done a mini-series. Well, that's not entirely true: I did "For Whom the Bells Toll" on *Playhouse 90*. But they didn't call it a mini-series; they called it a two-part *Playhouse 90*.

I had reservations about doing it because it was another story that took place in prison. I was becoming the maven of prison movies: *Birdman of Alcatraz, Attica* [finally called *Against the Wall*] and now *Andersonville*. But there was some very good writing in it and it was something I cared about.

The idea of doing *Andersonville* is such an epic one. There were 33,000 prisoners in a camp that was designed for 8,000, and 13,000 of them died. It all took place between February, 1864, and November of 1865. I suppose with the exception of Auschwitz it's the worst prison camp that's ever been perpetrated on mankind. It had no shelter; it had nothing. These people were out in the elements twenty-four hours a day. There was no drinking water; they had to drink out of a polluted stream.

But what I *didn't* want was a four-hour descent into hell. I didn't want to do a travelogue of horror. What I wanted to do was a picture about dignity, a picture about honor, a picture about the fact that man can sustain anything and still come out of it as perhaps a better human being.

The movie was hellaciously difficult to do. There were *thousands* of extras involved, and a really *huge* set, designed by Michael Hanan, who also did *Against the Wall* and *The Burning Season*.

A nine-acre set, I understand.

The set itself was nine acres. And then there were six acres outside, so the whole compound was fifteen acres. We had to deal with it every day, and it was very tough to stage scenes. There was no furniture; there were only tents. The actors were either standing up or sitting on the ground. And there were at least ten actors in every scene. Hellaciously difficult. The logistics of it were just overwhelming.

I just shot through all the weather. People said, "Hey, it's raining; we can't shoot." I said, "It rained at Andersonville; we'll shoot." We didn't lose an hour because of weather.

Were there key figures? I know there was a strange man who was the commandant.

Henry Wirtz, a Swiss, was later tried as a war criminal. He was convicted and hanged. There were those who say he was wrongfully hanged. We take the position that he was probably rightfully hanged.

Opposite page:
Ted Turner visits JF on the set of Andersonville *south of Atlanta, Georgia.*

"The project was impossible, it was so huge. Nobody could seem to get a handle on it. So I called John. He has the ability to take a big subject and put the personal story in front of it—and still manage to keep the big canvas. That's one of the things he does best. Without John, this project wouldn't have happened."
—Ethel Winant

From left: Longtime Frankenheimer associate, Ethel Winant, who brought the director to the project, producer/writer David Rintels and JF.

There *were* key figures. There was a guy who was head of a team of rogue prisoners who robbed all the other prisoners and who lived like a king. His name was Collins. There were six key leaders of the raiders, and they were tried, found guilty and hanged. The other prisoners did it themselves. That's all in our piece.

What sort of source material did Rintels have?

He had access to a lot of things. He had access to the head custodian of the national park at Andersonville. They had everything documented, a daily journal of everything that went on in the camp. There were a lot of records kept. Our characters are fictitious, except for Wirtz. Some of these guys did exist, but we don't know if they did what we say they did.

But the documentation gave you a kind of reality check.

We had a lot of research. And there were all these re-enacters, who are really well-versed in all that actually happened. Luckily we had one of those guys as technical advisor, and he was very good. And we had the great assistant director I had on *The Burning Season*. His name is Jim Sbardellati, and he's just brilliant. I had Frederic Forrest again, and he was terrific. And I had this young boy, Jarrod Emick, who's just won the Tony for *Damn Yankees* on Broadway. He played the other lead. And I had some other extraordinary actors, as you'll see. It was one of the best ensemble casts I've ever worked with, and one of the best crews I've ever had.

From a creative standpoint, it was a wonderful experience; from a logistical point of view, it was a horror. Just trying to get everything done. Every other week we worked six days, and we did the film in sixty days, which is amazing. It's actually three hours and twenty minutes, but it'll spread over four hours with the commercials.

You were already working on Andersonville *when you came back for the premiere of* The Burning Season.

It was a heady three days. The Emmy [for *Against the Wall*] was on Sunday and the premiere was on Monday. Incidentally I have to add that I really enjoyed working with David Puttnam on *The Burning Season*. One of the reasons I did it was that I had wanted to work with him. He's a man of great taste. He came into *The Burning Season* with a totally objective point of view.

When he saw the film cut together, knowing the material very well as he did, he said, "This doesn't work . . . this is slow . . . could you combine this . . . could you trim

The primary cast and hundreds of extras relax for a moment before shooting a key scene. Laying on the ground in front of the dugout are, from left, Andrew Kavovit, Ted Marcoux and Jarrod Emick. Frederic Forrest is sitting on the left edge of the dugout with Olek Krupa to his right and Justin Henry behind his head. Inside the dugout are Kris Kamm and Peter Murnik (with hat). Sitting on the right is Jayce Bartok, with Bruce Winant standing to the right.

The director said, "I shot through all the weather." People said, "Hey it's raining, we can't shoot." I said, "It rained at Andersonville; we'll shoot." Above, in the rain, Frankenheimer explains his shot to Robert David Hall, who had worked with him before.

JF in the cold, with Tony Award winning Broadway actor Jarrod Emick.

"It rained every day, there was mud, it was cold, it was physically hard. Yet the actors considered it the high point of their lives. John has the ability to engender this kind of loyalty and dedication and they all had a wonderful time. I had a wonderful time, and I'm too old for this!"

—Ethel Winant

this. . . ." In three days, two days really, in the cutting room with me, he accomplished more than anybody I ever worked with.

Ethel Winant was the one who kept the whole thing together. She was wonderful.

There are some other things I'd like to talk about in connection with this.

The long format really gave me a chance to work with the characters. I didn't feel constricted by the fact that I had to get it done in so many minutes. And the Turner people were very supportive, particularly their head of production, Nick Lombardo.

The extra problem was tremendous, to get the number of extras and re-enacters we needed. We had hundreds of re-enacters but then we needed hundreds more people, and I don't have to tell you that we had to get very thin, emaciated-looking people, particularly for the front of the scenes. We had to go to halfway houses; we had to go everywhere. We finally got quite a few guys from Fort Benning, whom we put in uniforms that were too big for them. They were good because above all these prisoners were soldiers.

I don't know; if I don't mess it up in the editing, I think it's very good. It's not compromised at all, this picture. They let me do the best I was capable of doing, whatever that is, and I had the tools to do it.

The cameraman, Ric Waite, did a very, very good job. You know, I shoot a lot with these extreme wide-angle lenses, and the camera is about six inches away from the actors, so it's very difficult to light this stuff; and he did a very good job.

I always move the camera around a lot, and I did that on this, and I did stuff as I did in *Against the Wall*. You remember the long Steadicam shot in the Yard that went all over the place?

I've got three or four of those shots in this one, and one of them is six minutes long. It goes around half the camp, and it takes in two and a half or three acres. The

Some of the thousands of extras on the nine-acre set.

Rehearsing a group of POWs arrival at the prison. From left: Kris Kamm, Tony Higgins, Tom Wilson, Jayce Bartok, Frederic Forrest, Jarrod Emick, JF and an unknown extra.

JF enjoying a lighter moment with Frederic Forrest.

Steadicam operator walked about three or four hundred yards to do the shot. It's terri-bly complicated.

It was a very tough movie. It takes a long time to get over it. I'm not sure that I still have. It was tough to come off it; it was a very intense experience, but a very gratify-ing one for myself, the actors and the crew.

What do you figure to do about music on this one?

I'm using the same guy, Gary Chang, who did *52 Pick-up* and later *The Burning Season*, who did *Against the Wall*. It pre-sents a big problem because to my thinking you should use instruments from the period. You can't use all period songs because a lot of them aren't appropriate. But some of them are for sure. The pris-oners had banjos, some of them even had fiddles. We used a lot of source music.

I don't know, by the time we finish the film I may have changed my mind, but I have one idea for a scene when these guys reject the Southern proposal to join the Confederate army. And Freddie Forrest starts it off by leading his detachment, who are our heroes, away from the massed group. He says, "About, face!" and each one of the detachments slowly does an about face, too.

I remember one of the most moving musical moments I ever experienced, which was at the Bobby Kennedy funeral. As we were walking out of the church, Andy Williams sang "The Battle Hymn of the Republic" very . . . very . . . slowly. "Mine eyes . . . have seen . . . the glory . . . of the . . . coming . . . of the Lord," and so on.

I thought of the scene in *Bridge on the River Kwai* when Guinness' troops march to the "Colonel Bogey" march. That's not appropriate but "The Battle Hymn of the Republic" is, starting out quietly, very quietly, and building to symphonic propor-tions.

Then, when they leave the camp at the end, it comes in again, slowly. They're being moved to another camp; it's not some victory that they've survived the camp. They're going to another camp, and a lot of the guys are dead.

The last image of the movie involves a guy we've come to identify with very strongly. He's married and he has six chil-dren and he plays the banjo. Throughout, you see that he's deteriorating, getting weaker. At a certain moment, when he knows that Sherman's army is going *that* way and the camp is this way, he says, "We're going to die in here." And he says, "There's one thing I want you to do when you bury me, and that is make sure I have a toe tag, because if you don't have a toe tag they don't know who you are, and I want my family to know."

And the last image is of Freddie Forrest and Jarrod Emick carrying this guy in the line with the thousands of prisoners, and the dead are way off to one side. They branch off from the line of prisoners and put this guy down with the rest of the dead. Jarrod Emick takes the toe tag and puts it

"Yul Brynner, who was a very, very dear friend of mine, said one thing to me which has seen me through a lot of very, very bad times. He said there's one thing you can be sure of. That no matter how things are now, whether they're good or bad, they're going to change. . . I've been around long enough to have had it both ways. . . What you have to be is a survivor."
—John Frankenheimer

209
ANDERSONVILLE

on. The camera moves in and you see, handwritten, the name "Martin Blackburn." Now you dissolve slowly to a headstone that says, "Martin Blackburn," engraved, and you pull back slowly and now you see 10,000 graves. That's the last thing you see, and as they come into view you hear again that slow, slow "Battle Hymn of the Republic."

It sounds overwhelming. It makes me wonder if the film is broken up into six acts or eight or whatever.

The simple answer is yes. But Ted Turner has seen 92 minutes of the film, and wants to go theatrical with it. My own feeling is that I'm not really for it. I think there are big pitfalls. I think we should make it an event for television, not a movie you're dependent on people lining up to see. This is not an upbeat thing, and I don't know that they'll sit there for three and a half hours.

It sounds like a tough one to sell to the theatrical audience, but a relatively easy one to persuade the television audience to look in on.

We were talking about age a while ago. There is this age barrier that exists, whether you want to admit or whether you don't. I saw Billy Wilder the other night. He's 88 but it looks as if he could get over there and direct a movie. His mind is very sharp.

And I think he'd like to, don't you?

Sure, but nobody asks him. One of the gratifying things for me now is that I'm being offered an awful lot of stuff. Things are going fairly well; I just hope it continues.

The problem that's going to present itself to you, I'm sure, is choosing among the kinds of projects offered to you by television and the kinds of projects offered by theatrical films.

It already presents itself. I'm offered a feature film right now that would pay me six times what I got for directing *Against the Wall,* and five times what I got for directing *The Burning Season,* and it's the same length of time. You have to ask yourself, what should I do? At the same time we know that sooner or later it's going to get released, and whoever Charles Champlin's successor as the critic is gets a shot at it. And there's nothing worse: you don't care what you're getting paid when you read the reviews. And when nobody comes. It's tough.

But I'd have thought you don't have to do what you don't want to do. You're in the ascendant, as they say.

I honestly think that if the postproduction on *Andersonville* goes well, from a sheer work point of view I feel better about it than I ever have. I'm not talking about public acceptance; that's out of my hands. But it's the freest I've ever felt, the most in command of the medium I've ever felt. The Movie God smiled upon us in terms of casting, weather, so many lucky decisions we made. It has everything to do with the Movie God, because sometimes the Movie God will crap all over you, and there's nothing you can do.

I had to make a moral decision the other day. I was offered a lot of money to do a film, play or pay, about a killer. He kills for a living, and this is a comedy. And he ends up with the girl at the end. It was a huge amount of money for me. Without thinking I said yes. And then I started to think: What am I doing here? This isn't right, you can't DO this. You can't justify what you're doing. So I turned it down.

The Director with his classic 1947 Oldsmobile '98 Club Sedan.

John and Evans Frankenheimer (December, 1993).

The director with the Emmy he received for *Against The Wall*, September 11, 1994.

Videography

The format is as follows: series title, episode title, network, air date, producer, director, associate director, original story, story adaptor, cast listing, brief plot description, live or tape, where produced, running time of show including commercials, if in color. The following abbreviations are used:

A =	adaptor of original, the teleplay writer
AD =	associate director
D =	director
E =	east
L =	live
LA =	Los Angeles
m =	minutes
NY =	New York
O =	original writer of story
P =	producer
T =	tape
W =	west

In 1952, John Frankenheimer, while still in the Air Force wrote and directed about 12 weekly one hour local shows called HARVEY HOWARD'S RANCH ROUNDUP, which was aired on channel 13 in Los Angeles. Also Frankenheimer made various films for the Air Force. He got out of the Air Force June 30, 1953. A short time later Frankenheimer went to work for CBS in New York as an associate director. He started on weather shows, news shows, THE GARY MOORE SHOW, PERSON TO PERSON and SEE IT NOW.

In 1954 CBS used the following studios/theatres: TV Production Center, 524 W. 57th St.; Studio 21, 49 E. 52nd St.; Studios 41-44, 15 Vanderbilt; Liederkrantz (45 & 46), 111 E. 58th St.; Studio 50, 1697 Broadway; Playhouse 51, 109 W. 39th St.; Playhouse 52, 254 W. 54th St.; Studio 57, 109 St. & 5th Ave.; Town #58, 851 9th(55th St.); Mansfield #59, 256 W. 47th St.; Lincoln Square #60, 1947 Broadway (66th St.); Monroe #61, 1456 1st (76th St.); Biltmore #62, 261 W. 47th St.

MAMA aired Fridays, 8:00 — 8:30 PM EST. Regulars were Peggy Wood, Judson Laire, Dick Van Patten, Rosemary Rice, Robin Morgan, Ruth Gates, and Kevin Coughlin.

MAMA: "Dagmar's Braces" (CBS, 2/12/54). Ralph Nelson — P., Sidney Lumet — D., John Frankenheimer — AD., Gail Ingram — O. *cast:* Janet Parker, Richard Trask, Gene Francis, Raymond Bailey, Frieda Altman.

Dagmar discovers that she must have braces put on her teeth. This unhappy event occurs just before her first date with the handsomest boy in school. L — NY 30m.

MAMA; "Katrin At The Exposition" (CBS, 2/19/54). Ralph Nelson — P., Sidney Lumet — D., John Frankenheimer — AD., Turner Bullock — O. *cast:* Joyce Van Patten, Betty Sinclair, Alex Clark.

Katrin takes a job at the San Francisco Exposition. Actual film clips of the 1915 Exposition were used. L — NY 30m.

DANGER aired Tuesdays, 10:00 — 10:30 PM EST.

DANGER: "Escape Route" (CBS, 4/27/54). John Frankenheimer — D., Donald Bevan — O., *cast* Philip Abbott, Robert Fortin, Frank Corsaro, Frank Maxwell, Mort Marshall, Iggie Wolfington.

A dramatization of the life of American POWs and their attempt to break out of prison by the co-author of STALAG 17. L — NY 30m.

YOU ARE THERE aired Sundays, 6:30 — 7:00 PM EST with Walter Cronkite as the reporter.

YOU ARE THERE : "The Plot Against King Solomon" (CBS 11/28/54). Charles W. Russell — P., John Frankenheimer — D., Kate Nickerson — O. *cast:* Walter Cronkite, Sylvia Saltman, Shepperd Strudwick, Mary Sinclair, Margaret Barker, Bruce Gordon, Mary Patten, Martin Brooks, Frederick Rolfe, Eliot Sharfe, Bert Berger, Jerry Eskow, Joseph Nathan.

The "plot" is Solomon's greatest triumph when he must pass judgment on the case of two women who appear in his court, each claiming to be the mother of the same child. L — NY 30m.

DANGER originally aired Tuesdays, 9:30–10:00 PM EST. Starting January 4, 1955, the show moved to 10:00 — 10:30 PM EST. John Frankenheimer replaced Byron Kelley as director, alternating with Tom Donovan.

DANGER: "Knife In the Dark" (CBS, 12/7/54). David Heilweil — P., John Frankenheimer — D., Evans Harrington — O., Rod Serling — A. *cast:* Paul Newman, James Gregory, William Harrington, Walter Burke, Joe Silver, John Connell.

An inmate with only six months to serve before going free, risks his life to defy a notorious gangster who bullies his fellow prisoners. L — NY 30m.

DANGER: "Treasure Of The Argo" (CBS, 12/21/54). David Heilweil —P., John Frankenheimer — D., Bret Harte — O., Frank P. DeFellitta — A. *cast:* Russell Collins, Larry Gates, Frank Marth, Inger Stevens, Al Hopson.

An old sea captain who always wanted to own his own boat, buys a ship which was used to carry gold during the Civil War and converts it into a bar. L — NY 30m.

DANGER: "Precinct Girl" (CBS, 1/4/55). David Heilweil —P., John Frankenheimer — D., James P. Cavanagh — O. *cast:* Peggy Ann Garner, Gene Saks, John Shay, Beatrice Pons, Frank Campanella, Irving Winters, Bert Berger, James Dolan, Myrtle Hebbard, Walter Mathews, John McDonald, Denise Morris, George Hoxie.

This semi-documentary dramatizes the work of a man and woman detective team combating the petty crimes in New York's subways. L — NY 30m.

DANGER: "No Passport For Death" (CBS, 1/18/55). David Heilweil — P., John Frankenheimer — D., Burton Rouche — O., Ben Radin — A. *cast:* John Cassavetes, Fred Sadoff, John Boruff, Leo Penn, Miriam Colon, Martin Newman, Don Keefer, Claire Kirby.

A South American, who has entered this country illegally, is unaware that he harbors the dreaded smallpox germ. L — NY 30m.

DANGER: "The Dark Curtain" (CBS, 2/1/55). David Heilweil — P., John Frankenheimer — D., Frank P. DeFellitta — O. *cast:* Beatrice Straight, Wesley Addy, Richard Waring, Adele Newton, Melba Rae, Ian Martin.

A kleptomaniac wife threatens to ruin her husband's career. L — NY 30m.

Joe Scibetta replaced John Frankenheimer on DANGER as a regular alternating director with Tom Donovan. Frankenheimer moved to CLIMAX, which was produced in Hollywood and aired Thursday nights, 8:30–9:30 PM EST. William Lundigan was the host introducing each show while Mary Costa did the Chrysler car commercials.

CLIMAX: "South Of The Sun" (CBS, 3/3/55). Edgar Peterson — P., John Frankenheimer — D., Wade Miller — O., Jack Newman — A. *cast:* Margaret O'Brien, Jeffrey Hunter, Edward Arnold, Natalie Schafer, Thomas Gomez.

Jack Fathian, a Las Vegas racketeer, spends an enforced vacation in Acapulco, Mexico with his daughter, Kathy. She falls in love with an American pilot, and is torn between this new love and her allegiance to her father. L — LA 60m.

CLIMAX: "The Darkest Hour" (CBS, 3/24/55). Martin Manulis — P., John Frankenheimer — D., Adrian Spies — O. *cast:* Joanne Dru, Zachary Scott, Peter Votrian, B. G. Norman.

A widow and widower, both of whom have sons, meet and marry expecting to find happiness, but the widower's desire to make his son a great athlete comes between them. L — LA 60m.

CLIMAX: "Private Worlds" (CBS, 4/7/55). Martin Manulis — P., John Frankenheimer — D., Phyllis Bottome — O., Mel Dinelli — A. *cast:* Claudette Colbert, Lorne Green, Marilyn Erskine, Warren Stevens, Marguerite Chapman, Katharine Warren, Eve Marsh, Mike Ross, Peter Camlin, Glenn Vernon, Bill Tauman.

A woman doctor probes the twisted minds of her patients in a mental institution. (Colbert also starred in the 1935 Paramount feature.) L — LA 60m.

CLIMAX: "The First And The Last" (CBS, 4/28/55). Martin Manulis, — P., John Frankenheimer — D., John Galsworthy — O., William Kozlenko — A. *cast:* Robert Newton, John Agar, Peggy Ann Garner, John Carradine, Kathryn Beaumont, Lumsden Hare.

The threat of a scandal revolving around the death of a man in London, prompts an ambitious lawyer to disregard both legal and moral principles. L — LA 60m.

CLIMAX: "No Stone Unturned" (CBS, 5/19/55). Martin Manulis — P., John Frankenheimer — D., Ian Hamilton — O., Whitfield Cook — A. *cast:* Dan O'Herlihy, Sir Cedric Hardwicke, Jeff Donnell, Tom Drake.

A Scottish student possesses the historical Stone of Scone, stolen from Westminster Abbey to force England to recognize Scotland's independence. L — LA 60m.

CLIMAX: "The Unimportant Man" (CBS, 6/2/55). Martin Manulis — P., John Frankenheimer — D., Marie Baumer and James P. Cavanagh — O., James P. Cavanagh — A. *cast:* MacDonald Carey, Ruth Hussey, Elliot Reed, Tommy Ivo, Robert F. Simon, Larry Blake, Tyler McVey, Berry Kroeger.

The life of a very mild mannered man is changed when he identifies the murderer of his employer's brother. L — LA 60m.

CLIMAX: "To Wake At Midnight" (CBS, 6/23/55). Martin Manulis — p., John Frankenheimer — d., Rod Serling — O. *cast:* Wendell Corey, Akim Tamiroff, Maria Riva, Peter Votrian, George Voskovec.

All the pent-up prejudices and hatreds of post-war Europe are revived when a Nazi lieutenant, in a coma for years, regains consciousness in a British hospital. L — LA 60m.

Associate producer Edgar Peterson becomes producer for seven weeks, replacing Martin Manulis, effective June 30. Manulis is developing fall dramas for the program.

CLIMAX: "Edge Of Terror" (CBS, 8/11/55). Edgar Peterson — P., John Frankenheimer — D., Irving Elman — O. *cast:* Dennis O'Keefe, Phyllis Kirk, Lloyd Bridges, Ed Binns, Karen Steele, Tom Laughlin, Joe Downing, Raymond Greenleaf, Jean Porter.

A small town bank official finds his life placed in the balance by a ruthless criminal, who threatens to kill him and his family if the police are given the thief's identity. L — LA 60m.

CLIMAX: "Deal A Blow" (CBS, 8/25/55). Martin Manulis — P., John Frankenheimer — D., Robert James Dozier — O. *cast:* MacDonald Carey, Phyllis Thaxter, James MacArthur, Edward Arnold, Margaret Hayes, Whit Bissell, Jeff Silver, Byron Foulger.

A teen-age boy has a dispute with an abusive movie theatre manager. The boy's father accepts the manager's somewhat twisted version of the incident and doesn't give his son a chance to explain his side of the matter. (This was the basis for Frankenheimer's first feature, THE YOUNG STRANGER.) L — LA 60m.

CLIMAX: "Silent Decision" (CBS, 9/15/55). Martin Manulis — P., John Frankenheimer — D., Laura Z. Hobson — O., Adrian Spies — A. *cast:* Franchot Tone, Betty Furness, John Baragrey, Katharine Bard.

A successful surgeon is told that his wife is unfaithful. At first, he refuses to believe the story, but events occur which force him to reconsider. L — LA 60m.

CLIMAX: "Sailor On Horseback" (CBS, 9/29/55). Martin Manulis — P., John Frankenheimer — D., Irving Stone — O., Paul Monash — A. *cast:* Lloyd Nolan, Mercedes McCambridge, Mary Sinclair, Mario Siletti, Michael Ross.

Jack London and his wife, Charmain, return to their San Francisco ranch, where their lavish spending and entertaining leads to mounting expenses. The author's sister, Eliza pleads with the couple to act more reasonably and circumstances lead to a crisis. L — LA 60m.

CLIMAX: "House Of Shadows" (CBS, 10/20/55). Martin Manulis — P., John Frankenheimer — D., Nona Coxhead — O., Devery Freeman — A. *cast:* Diana Lynn, James Daly, Ernest Truex, Jane Darwell.

Small town gossip has it that a young woman holds her aged uncle a virtual prisoner in his own home. A visiting artist, looking for a colorful subject to paint, becomes involved when he tries to discover the truth of the strange situation. L — LA 60m. Color

CLIMAX: "Scheme To Defraud" (CBS, 11/10/55). Martin Manulis — P., John Frankenheimer — D., Marc Brandel — O. *cast:* Dennis O'Keefe, Phyllis Thaxter, Marilyn Erskine, Whit Bissell, Paul Harvey.

A married insurance underwriter and his secretary, disgruntled over their dull, monotonous routine, fall in love and discover a way to cash in a $70,000 insurance claim. L — LA 60m. Color

CLIMAX: "Portrait In Celluloid" (CBS, 11/24//55). Martin Manulis — P., John Frankenheimer — D., Rod Serling — O. *cast:* Jack Carson, Kim Hunter, Don Taylor, Audrey Totter, Robert F. Simon, John Gallaudet.

Art Shaddick was a writer but is now a writer's agent. On his bookcase is an Oscar he won in 1929. Since then he has gone steadily downhill, shouting all the way. Suddenly a young writer appears with a great script, offering Art a golden opportunity to rise again to greatness. L — LA 60m. Color

CLIMAX: "The Passport" (CBS, 12/8/55). Martin Manulis — P., John Frankenheimer — D., Elliot West — O. *cast:* Frank Lovejoy, Viveca Lindfors, Charles Korvin.

Following World War II, an American correspondent is offered a fortune in confiscated gems by an ex-Nazi officer for the use of the American's passport. (Viveca Lindfors was a last minute replacement for Katy Jurado.) L — LA 60m. Color

CLIMAX: "Bail Out At Forty-Three Thousand" (CBS, 12/29/55). Martin Manulis — P., John Frankenheimer — D., Paul Monash — O. *cast:* Charlton Heston, Richard Boone, Nancy Davis, Lee Marvin.

Three men prepare to test the ejector seat of a high altitude jet bomber. As they wait for favorable weather conditions, each reacts differently. L — LA 60m.

CLIMAX: "The Hanging Judge" (CBS, 1/12/56). Martin Manulis — P., John Frankenheimer — D., Raymond Massey — O., Whitfield Cook — A. *cast:* Raymond Massey, Sir Cedric Hardwicke, John Williams, John Carradine, Hurd Hatfield, Alan Marshal, Reginald Denny.

One of the most despised men in the legal profession clings tenaciously to the belief that English law is infallible and even stands trial for a murder he did not commit. L — LA 60m.

CLIMAX: "Gamble On A Thief" (CBS, 2/2/56). Martin Manulis — P., John Frankenheimer — D., Frank Cameron — O., James P. Cavanagh — A. *cast:* MacDonald Carey, Dewey Martin, Phyllis Kirk, Elizabeth Patterson, Tom Laughlin, Mickey Palmer, Tyler McVey.

This is a true story from the files of the California parole office. George Webster, thief, two-time loser and parole violator, becomes involved once more in crime, in spite of new-found happiness. L — LA 60m.

CLIMAX: "Nightmare By Day" (CBS, 2/23/56). Martin Manulis — P., John Frankenheimer — D., James P. Cavanagh — O. *cast:* Gene Nelson, Katy Jurado, Coleen Gray, Warner Anderson, Mary Astor.

The parents of a newlywed daughter suspect their son-in-law of treachery when he claims the girl has taken a trip to New York. L — LA 60m.

CLIMAX: "The Gay Illiteraterate: The Louella Parsons' Story" (CBS, 3/8/56). Martin Manulis — P., John Frankenheimer — D., Louella Parsons — O., Whitfield Cook — A. *cast:* Teresa Wright, Whit Bissell, William Tallman, Helen Winston, Addison Richards, William Roerich, Nestor Paiva, Sid Kane, Harriet Best, Jeri Lou James, Gracie Allen, Eve Arden, Jean Pierre Aumont, Gene Autry, Joan Bennett, Jack Benny, Charles Boyer, George Burns, Eddie Cantor, Dan Dailey, Howard Duff, Joan Fontaine, Zsa Zsa Gabor, Susan Hayward, Rock Hudson, Jack Lemmon, Ida Lupino, Jeanette MacDonald, Robert Mitchum, Fred MacMurray, Kim Novak, Merle Oberon, Ginger Rogers, Gilbert Roland, Red Skelton, Bob Stack, Lana Turner, Robert Wagner, John Wayne.

Teresa Wright portrays Miss Parsons in the drama covering the years from the early Twenties to 1948. As a climax to the drama, there was a tribute from the stars of the movie industry with Jack Benny as emcee. L — LA 60m.

CLIMAX: "Pale Horse, Pale Rider" (CBS, 3/22/56). Martin Manulis — P., John Frankenheimer — D., Katherine Anne Porter — O., F.W. Durkee, Jr. — A. *cast:* Dorothy McGuire,

John Forsythe, Ann Rutherfield, Lili Darvas, Byron Foulger, Ralph Dumke.

A young woman lives in fear that a recurrent dream foretells real tragedy. The premonition persists when she falls in love with a young soldier about to leave for overseas duty. L — LA 60m.

CLIMAX: "Spin Into Darkness" (CBS, 4/5/56). Martin Manulis — P., John Frankenheimer — D., Hagar Wilde — O. *cast:* Ruth Roman, Vincent Price, Charles Drake, Virginia Grey.

After gambling away the money given her by her pilot husband as a down payment on a plane, a young wife finds a position as a nurse to an alcoholic. In a drunken stupor the patient gives her $5,000, to recoup her losses; but when he sobers up, he reports to the police that the money has been stolen. L — LA 60m.

Edgar Peterson replaces Martin Manulis as producer of CLIMAX, effective with the program of April 19, 1956.

CLIMAX "Sit Down With Death" (CBS, 4/26/56). Edgar Peterson — P., John Frankenheimer — D., William Irish — O., James P. Cavanagh — A. *cast:* Ralph Bellamy, William Tallman, John Williams, Vicki Cummings, Constance Ford, Dan Barton, Tom Pitman, Irene Tedrow, Helen Kleeb, Charles Davis.

When one of the victims of an elevator mishap is pulled out of the wreckage, it's discovered he has been shot. L — LA 60m.

CLIMAX: "Flame-Out On T-6" (CBS, 5/17/56). Edgar Peterson — P., John Frankenheimer — D., George Lowther — O. *cast:* Richard Carlson, Kevin McCarthy, Sidney Blackmer, Jack Warden, Shepperd Strudwick, Royal Dano, Warren Stevens.

Ten men are assigned to mission T-6 in the sub-zero region of the North Pole. One of the men goes berserk and wrecks the radio, the group's only means of contact with the outside world. Now there is no way to notify headquarters of the location of the drifting ice flow. L — LA 60m.

CLIMAX: "Figures In Clay" (CBS, 5/31/56). Edgar Peterson — P., John Frankenheimer — D., Howard Leeds and Jerry Davis — O. *cast:* Edmond O'Brien, Lloyd Bridges, Georganne Johnson, Henry Hull.

Without informing his firm, a lawyer takes on the case of an irrational old man accused of killing a B-girl. His partner is shocked to think the attorney wants the case only to make headlines. L — LA 60m.

CLIMAX: "To Scream At Midnight" (CBS, 6/14/56). Edgar Peterson — P., John Frankenheimer — D., Patricia Highsmith — O., John McGreevey — A. *cast:* Diana Lynn, Dewey Martin, Karen Sharpe, Richard Jaeckel.

A wealthy young woman is so upset when she is thrown over by the man she loves, she is placed in a sanitarium. Her psychiatrist is suspicious when the boyfriend reappears unexpectedly and claims he wants to marry her. L — LA 60m.

During the summer hiatus, John Frankenheimer shot his first feature, THE YOUNG STRANGER, based on the CLIMAX show "Deal A Blow". The movie was shot from July, 9 to August 10, 1956. James MacArthur and Whit Bissell repeated their roles.

PLAYHOUSE 90 debuted on Thursday October 4, 1956, in the 9:30 — 11:00 PM EDT time slot. This was a weekly drama anthology series, all starring major talent in original and adaptations of novels, short stories and plays by first rank writers. An interesting gimmick was used, at least at the beginning of the series, a star from the next week's show would be the host for the current week. Basically the program was live originating in Los Angeles. In the first season eight filmed productions airing one every fourth Thursday were produced by Screen Gems, for CBS-TV. The production team consisted of Martin Manulis as producer with John Frankenheimer, Arthur Penn, Ralph Nelson, Vincent Donehue as alternating directors. The associate director on "Forbidden Area" was Jack Orbison, with Walter Scott Herndon as art director and Peter Kortner as script editor.

PLAYHOUSE 90: "Forbidden Area" (CBS, 10/4/56). Martin Manulis — P., John Frankenheimer — D., Pat Frank — O., Rod Serling — A. *cast:* Charlton Heston, Tab Hunter, Diana Lynn, Vincent Price, Victor Jory, Charles Bickford, Jackie Coogan, David Lewis, Tyler McVey, William Schallert, Lamont Johnson, Robert Middleton (narrator), Jack Palance (host).

This is a spy story set in the future when both the United States and Soviet Union have acquired the ability to knock out any enemy completely. In the Pentagon, two men and a woman assigned to study the enemy's intentions became convinced that an atomic attack is imminent. They grow desperate when the military brass refuses to credit their story. L — LA 90m.

PLAYHOUSE 90: "Rendezvous In Black" (CBS, 10/25/56). Martin Manulis — P., John Frankenheimer — D., Cornell Woolrich — O., James P. Cavanagh — A. *cast:* Franchot Tone, Laraine Day, Boris Karloff, Tom Drake, Viveca Lindfors, Elizabeth Patterson, Whit Bissell, Irene Tedrow, Andrew Duggan, Jerry Paris, Jennifer Howard, Reba Tassell, Jan Cheney, Jack Kruschen, Frank Lovejoy (host).

A young man makes a date with his fiancee to meet her on a street corner, and when he gets there she is dead. Neither he nor the authorities are able to find any motive for the mysterious murder of the girl. This first unexplainable death sets off a series of seemingly unrelated murders in the city. L — LA 90m.

PLAYHOUSE 90: "Eloise" (CBS, 11/22/56). *cast:* Evelyn Rudie, Kay Thompson, Louis Jourdan, Hans Conried, Ethel Barrymore, Monty Woolley, Conrad Hilton, Mildred Natwick, Jack Mullaney, Charlie Ruggles, Maxie Rosenbloom.

"Eloise" is a six-year-old who lives at New York's fashionable Plaza Hotel, and is always doing, doing, doing things to upset the management and it's guests. L — LA 90m.

PLAYHOUSE 90: "The Family Nobody Wanted" (CBS, 12/20/56). Martin Manulis — P., John Frankenheimer — D., Helen Doss — O., George Bruce — A. *cast:* Tim Hovey, Lew Ayres, Nanette Fabray, Tyler McVey, Bill Goodwin, Candace Lee, Deborah Hengen, Warren Hsieh, Dick Hong, Steven Ing, John Ing, Clifford Botello, Philip Coolidge, Helen Kleeb, Dale Evans (narrator).

After Helen and Carl Doss learn they cannot have children of their own, they decide to adopt a child. It seems they have everything to offer a child except financial standing in the community. Helen begins writing to adoption agencies and foundling homes throughout the country. The Dosses start their family with Donny, as six-week-old boy of American parentage and, over a period of years, their family grows until it includes 12 youngsters of mixed racial backgrounds, all of whom had been denied adoption through regular channels. L — LA 90m.

PLAYHOUSE 90: "The Ninth Day" (CBS, 1/10/57). Martin Manulis — P., John Frankenheimer — D., Dorothy Baker and Howard Baker — O. *cast:* John Kerr, Piper Laurie, Sir Cedric Hardwicke, Victor Jory, Mary Astor, Elizabeth Patterson, Audra Lindley, James Dunn, Nehemiah Persoff.

A small group of people living in an isolated section of the desert for 20 years believe they are the sole survivors of nuclear war, and the future existence of the human race depends on the two young people among them. (This show was publicized as "Mr. and Mrs. McAdam" but aired under the title, "The Ninth Day".) L — LA 90m.

PLAYHOUSE 90: "The Comedian" (CBS, 2/14/57). Martin Manulis — P., John Frankenheimer — D., Ernest Lehman — O., Rod Serling — A. *cast:* Mickey Rooney, Edmond O'Brien, Kim Hunter, Mel Torme, Constance Ford, Whit Bissell, King Donovan, Eddie Ryder, H.M. Wynant.

Sammy Hogarth has reached the top of his profession as a TV comedian. Although his audience loves him, he is an egotistical petty tyrant. In fact, Sammy threatens to fire his head writer unless he comes up with some especially clever and unusual material for the next show. L — LA 90m.

PLAYHOUSE 90: "The Last Tycoon" (CBS, 3/14/57). Martin Manulis — P., John Frankenheimer — D., F. Scott Fitzgerald — O., Don M. Mankiewicz — A. *cast:* Jack Palance, Keenan Wynn, Peter Lorre, Viveca Lindfors, Lee Remick, Robert F. Simon, John Hudson, Tom Laughlin, Reginald Denny.

Monroe Stahr heads a movie studio that seems headed for financial trouble and is under pressure from the stockholders to turn out a box-office hit. (This was the vehicle in which Humphrey Bogart had hoped to star but was unable to because of his fatal illness.) L — LA 90m.

PLAYHOUSE 90: "If You Knew Elizabeth" (CBS, 4/11/57). Martin Manulis — P., John Frankenheimer — D., Tad Mosel — O. *cast:* Claire Trevor, Gary Merrill, Ernest Truex, Natalie Schafer, Joe Sweeney, Doro Merande, Stephen Wootton, Joi Lansing, Nancy Marchand.

At her engagement party, Elizabeth Owen learns that Walter Hubbard is marrying her simply to enhance his chances for the position as president of the university. She vanishes, and Hubbard, in his search for her, finds out that each of her acquaintances knows a very different facet of her character. (The producers first signed Bette Davis, who pulled out because she became "too tired," and then Anne Baxter became ill.) L — LA 90m.

PLAYHOUSE 90: "Winter Dreams" (CBS, 5/23/57). Martin Manulis — P., John Frankenheimer — D., F. Scott Fitzgerald — O., James P. Cavanagh — A. *cast:* John Cassavetes, Dana Wynter, Mildred Natwick, Darryl Hickman, Edmund Gwenn, Phyllis Love, Lana Wood, Joe Sweeney, Robert F. Simon, Raymond Bailey, Howard Wendell, Peter Votrian.

For most of his young life Dexter Green has been molded by the dreams and ambitions of his mother, who wanted him to achieve financial success, and his father, who wanted his son to be content with a peaceful way of life. As the play opens, Dexter has just announced his engagement to Irene Hedrich. The sudden reappearance of Judy Holt, the rich girl he has dreamed of and loved for years starts him remembering the past years and his own dreams. (Martin Manulis wanted Dana Wynter so much, that he moved the show back five months so that she could be borrowed from 20th Century-Fox.) L — LA 90m.

PLAYHOUSE 90: "Clash By Night" (CBS, 6/13/57). Martin Manulis — P., John Frankenheimer — D., Clifford Odets — O., F. W. Durkee, Jr. — A. *cast:* Kim Stanley, Lloyd Bridges, E. G. Marshall, Edgar Sthel, John Bleifer, Peggy Maurer.

Jerry Wilenski loves his young wife and daughter, feels his happiness is a great achievement and isn't bothered by his ramshackle house or shaky finances. His wife Mae is restless, and longs for something better. Into this explosive situation walks Earl Pfeiffer, an old friend of Jerry's. L — LA 90m.

PLAYHOUSE 90: "The Fabulous Irishman" (CBS, 6/27/57). Martin Manulis — P., John Frankenheimer — D., Erick Moll — O. *cast:* Art Carney, Katharine Bard, Michael Higgins, Charles Davis, Eli Mintz, George Mathews, David Opatosheu, Berta Gersten, Peter Lorre, Eddie Cantor (host).

In 1918, at the age of 23, Robert Briscoe is swept up in the fever of the Irish rebellion against Britain and joins the Irish Republican army. By day he works as a respectable wool salesman, by night as the notorious arms smuggler, "Captain Swift." A truce with England results in a split between the Sinn Fein and the Irish Republican Army which sets Irishman against Irishman. L — LA 90m.

PLAYHOUSE 90's second season debuted on Thursday September 12, 1957 (9:30 — 11:00 PM EDT). The program originated live from Los Angeles, with some filmed dramas. The production team consisted of Martin Manulis as producer, Peter Kortner as associate producer, with John Frankenheimer, Vincent J. Donehue, George Roy Hill, Arthur Hiller, Arthur Penn, and Franklin Schaffner the alternating directors. The story editor was Del Reisman.

PLAYHOUSE: "The Death of Manolete" (CBS, 9/12/57). Martin Manulis — P., John Frankenheimer — D., Barnaby Conrad — O., Paul Monash — A. *cast:* Jack Palance, Suzy Parker, Robert Middleton, Ray Danton, Nehemiah Persoff, Esther Minclotti, H.M. Wyant, Ricky Vera.

Discovered at 16 by an ex-torero, Manolete spends two years in training. He is placed in competition with Marquez, a once-famous man. The old man insists on entering the arena even though he is afraid and is killed. Marquez's manager blames Manolete. Actual films of Manolete bull fighting were integrated into the drama. L — LA 90m.

PLAYHOUSE 90: "A Sound Of Different Drummers" (CBS, 10/3/57). Martin Manulis — P., John Frankenheimer — D., Robert Alan Aurthur — O. *cast:* Sterling Hayden, Diana Lynn, John Ireland, David Opatoshu, Adam Williams, James Edwards, Paul Lambert.

In a totalitarian state of the future, a young officer of the government police organization sees an attractive young librarian hastily hide an illegal volume. L — LA 90m.

PLAYHOUSE 90: "The Troublemakers" (CBS, 11/21/57). Martin Manulis — P., John Frankenheimer — D., George Bellak — O. *cast* Ben Gazzara, Keenan Wynn, Barbara Rush, Robert Vaughn, Mary Astor, Jackie Coogan, Nick Adams, Harry Guardino, Tom Laughlin, Jack Mullaney, Malcolm Atterbury.

A college journalist has made enemies of some students because of his outspoken editorials. A group of boys harass and beat him until he falls to the floor dead. One boy struggles with his conscience, to report the death or remain silent. L — LA 90m.

PLAYHOUSE 90: "The Thundering Wave" (CBS, 12/12/57). Martin Manulis — P., John Frankenheimer — D., Robert Alan Arthur — O. *cast:* James Mason, Franchot Tone, Joan

Bennett, Pamela Mason, Susan Oliver, Jack Klugman.

Actor Allen Grant and his actress-wife Vickie Maxwell, after a marital and professional separation of many years, are asked to do a play together, and Allen is insulted to learn that his role will be that of Vickie's father. L — LA 90m.

PLAYHOUSE 90: "The Last Man" (CBS, 1/9/58). Martin Manulis — P., John Frankenheimer — D., Aaron Spelling — O. *cast:* Sterling Hayden, Carolyn Jones, Lee Phillips, Wallace Ford, Hurd Hatfield, Mark Richmond.

After the long, exhausting trip from California to frontier Arizona, Mitch Barrett's wife gives birth to a child and is in critical condition. The doctor sends Barrett for medicine, but the storekeeper, annoyed at being awakened late at night, demands full payment and Barrett is 87 cents short. He returns to find both his wife and child dead. L — LA 90m.

PLAYHOUSE 90: "The Violent Heart" (CBS, 2/6/58). Martin Manulis — P., John Frankenheimer — D., Daphne du Maurier — O., Leslie Stevens — A. *cast:* Dana Wynter, Ben Gazzara, Pamela Brown, Charles Korvin, Vivian Nathan, Mimi Gibson, William Roerick.

On the Riviera, a young marquise searching for a camera, buys one from a photographer who is drawn to the marquise's beauty. The marquise's husband leaves for Paris and she goes for a walk and finds herself back in the photographer's shop. L — LA 90m.

PLAYHOUSE 90: "Rumors Of Evening" (CBS, 5/1/58). Martin Manulis — P., John Frankenheimer — D., F.W. Durkee, Jr. — O., Leslie Stevens — A. *cast:* John Kerr, Barbara Bel Geddes, Robert F. Simon, Pat Hitchcock, Robert Loggia, Ron Soble, Mimi Gibson, The Kingston Trio.

A young American pilot, stationed at an air force base in England during World War II, is attracted to a girl who rebuffs his overtures. He learns that a dangerous mission is scheduled, and though he is due to return to the States on leave, he feels it is his duty to stay. (This show was to be telecast April 10, 1958, but was delayed by the IBEW strike.) L — LA 90m.

PLAYHOUSE 90: "Bomber's Moon" (CBS, 5/22/58). Martin Manulis — P., John Frankenheimer — D., Rod Serling — O. *cast:* Robert Cummings, Hazel Court, Rip Torn, Martin Balsam, Larry Gates, J. Patrick O'Malley, Malcolm Atterbury, Ron Soble, Tim Lyon, Mike Masters, Rick Ellis.

The pilots of an American bomber wing in England in 1943 feel their commander, as a man devoid of human emotion or understanding. After a mission when one of the best pilots was shot down, the overwrought colonel singles out a young flier and publicly accuses him of cowardice. L — LA 90m.

PLAYHOUSE 90: "A Town Has Turned To Dust" (CBS, 6/19/58). Martin Manulis — P., John Frankenheimer — D., Rod Serling — O. *cast:* Rod Steiger, William Shatner, Fay Spain, James Gregory, Martin Garralaga, Mario Alcalde, Eugene Iglesias, Gregg Holt, Paul Lambert, Malcolm Atterbury, Sandy Kenyon.

In a small southwestern town, a Mexican boy is jailed, accused of robbing a general store and attacking the storekeeper's wife. A mob sets out to lynch the youth without waiting for a trial. The sheriff tries to reason with the mob, but finally sees his efforts are in vain. (Originally called "Aftermath," it dealt with a Negro lynching in the South and was deemed too hot to handle without rewriting.) L — LA 90m.

STUDIO ONE IN HOLLYWOOD aired Mondays, 10:00 — 11:00 PM EST as a summer substitute for STUDIO ONE.

STUDIO ONE IN HOLLYWOOD: "The Last Summer" (CBS, 8/4/58). John Frankenheimer — D., Frank Gilroy — O. *cast:* Dennis Hopper, Vivian Nathan, Claire Griswold, Malcolm Atterbury.

Teenager Harry Wales has worked to save for his college tuition. He meets a spoiled girl and in an effort to impress her finds himself using some of his precious savings. L — LA 60m.

PLAYHOUSE 90's third season debuted on Thursday September 25, 1958 (9:30 — 11:00 PM EDT). The program originated live from Los Angeles, with no filmed dramas. Martin Manulis was replaced by Fred Coe, Herbert Brodkin, and John Houseman. The directors for the third season were: Daniel Mann, John Frankenheimer, Franklin Schaffner, Ralph Nelson, Alex Segal, George Roy Hill, and Buzz Kulik.

PLAYHOUSE 90: "The Days Of Wine And Roses" (CBS, 10/2/58). Fred Coe — P., John Frankenheimer — D., J.P. Miller — O. *cast:* Piper Laurie, Charles Bickford, Cliff Robertson, Malcolm Atterbury, Marc Lawrence, Martha Wentworth, Doug Henderson, Mimi Gibson, Dick Elliot, Ellen Hardies, Richard LePore.

Joe Clay, a once-successful businessman and his wife have become alcoholics. In an effort to get help Joe goes to a meeting of Alcoholics Anonymous where he is asked to recount how he became an alcoholic. L — LA 90m. (Repeated 9/17/59)

PLAYHOUSE 90: "Old Man" (CBS, 11/20/58). Fred Coe — P., John Frankenheimer — D., William Faulkner — O., Horton Foote — A. *cast:* Sterling Hayden, Geraldine Page, James Westerfield, Sandy Kenyon, George Mitchell, Malcolm Atterbury, Richard LePore, Marc Lawrence, Milton Selzer, Bob O'Connor, Len Lesser, Naomi Stevens, Stafford Repp, Jamie Foster, Alvin Childress, Cleff Hoyt, Bob Dugan, Ned Roberts.

In 1927, to fight a Mississippi flood, a prison farm releases some convicts. Some see the flood as an opportunity to escape, others feel honor-bound to carry out the work and return. L — LA 90m. (Repeated 09/19/61)

PLAYHOUSE 90: "Face Of A Hero" (CBS, 1/1/59). John Houseman — P., John Frankenheimer — D., Pierre Boulle — O., Robert L. Joseph — A. *cast:* Jack Lemmon, James Gregory, Rip Torn, Henry Hull, Anne Meacham, Larry Gates, William Hansen, Malcolm Atterbury, Whit Bissell, Bryon Foulger, Richard LePore, Stanley Adams, Jamie Foster, Charles Aidman, Carol Kelly, Leonard Bell, Burt Reynolds.

The prosecuting attorney in a Southern town is virtually a hero in the town's eyes. The play opens with two seemingly unrelated events. The prosecutor is expounding to a jury his belief that concentration on the truth and the facts must lead to justice. Flashback to a tragic scene several months earlier, when he stood helplessly by while a girl drowned. L — LA 90m. (Repeated 07/04/62)

PLAYHOUSE: "The Blue Men" (CBS, 1/15/59). Herb Brodkin — P., John Frankenheimer — D., Alvin Boretz — O. *cast:* Edmond O'Brien, Jack Warden, Eileen Heckart, Cameron Prud'homme, James Westerfield, David Lewis, Rafael Campos, Richard LePore.

A police detective has a long and distinguished service record but his integrity is questioned after he refuses to arrest a youth who has been accused of theft. L — LA 90m.

PLAYHOUSE 90: "For Whom The Bells Toll" Part 1 (CBS, 3/12/59). Fred Coe — P., John Frankenheimer — D., Ernest Hemingway — O., A.E. Hotchner — A. *cast:* Maria Schell, Jason Robards, Jr., Maureen Stapleton, Eli Wallach, Nehemiah Persoff, Steven Hill, Vladimir Sokoloff, Joseph Bernard, Milton Selzer, Sydney Pollack, Nicholas Colasanto, Marc Lawrence, Herbert Berghof.

1937 Spain is in the midst of civil war. Robert Jordan, an American, has come to Spain to fight with Loyalists against the insurgent forces which are trying to take over the country. T — NY 90m.

PLAYHOUSE 90: "For Whom The Bells Toll" Part 2 (CBS, 3/19/59). Credits and cast are the same as Part I.

Robert Jordan and his group are planning the destruction of a bridge. (Budgeted at $300,000 for both parts the final cost was approximately $500,000. There were five weeks of intensive rehearsal and ten days of taping. Part of this expense was Frankenheimer's insistence for taping retakes.) T — NY 90m.

The DUPONT SHOW OF THE MONTH aired Thursdays, 8:00–9:30 PM EST.

DUPONT SHOW OF THE MONTH: "The Browning Version" (CBS, 4/23/59). David Susskind — P., John Frankenheimer — D., Terence Rattigan — O., Jacqueline Babbin, and Audrey Gellen — A. *cast:* Sir John Gielgud, Margaret Leighton, Cecil Parker, Robert Stephens, Rhoden Streeter, James Valentine, Iola Lynn, Donald Moffat, Carson Woods.

John Gielgud portrays an English schoolteacher who has lost the respect of his pupils, his colleagues and his wife. L — NY 90m.

The SUNDAY SHOWCASE aired Sundays, 8:00 — 9:00 PM EST.

SUNDAY SHOWCASE: "People Kill People Sometimes" (NBC, 9/30/59). John Frankenheimer — P./D., S. Lee Pogostin — O. *cast:* Jason Robards, Jr., Geraldine Page, George C. Scott, Nan Martin, Zina Bethune, Irving Steinberg, Kate Harkin.

Alex and Virginia Reed have lost interest in their marriage. Alex is loved by Nancy, who he met in Mexico. Richard Bryan, a psychoanalyst, has fallen in love with his patient Virginia. The four come together at a party in the Reed's house, in a neighborhood plagued by a prowler. L — NY 60m. Color

The FORD STARTIME aired Tuesdays, 9:30 — 11:00 PM EST.

FORD STARTIME: "The Turn Of The Screw" (NBC, 10/20/59). John Frankenheimer — P./D., Henry James — O. James Costigan — A. *cast:* Ingrid Bergman, Isobel Elsom, Haywood Morse, Alexandra Wagner, Paul Stevens, Laurinda Barrett, Carla Patricia Challoner.

A governess arrives at a country estate to care for two orphans. One day she is frightened when a strange man suddenly materializes, stares fixedly at her, then disappears. T — 90m. Color

The BUICK ELECTRA PLAYHOUSE aired Fridays, 8:30 — 11:00 PM EST.

BUICK ELECTRA PLAYHOUSE: "The Fifth Column" (CBS, 1/29/60). Gordon Duff — P., John Frankenheimer — D., Ernest Hemingway — O., A.E. Hotchner — A. *cast:* Richard Burton, Maximilian Schell, Sally Ann Howes, Betsy von Furstenburg, George Rose, Milton Selzer, Shai K. Ophir, Elisa Loti, Tonio Selwart, Sydney Pollack, Robert

Dowdell, Alfred De La Fuente, R. G. Brown, Philip Kenneally, Andreas Voutsinas, Clifford David.

Journalist Philip Rawlings is posing as a playboy who is bored by the Spanish Civil War, risking his life as a counterespionage agent for the Loyalists. T — 90m.

BUICK ELECTRA PLAYHOUSE: "The Snows Of Kilimanjaro" (CBS, 3/25/60). Gordon Duff — P., John Frankenheimer — D., Ernest Hemingway — O., A.E. Hotchner — A. *cast:* Robert Ryan, Ann Todd, Janice Rule, Norma Crane, Mary Astor, James Gregory, Liliane Montevecchi, Brock Peters, Frank Puglia, Clancy Cooper, Cleg Hoyt, Albert Paulson.

Harry Walters feels death closing in. Injured on a hunting trip, he is attended by his wife as he lies on an African plain in the shadow of snow capped Mount Kilimanjaro. (Norma Crane substituted for Jean Hagen.) T — 90m. Color

SUNDAY SHOWCASE: "The American" (NBC, 3/27/60). John Frankenheimer — P./ D., Merle Miller — O. *cast:* Lee Marvin, Steven Hill, Frank Overton, Milton Selzer, Thomas Carlin, Frank Corsaro, Sydney Pollack.

Ira Hayes, a Pima Indian, one of the Marines who raised the American flag on Iwo Jima in 1945, got a hero's welcome when he returned to his Arizona reservation. Eleven years later, Hayes was dead at the age of 32. This show was taped on location mostly in Arizona. T —60m. Color

PLAYHOUSE 90 now aired Fridays, 9:00 — 10:30 PM EST.

PLAYHOUSE 90: "Journey To The Day" (CBS, 4/22/60). Fred Coe — P., John Frankenheimer — D., Roger O. Hirson — O. *cast:* Mary Astor, Mike Nichols, Janice Rule, Steven Hill, James Dunn, Vivian Nathan, James Gregory, Peter Votrian, David J. Stewart, Helen Kleeb.

In a state mental hospital, six patients are brought together for group psychotherapy. L — LA 90m.

THE GOLDEN AGE OF TELEVISION: Playhouse 90: "The Comedian" (PBS, 2/6/82). Sonny Fox — P., *cast:* John Frankenheimer, Mickey Rooney, Kim Hunter, Mel Torme.

This series produced by Sunny Fox for Public Television consisted of the original show, in black and white, without commercials. New interview footage with the above "cast" talking about the making of the original show was shot in color. 90m. B&W and Color.

HBO THEATRE: "The Rainmaker" (HBO, 10/24/82). Marcia Govons — P., John Frankenheimer — D., N. Richard Nash — O. *cast:* Tommy Lee Jones, Tuesday Weld, William Katt, Lonny Chapman, James Cromwell, Taylor Lacher, William Traylor.

At a time of severe drought in 1922, a brash young con artist promises to make rain descend upon the Curry family creating a storm of discord. T — 135m. Color

TALES FROM THE CRYPT: "Maniac At Large" (HBO 8/19/92). John Frankenheimer — D., Mae Woods — S. *cast:* Blythe Danner, Adam Ant, Clarence Williams, III, Salome Jens.

There's a maniac at large when a serial killer leaves a trail of dead men in the park near the library. After a nervous librarian gets a tip about the next victim, she becomes very suspicious. 30m. Color

HBO SPECIAL: "Against The Wall" (HBO 3/26/94). Jonathan Axelrod, Irwin Meyer, Harvey Bibicoff — Ex. P., Steven McGlother — P., John Frankenheimer — D., Ron Hutchinson — S. *cast:* Kyle MacLachlan, Samuel L. Jackson, Harry Dean Stanton, Clarence Williams, III, Frederic Forrest, Philip Bosco, Tom Bower, Anne Heche, Carmen Argenziano, Peter Murnik, Steve Harris, David Ackroyd, Mark Cabus, Bruce Evers, Joey Anderson, Richard Cowl, Bud Davis, Danny Drew, Jeffrey Ford, Denis Forest, Juan Garcia, Al Garrison, Vincent Harris, Vincent Henry, Scott Higgins, Rand Hopkins, James Mayberry, James "Sonny" Moore, Danny Trejo, Bart Whiteman, Craig Hoskins.

Based on the terrifying true experiences of novice guard Michael Smith, this tells a story of courage and moral conviction amid the chaos and horror of the 1971 Attica prison rebellions. 110m. Color.

HBO SPECIAL: "The Burning Season" (HBO 9/17/94). David Puttnam — Ex. P., Thomas M. Hammel, John Frankenheimer — P., Diane Smith — Co. P., John Frankenheimer — D., Andrew Revkin — O., William Mastrosimone — O., William Mastrosimone, Michael Tolkin, Ron Hutchinson — S. *cast:* Raul Julia, Carmen Argenziano, Sonia Braga, Kamala Dawson, Luis Guzman, Nigel Havers, Tomas Milian, Esai Morales, Edward James Olmos.

Spurred to action by soft-spoken but charismatic Chico Mendes, the peasants form a union and mass to prevent construction of a road that will allow easy access to their forest by speculators and cattlemen. Fighting the union are corrupt Brazilian politicians and capitalists. 150m. Color.

ANDERSONVILLE (Turner Pictures Inc., 1995). Ethel Winant—Ex.P., David Rintels — P., Diane Smith — Co. P., John Frankenheimer — P./D., David Rintels — S. *cast:* Jarrod Emick, Frederic Forrest, Cliff de Young, Ted Marcoux, Kris Kamm, Tony Higgins, Jan Triska.

Andersonville was the crude, open-air Confederate prison stockade where Union captives, exposed to the elements, overcrowding and staggering deprivation waited out the war. At its peak, the camp held some 32,000 prisoners, of whom 12,000 died — more than 100 a day during the summer of 1864. The story, as seen through the eyes of young Josiah Day, is an extraordinary tale of friendship, survival and the triumph of hope. 200m. Color.

Filmography

The following abbreviations are used:

A = adaptor
D = director
O = original
P = producer
S = screenplay

THE YOUNG STRANGER (RKO-Universal International, 4/8/57). Stuart Millar — P., John Frankenheimer — D., Robert Dozier — S. *cast:* James MacArthur, Kim Hunter, James Daly, James Gregory, Whit Bissell, Jeff Silver, Jack Mullaney, Tom Pittman, Charles Davis, Marian Seldes, Eddie Ryder. 84m. B&W Flat.

THE YOUNG SAVAGES (United Artists, 5/24/61). Pat Dugan — P., John Frankenheimer — D., Evan Hunter — O., Edward Anhalt, J.P. Miller — S. *cast:* Burt Lancaster, Dina Merrill, Shelley Winters, Edward Andrews, Vivian Nathan, Larry Gates, Telly Savalas. 103m. B&W Flat.

BIRDMAN OF ALCATRAZ (United Artists, 7/3/62). Stuart Millar, Guy Trosper — P., John Frankenheimer — D., Thomas E. Gaddis — O., Guy Trosper — S. *cast:* Burt Lancaster, Karl Malden, Thelma Ritter, Neville Brand, Betty Field, Telly Savalas, Edmond O'Brien, Hugh Marlowe, Whit Bissell. 147m B&W Flat.

ALL FALL DOWN (MGM, 3/28/62). John Houseman — P., John Frankenheimer — D., James Lee Herlihy — O., William Inge — S. *cast:* Eve Marie Saint, Warren Beatty, Karl Malden, Angela Lansbury, Brandon DeWilde, Constance Ford, Barbara Baxley, Evans Evans, Jennifer Howard, Madame Spivy, Albert Paulson. 111m B&W Flat.

THE MANCHURIAN CANDIDATE (United Artists, 10/24/62). George Axelrod, John Frankenheimer — P., John Frankenheimer — D., Richard Condon — O., George Axelrod — S. *cast:* Frank Sinatra, Laurence Harvey, Janet Leigh, Angela Lansbury, Henry Silva, James Gregory, Leslie Parrish, John McGiver, Knigh Dhiegh, James Edwards, Douglas Henderson, Albert Paulsen, Madame Spivy, Barry Kelly.

SEVEN DAYS IN MAY (Paramount, 2/12/64). Edward Lewis — P., John Frankenheimer — D., Fletcher Knebel, Charles W. Bailey II — O., Rod Serling — S. *cast:* Burt Lancaster, Kirk Douglas, Fredric March, Ava Gardner, Edmond O'Brien, Martin Balsam, George Macready, Whit Bissell, Hugh Marlowe, Bart Burns, Richard Anderson, Jack Mullaney, Andrew Duggan, John Larkin, Malcolm Atterbury, Helen Kleeb, John Houseman, Colette Jackson. 117m B&W Flat.

THE TRAIN (United Artists, 3/17/65). Jules Bricken — P., John Frankenheimer — D., Rose Valland — O., Franklin Coen, Frank Davis — S. *cast:* Burt Lancaster, Paul Scofield, Jeanne Moreau, Michel Simon, Suzanne Flon, Wolfgang Preiss, Richard Munch, Albert Remy, Charles Millot, Jacques Marin. (Arthur Penn was the original director and Frankenheimer replaced him. This film was released in France first in September of 1964.) 133m B&W Flat.

SECONDS (Paramount, 9/14/66). Edward Lewis — P., John Frankenheimer — D., Lewis John Carlino — S. *cast:* Rock Hudson, Salome Jens, John Randolph, Will Geer, Jeff

Corey, Richard Anderson, Murray Hamilton, Karl Swenson, Knigh Dhiegh, Frances Reid, Wesley Addy, Francoise Ruggieri. 106 m B&W Flat.

GRAND PRIX (MGM, 12/22/66). Edward Lewis — P., John Frankenheimer — D., Robert Alan Aurthur — S. *cast:* James Garner, Eva Marie Saint, Yves Montand, Toshiro Mifune, Brian Bedford, Jessica Walter, Antonio Sabato, Francoise Hardy, Adolfo Celli, Claude Dauphin, Phil Hill, Graham Hill. 167m Metrocolor Cinerama Super Panavision.

THE EXTRAORDINARY SEAMAN (MGM, 1/22/69). Edward Lewis, John H. Cushingham — P., John Frankenheimer — D., Phillip Rock — O., Phillip Rock, Hal Dresner — S. *cast:* David Niven, Faye Dunaway, Alan Alda, Mickey Rooney, Jack Carter, Juano Hernandez, Manu Tupou, Barry Kelley. (This picture was produced before THE FIXER.) 79m Metrocolor Panavision.

THE FIXER (MGM, 12/8/68). Edward Lewis — P., John Frankenheimer — D., Bernard Malamud — O., Dalton Trumbo — S. *cast:* Alan Bates, Dirk Borgarde, Georgia Brown, Hugh Griffith, Elizabeth Hartman, Ian Holm. David Warner, Carol White. 132m Metrocolor Flat.

THE GYPSY MOTHS (MGM, 8/28/69). Hal Landers, Bobby Roberts — P., John Frankenheimer — D., James Drought — O., William Hanley — S. *cast:* Burt Lancaster, Deborah Kerr, Gene Hackman, Scott Wilson, William Windom, Bonnie Bedelia, Sheree North, Carl Reindel, Ford Rainey, John Napier. 107m Metrocolor Flat.

I WALK THE LINE (Columbia, 10/12/70). Harold Cohen — P., John Frankenheimer — D., Madison Jones — O., Alvin Sargent — S. *cast:* Gregory Peck, Tuesday Weld, Estelle Parsons, Ralph Meeker, Lonny Chapman, Charles Durning, Jeff Dalton, Freddie McCloud, Jane Rose, J.C. Evans, Margaret A. Morris, Bill Littleton, Leo Yates, Dodo Denney. 96m Eastmancolor Panavision.

THE HORSEMAN (Columbia, 6/23/71). Edward Lewis — P., John Frankenheimer — D., Joseph Kessel — O., Dalton Trumbo — S. *cast:* Omar Sharif, Leigh Taylor-Young, Jack Palance, David De, Peter Jeffrey, Mohammed Shamsi, George Murcell, Eric Pohlmann. 109m Color Super Panavision.

THE IMPOSSIBLE OBJECT (Valoria Films, 5/18/73). John Frankenheimer — D., Nicolas Mosley — S. *cast:* Alan Bates, Dominique Sanda, Evans Evans, Lea Massari, Michel Auclair, Laurence De Monaghan. (A French film with an English soundtrack was shown out of competition at the 1973 Cannes Film Festival. Also known as THE STORY OF A LOVE STORY.) 110m Eastmancolor Flat.

THE ICEMAN COMETH (AFT, 10/29/73). Ely A. Landau — P., John Frankenheimer — D., Eugene O'Neill — O., Thomas Quinn Curtiss — S. *cast:* Lee Marvin, Fredric March, Robert Ryan, Jeff Bridges, Bradford Dillman, Sorrell Booke, Hildy Brooks, Nancy Juno Dawson, Evans Evans, Martyn Green, Moses Gunn, Clifton James, John McLaim, Stephen Pearlman, Tom Pedi, George Voskovec, Bart Burns, Don McGovern. 239m Technicolor Flat.

99 AND 44/100 % DEAD (20th Century-Fox, 6/26/74). Joe Wizan — P., John Frankenheimer — D., Robert Dillon — S. *cast:* Richard Harris, Edmond O'Brien, Bradford Dillman, Ann Turkel, Constance Ford, David Hall, Kathrine Baumann, Janice Heiden, Roy Jenson, Chuck Roberson, Chuck Connors. 97m Deluxe color Panavision.

FRENCH CONNECTION II (20th Century-Fox, 5/18/75). Robert L. Rosen — P., John Frankenheimer — D., Robert Dillon, Laurie Dillon — O., Robert Dillon, Laurie Dillon, Alexander Jacobs — S. *cast:* Gene Hackman, Fernando Rey, Bernard Fresson, Jean-Pierre Castaldi, Charles Millot, Cathleen Nesbitt, Pierre Collet, Alexandre Fabre, Ed Lauter. 119m Deluxe color. Flat.

BLACK SUNDAY (Paramount, 3/31/77). Robert Evans — P., John Frankenheimer — D., Thomas Harris — O., Ernest Lehman, Kenneth Ross, Ivan Moffat — S. *cast:* Robert Shaw, Bruce Dern, Marthe Keller, Fritz Weaver, Steven Keats, Bekim Fehmiu, Michael V. Gazzo, William Daniels. 143m Movielab color. Panavision.

PROPHECY (Paramount, 6/15/79). Robert L. Rosen — P., John Frankenheimer — D., David Selzer — S. *cast:* Talia Shire, Robert Foxworth, Armand Assante, Richard Dysart, Victoria Racimo, George Clutesi. 102 m Movielab color Panavision.

THE CHALLENGE (Embassy Pictures, 7/23/82). Robert L. Rosen, Ron Beckman — P., John Frankenheimer — D., Richard Maxwell, John Sayles — S. *cast:* Scott Glenn, Toshiro Mifune, Donna Kei Benz, Atsuo Nakamura, Calvin Jung, Clyde Kusatsu. 110m Eastmancolor Flat.

THE HOLCROFT COVENANT (Universal, 10/18/85). Edie Landau — P., John Frankenheimer — D., Robert Ludlum — O., George Axelrod, Edward Anhalt, John Hopkins — S. *cast:* Michael Caine, Anthony Andrews, Victoria Tennant, Lilli Palmer, Mario Adorf, Michael Lonsdale, Bernard Hepton, Richard Munch. 112m Color Flat.

52 PICK-UP (Cannon, 11/7/86). Menahem Golan, Yoram Globus — P., John Frankenheimer — D., Elmore Leonard — O., Elmore Leonard, John Steppling — S. *cast:* Roy Scheider, Ann-Margret, Vanity, John Glover, Robert Trebor, Lonny Chapman, Kelly Preston, Clarence Williams, III, Doug McClure. 114m TVC Color Flat.

DEAD BANG (Lorimar/Warner Bros., 3/24/89). Steve Roth — P., John Frankenheimer — D., Jerry Beck, Robert Foster — O., Robert Foster — S. *cast:* Don Johnson, Penelope Ann Miller, William Forsythe, Bob Balaban, Frank Military, Tate Donovan, Tim Reid. 105m Alpha-Cine Color Flat.

THE FOURTH WAR (Cannon, 3/23/90). Wolf Schmidt — P., John Frankenheimer — D., Stephen Peters — O., Stephen Peters, Kenneth Ross — S. *cast:* Roy Scheider, Jurgen Prochnow, Tim Reid, Lara Harris, Harry Dean Stanton, Dale Dye, Bill MacDonald. 91m Alpha-Cine Color Flat.

YEAR OF THE GUN (Triumph, 11/1/91). Edward R. Pressman — P., John Frankenheimer — D., Michael Mewshaw — O. David Ambrose — S. *cast:* Andrew McCarthy, Valeria Golino, Sharon Stone, John Pankow, George Murcell, Lou Castel, Francesca Prandi. 111m Color.

Sources

P. 3 "I was always a very introverted child . . .," Pratley, Gerald, *The Cinema of John Frankenheimer.* (A.S. Barnes & Co., New York, 1969.)

P. 4 "Soon after he discovered . . .," from C. Robert Jennings article in *Horizon* Magazine March, 1963.

P. 6 "I had men in that squadron . . .," *Pratley* p. 19.

P. 7 "I shot a whole short subject . . .," *Pratley,* p. 19.

P. 7 "We knew nothing about cameras but . . .," Champlin interview.

P. 14 "What I remember as an actor . . .," Lisa Mitchell interview with Betsy Palmer, February, 1995.

P. 18 "I remember sitting up for nights . . .," *Pratley* p. 26.

P. 20-21 "I learned a great deal . . .," *Action* Magazine, 1973.

P. 21 "(John Frankenheimer) is the most talented . . .," *Horizon* Magazine, March, 1963.

P. 28 "I was panic-stricken . . .," *Pratley,* p.42.

P. 36 "He used his own face . . .," Mitchell interview with Marc Lawrence, November, 1994.

P. 39 "I remember during an on-air show . . .," and "someone once compared . . ." J.F. quoted in *Television* by Michael Winship (Random House, 1988).

P. 40 "The best thing I've ever done . . .," Robert Ryan in *Films and Filming* Magazine, August, 1961.

P. 41 "For Whom The Bell Tolls" was the longest . . . etc., *Newsweek,* March 16, 1959.

P. 41 "John Frankenheimer was *the* man . . .," Mitchell interview with Mark Rydell, March, 1995.

P. 44 "John Frankenheimer . . . was so long the 'child prodigy' . . .," *Show* Magazine, August, 1961.

P. 59 "*Birdman of Alcatraz* was something I'd wanted to do . . .," JF *Action* Magazine, 1973.

P. 71 "It was one of the best film experiences . . .," Sinatra quoted in Army Archerd's column, *Variety,* February 26, 1988.

P. 72 "Frankenheimer, who loses weight . . .," from C. Robert Jennings article in *Horizon* Magazine, March 1963.

P. 75 "This was one film that really marked what I wanted to do . . .," from *Horizon* Magazine, March, 1963.

P. 82 "There was a conflict of personalities . . .," *Pratley*, p. 123.

P. 85 "Smashing up the trains . . .," *Pratley*, p. 126.

P. 87 "Frankenheimer's use of locations . . .," *Pratley*, p. 122.

P. 88 "Frankenheimer cut *The Train* himself . . .," *Kansas City Star*, August 1, 1965.

P. 94 "When we talk about life . . .," *Pratley*, p. 148.

P. 94 "John was conscious of the fact that I had been blacklisted . . .," Mitchell interview with John Randolph, March, 1995.

P. 100 ". . . I hoped (Garner) would be as good as he was in . . .," *Pratley*, p. 161.

P. 101 "All of the cars in *Grand Prix* were real . . .," *Pratley*, p. 156 & 161.

P. 107 "I feel better about *The Fixer* than anything . . .," *Pratley*, p. 183.

P. 109 "*The Fixer* was something that had the same . . .," JF in *Action* Magazine, 1973.

P. 111 "We didn't have any fades . . .," *Pratley*, p. 208.

P. 118 "John Frankenheimer likes and believes in actors . . .," from The *Long Island Press*, September 7, 1969.

P. 133 "When March died, his family . . .," from The *Boston Globe*, May 18, 1975.

P. 152 Frankenheimer used ten cameras . . ., From JF interview on *Later — With Bob Costas*, NBC TV, November, 1991.

P. 154 "When you've been blasted critically . . .," JF on *Later — With Bob Costas*.

P. 169 "When you say that film is a director's medium . . .," JF in *Action Magazine*, 1973.

P. 174 "Frankenheimer told film critic Kirk Honeycutt . . .," *Movie Talk From The Front Lines* edited by Jerry Roberts and Steven Gaydos (McFarland, 1995) pp. 277, 279.

P. 175 Roy Scheider's quote from interview with Kirk Honeycutt in *Movie Talk From The Front Lines*, p. 285.

P. 180 ". . .I would like Sharon Stone . . .," JF on *Later —With Bob Costas*.

P. 184 ". . . directing a film . . .," JF on *Later — With Bob Costas*.

P. 184 "I have no great secrets . . .," JF in Kodak Professional Forum.

P. 187 "I don't know how you can say . . .," JF to Charles Champlin, *Los Angeles Times*, April 10, 1977.

P. 191 "If this was a major studio feature . . ." JF interview with Michael McCall, *Los Angeles Times*, June 20, 1993.

P. 192 "I guess people will see different things . . .," — Michael Smith quoted in *On Set* Magazine; "When they filmed a couple of violent scenes . . ." — Michael Smith quoted in *The Buffalo News*, March 23, 1994.

P. 193 "Since I directed *Against The Wall* . . .," JF interview in *DGA News*, Aug. - Sept. '94.

P. 194 "I think that people want to see heroes . . .," — JF in Kodak Professional Forum.

P. 198 "Frankenheimer is the best director . . .," Esai Morales as quoted in *Premiere* Magazine, November, 1994.

P. 202 "The project was impossible, it was so *huge* . . .," Mitchell interview with Ethel Winant, March 10, 1995.

P. 206 "It rained every day . . .," Mitchell interview with Winant.

P. 208 "John is like a bottle of Lafitte Rothschild . . .," Mitchell interview with Winant.

P. 209 "Yul Brynner, who was a very, very dear friend . . .," JF on *Later — With Bob Costas*.

A Matter of Conviction, 49, 51
A Place in the Sun, 184
"A Portrait in Celluloid" *(Climax),* 24
"A Town Has Turned to Dust" *(Playhouse 90),*
    32, 33
ABC, 9, 11
Abrahams, Mort, 167, 168
Academy Award, 101
Adam, Ken, 177
Adelson, Merv, 159
Adler, Gil, 187
Adler, Renata, 107
Against the Wall, 133, 187, 188–191, 195,
    196, 198, 201, 202, 207, 208, 209
Air Force,
    motion picture squadron, —see also
        Howard, Harvey.
    television squadron, 9
Alcatraz, 54, 57
Alda, Alan, 103
All Fall Down, 62–65, 67, 70, 201
Allen, Jay Presson, 181
Alonzo, John, 148
Ambassador Hotel, 113, 114
American Civil Liberties Union, 75
American Express, 135
American Film Theater, 133
"American, The," *(Producer's Showcase),* 135
Andrews, Edward, 50
An Exile, 121
Andersonville, 200–209
Anka, Paul, 49
Ann-Margret, 171, 173, 174
Ant, Adam, 186, 187
Antonowsky, Marvin, 169
Argenziano, Carmine, 191, 195
Arnold, Edward, 23
Ashley, Ted, 22
Assante, Armand, 157, 158
Astor, Mary, 40, 42
Atlanta Film Festival, 131
Aubrey, James, 118
Aurthur, Robert Alan, 35, 97
Axelrod, George, 47, 67–69, 73, 75, 167, 169
Axelrod, Jonathan, 192

Bacall, Lauren, 34
"Bail Out at 43,000" *(Climax),* 23, 135
Bailey, Charles II, 75
Baker, Rick, 157
Ball, Lucille, 67, 70
Balsam, Martin, 35, 77
Baltimore Colts, 150
Bankhead, Tallulah, 13
Bard, Katharine, 22

Barker, Katherine, 18
Barker, Margaret, 19
Barry, Tim, 155
Bart, Peter, 159
Bartok, Jayce, 203, 207
Bates, Alan, 107, 108, 110, 131
Baumann, Kathrine, 137
Beatty, Warren, 63–65
Beck, Jerry, 177
Bedelia, Bonnie, 118
Bedford, Brian, 98
Begelman, David, 76
Begley, Ed, 58
Bell, Book and Candle, 168, 169
Bell, Tom, 108
Benny, Jack, 24
Benson, Sheila, 174
Benz, Donna Kei, 163
Berg, Jeff, 147, 159, 171, 177
Bergman, Ingrid, 44, 45, 50
Bernstein, Walter, 19, 20, 83
Berwick, Ray, 54
Best of Broadway, The, 21
Bill and Cora Baird's puppets, 25
Birdman of Alcatraz, 47, 52, 53–60, 63, 64,
    81, 139, 196, 201
Birmingham, Stephen, 3
Bissell, Whit, 28
Black Sunday, 145, 147–153, 161, 175, 179,
    184, 185
Blacklist, 18, 39, 57, 75, 77, 83, 112
Blackmer, Sidney, 24
Blue Moon, 5
Bogarde, Dirk, 108, 110, 112
Bogart, Humphrey, 34
"Bomber's Moon" *(Playhouse 90),* 35
Bondurant, Bob, 98
Boone, Richard, 23, 24, 135
Bradford, Barbara Taylor, 131
Bradford, Robert, 131
Braga, Sonia, 195, 197, 198
Brand, Neville, 57
Brando, Marlon, 133
Breakfast at Tiffany's, 47, 67
Bricken, Jules, 81
Bridges, Jeff, 133, 134
Bridges, Lloyd, 35
Brillstein, Bernie, 177
Brink's Job, The, 153
Brodkin, Herbert, 35, 36, 184
Brooks, Marty, 18, 19
Brooks, Mel, 131
Brown, Georgia, 108
Brown, Kay, 44
Brown, Tom, 32

"Browning Version, The," *(DuPont Show of the Month)*, 16, 43
Bureau of Prisons, 52, 54
Burman, Thomas H., 157
Burning Season, The, 194–197, 201, 202, 208, 209
Burns, George, 24
Burton, Richard, 40
Burton, Sir Richard, (explorer), 129
Buzkashi, 123–124

Caan, James, 167, 168
Caine, Michael, 166, 168, 169
Campbell, Vernon, 16
Canby, Vincent, 69, 140, 158
Cannon Pictures, 171, 174, 179
Carey, MacDonald, 24
Carlino, Lewis John, 91
Carlson, Richard, 24
Carroll, Cathleen, 107, 131
Carson, Jack, 24
Cassavetes, John, 15, 20, 21, 38, 39
Cat Ballou, 135
Cavanagh, James, 38
CBS Theatrical Films, 159, 161
CBS, 9–25, 31–45, 52, 185
        Studio 55, 16
Challenge, The, 159, 160–163, 165
Chandler, John Davis, 49
Chang, Gary, 208
Chapman, Colin, 100
Chateau Marmont, 53
Chayevsky, Paddy, 35
"Clash By Night" *(Playhouse 90)*, 35
Cleaves, Helen, 43
Climax, 19–25, 27, 35, 36, 39
Clurman, Harold, 19
Cocks, Jay, 107, 141
Coe, Fred, 12, 13, 35, 36, 38, 43, 63, 184
Coen, Franklin, 83
Cohn, Harry, 183
Collingwood, Charles, 18
Colon, Miriam, 20
Columbia Pictures, 126, 127, 129, 181, 183, 185
"Comedian , The," *(Playhouse 90)*, 32, 34, 36, 77
Condon, Richard, 67, 69
Connors, Chuck, 137
Cook, Whitfield, 25
Cooper, Clancy, 40
Cooper, Robert, 190, 192, 198
Cordon Bleu, 129
Corey, Jeff, 94
Corey, Wendell, 24

Costigan, James, 45
Crane, Norma, 40
Crawford, Joan, 24
Creach, Everett, 151
Crichton, Charles, 52
Crone, David, 191
Cronkite, Walter, 14, 18
Crowther, Bosley, 51, 68
Cummings, Robert, 35
Curtis, Tony, 67
Curtiss, Thomas Quinn, 135
Curtiz, Michael, 40, 43
Cushingham, John, 103

Daily News, 107
Daly, James, 28
Daly, Robert, 177
Danger, 14–21
Danner, Blythe, 187
Dare, Michael, 173
Davis, Bud, 182
Davis, Frank, 83
Davis, Geena, 185
Davis, Kristi Frankenheimer, 182
Davis (Reagan), Nancy, 23, 24 —see also
        Reagan, Nancy Davis
Day, Laraine, 32
Days of Wine and Roses (feature film), 47
"Days of Wine and Roses" *(Playhouse 90)*, 35–38, 63
"Death in My Neighborhood" *(Danger)*, 14
De Felitta, Frank, 20
de Hartog, Jan, 183
De Laurentiis, Dino, 153
de Wilde, Brandon, 63, 64, 65
Dead-Bang, 176–177, 181, 183, 191
"Deal A Blow" *(Climax)*, 26, 27
Dean, James, 14
"Death of Manolete, The," *(Playhouse 90)*, 32, 34
Defiant Ones, The, 75, 83
Dehn, Paul, 73
Dennis Day Show, The, 9
Denny, Reginald, 34
Dern, Bruce, 149
Devil Drives, The, 129
Digest of Bird Diseases, 57
Diller, Barry, 147, 185
Dillman, Bradford, 133, 134, 137
Dillon, Robert, 137, 139
Dimsdale, Howard, 83
Donohue, Vincent, 36
Douglas, Kirk, 75–79, 91
Dozier, Robert (Bob), 26, 27, 29
Dozier, William (Bill), 23, 26, 27

Dresner, Hal, 103
Dreyfuss, Richard, 165
Drought, James, 117
Dru, Joanne, 24
Duff, Gordon, 39
Dunaway, Faye, 103, 104
Dunn, James, 42
Dunne, Dominick, 121
Dunnock, Mildred, 38
Dutton, Fred, 114
Dysart, Richard, 157

Eady Plan, 168, 169
Ebert, Roger, 131, 175
Edwards, Blake, 47, 63
Eisenstein, Sergei, 6
Eisner, Michael, 157, 185
Elliott, Sumner Locke, 35, 47
Ely, David, 91
Embassy Pictures, 161
EMI, 169
Emick, Jarrod, 202, 203, 206–208
Emmy Award, 24, 31, 40, 77, 189, 193, 202, 211
Evans, Robert, 148, 149, 152, 161, 184, 187
Evans, Evans (Mrs. John Frankenheimer), 52, 60, 63, 65, 86, 88, 94, 99, 114, 126, 131, 133, 137, 153, 169, 184, 210
Evans, J. C., 121
Evans, Joanne, (former Mrs. John Frankenheimer), 5, 11
Evans, Robert, 147
Executive Action, 185
Extraordinary Seaman, The, 103–105
"Face of a Hero" *(Playhouse 90),* 63

Factory, The, 114
Farmer, Michael, 51
Faulkner, Robert, 177
Faulkner, William, 35, 38
FCC, 7
Fehmiu, Bekim, 150
Ferber, Mel, 14
Feret, Liv, 165
Ferguson, Bob, 129
Ferrer, Mel, 47
Field, Betty, 57
Fields, Freddie, 76
Fields, Freddie, Mrs., 97
"Fifth Column, The," *(Buick Electra Playhouse),* 40, 47
52 Pick-Up, 170–175, 208
Fitzgerald, F. Scott, 34, 38

Fixer, The, 103, 105, 107–112
"Flame-Out on T-6" *(Climax),* 24
Fonda, Henry, 4
Fonda, Jane, 49
Fontanne, Lynn, 22
Foote, Horton, 35
"For Whom the Bell Tolls" *(Playhouse 90),* 35, 36, 38, 39, 41, 50, 201
"Forbidden Area, The," *(Playhouse 90),* 31
Ford, Glenn, 91
Foreign Correspondent, 68
Foreman, Carl, 183
Foreman, John, 91
Forrest, Frederic, 192, 202, 203, 207, 208
Forsyth, Frederick, 169
Forsythe, John, 24
Four Horsemen of the Apocalypse, The, 65
Fourth Protocol, The, 169
Fourth War, The, 179
Fox —see 20th Century-Fox
Foxworth, Robert, 157, 158
Frank, Pat, 31
Frazee, Logan, 143
Freed, Donald, 185
Freeman, David, 165
French Academy Award (Cesar), 129
French Army, 86
French Connection I, 139
French Connection II, 138–145, 149
Fresson, Bernard, 139, 141, 144
Friedkin, William, 143, 153
Fritz the Cat, 11
Front, The, 19

Gaddis, Thomas, 52
Gardner, Ava, 77
Garland, Robert, 165
Garner, James, 97–100
Gay Illiterate, The, 25
Gazzara, Ben, 15
Geer, Will, 94, 95, 121, 185
Gielgud, John, 16, 38, 43
Gilroy, Frank, 49
Giurato, Blasco, 181
Glenn, Scott, 161–163
Globus, Yoram, 171, 173, 174
Glover, John, 173
Godfrey, Lionel, 64
Golan, Menachem, 171–174
Goldmark, Peter, 25
Goldsmith, Jerry, 44
Golino, Valeria, 181
Gomez, Thomas, 23
Goodman, Benny, 13

Goodwin, Dick, 114–115
Goodyear Tire and Rubber Company, 147–150
    Goodyear blimp, 147, 148
Grand Prix, 64, 88, 96–100, 103, 117, 123, 135, 148, 185
Grant, Cary, 72
Grant, Lee, 49
Greene, Lorne, 18
Gregory, James, 20, 28, 32, 33, 40, 43, 47
Griffith, Hugh, 110
Griswold, Claire, 50
Guardino, Harry, 15
"Guardsman, The," 22
Guffey, Bernard, 54
Guiding Light, 13
Gunfight at the OK Corral, 76
Gunn, Moses, 133
Guzman, Luis, 195
Gypsy Moths, The, 115, 116–119, 121

HBO —see Home Box Office
Hackman, Gene, 117, 118, 121, 133, 139–145
Hall, Robert David, 206
Hampden, Walter, 14
Hamill, Pete, 139
Hanks, Tom, 185
Hanley, William, 117
Hannon, Michael, 190, 196, 201
Hardwicke, Sir Cedric, 39
Harris, Lara, 179
Harris, Richard, 137
Harris, Robert H., 23, 24
Harris, Steve, 191, 192
Harrison, Rex, 168, 169
Hartman, Elizabeth, 110
Harvey, Laurence, 66–68, 73
Havers, Nigel, 196
Hayes, Helen, 27, 38
Hayes, Ira, 135
Hays Code, 94
Hayward, Susan, 24
Heche, Anne, 192
Hecht, Harold, 49, 54, 57, 60, 184
Hecht, Harold Jr., 155
Hecht-Hill-Lancaster, 49
Heilweil, David, 21
Hellman, Jerome, 22
Hemingway Playhouse, The, 39
Hemingway, Ernest, 39, 40, 47
Henry, Justin, 203
Hepburn, Audrey, 47
Herlihy, James Leo, 62, 63
Heston, Charlton, 23, 24, 31, 135
Hickman, Darryl, 38

Higgins, George V., 153
Higgins, Tony, 207
Hill, Phil, 98
Hill, Steven, 40–43, 49
Hirschman, Herb, 13
Hirson, Roger O., 35, 43
Hitchcock, Alfred, 68, 183
Holcroft Covenant, The, 166–169
Holm, Ian, 108, 110
Home Box Office (HBO), 133, 165, 187, 189, 192, 193, 195, 199, 201
Honeycutt, Kirk, 174
Hopkins, John, 167
Hopper, Dennis, 50
Horseman, The, 122–129, 145, 185
Hotchner, A. E., 40
Houseman, John, 35, 36, 63–65, 184, 201
Howard, Harvey, 6, 7, 12
Howe, James Wong, 92, 94, 95
Howes, Sally Ann, 40
Hudson, John, 34
Hudson, Rock, 24, 91–98, 105
Humphrey, Hubert, 113
Hunter, Evan, 49, 51
Hunter, Jeffrey, 23
Hunter, Kim, 27, 28, 30, 34, 38
Hunter, Tab, 31
Hussey, Ruth, 24
Hutchinson, Ron, 191, 192, 195

I Walk the Line, 120–129, 165, 185
I Want to Live, 27
Iceman Cometh, The, 132–136, 167, 191
ICM, 147, 177
Importance of Being Earnest, The, 169
Impossible Object, The, 129, 130–131, 145
Inge, William, 62–65
Ipana toothpaste commercial, 15

Jackson, Samuel L., 189, 190
Jackter, Norm, 129
Jacobs, Alex, 139
Jaffe, Leo, 183
James, Henry, 44
Jarre, Maurice, 101
Jennings, Robert C., 4, 21, 72
Jens, Salome, 89, 187
Jeter, Michael, 176
Johnson, Don, 176, 177, 179, 181, 191
Johnston, Denis, 4
Jones, Jennifer, 47, 49
Jones, Tommy Lee, 165
Jory, Victor, 24, 31
"Journey to the Day" *(Playhouse 90),* 38, 43, 44

Joyce, James, 133
Judgment at Nuremberg, 60
Julia, Raul, 194–197, 199
Jurow, Martin, 47

Kamm, Kris, 203, 207
Kaplan, William, 98
Karloff, Boris, 31, 32
Kaskle and Kaskle, 3
Kaufman, Dave, 34
Kavovit, Andrew, 203
Kazan, Elia, 64
Keller, Marthe, 149
Kelly, Barry, 71
Kennedy, Edward, 115
Kennedy, Ethel, 113, 114
Kennedy, John Fitzgerald, 67, 72, 185
Kennedy, Robert, 113–115, 129, 192, 193, 208
Kerr, Deborah, 117, 118
Kessel, Joseph, 123
Key, The, 183
Kilmer, Ned, 18
Kirk Douglas Company, 75
Knebel, Fletcher, 75
Knight, Arthur, 107
Knight, Shirley, 167
Knox Hats, 3
Kodiak Films, 179
Korda, Alexander, 184
Korean War, 4
Kraft Theater, 13
Krantz, Judith, 11
Krantz, Steve, 11
Krim, Arthur, 183
Kristien, Stanley, 49, 51
Krupa, Olek, 203
Kurland, Gil, 54

Lancaster, Burt, 49–51, 53–55, 57, 58, 60, 76, 77, 79, 81–88, 117, 118, 139, 185
Landau, Edie, 166–168
Landau, Ely, 133, 135, 167
Landers, Hal, 117
Lane, Mark, 185
Lane, Robert, 148, 149
Lansbury, Angela, 47, 49, 58, 63–65, 67–70
"Last Summer, The," *(Studio One),* 49–50
"Last Tycoon, The," *(Playhouse 90),* 32, 34, 36
Laurie, Piper, 36
Lauter, Ed, 133
Lawrence, Marc, 36–38
Lawrence of Arabia, 184
Lazar, Irving, 67, 147

League of Their Own, A, 185
Le Mans, 97, 165
Lean, David, 101, 184
Legrand, Michel, 131
Lehman, Ernest, 34, 147
Leigh, Janet, 70
Leighton, Margaret, 43
Lemay, General Curtis, 7, 8
Lemmon, Jack, 38, 63
Leonard, Elmore, 171, 175
Leonetti, John, 187, 190, 193, 196
Levy, Michael, 161
Lewis, Edward, 75, 91, 97, 98, 103, 104, 107, 108, 113, 117, 121, 123, 127, 129, 133, 184, 185
Lindfors, Viveca, 32, 34
Lindon, Lionel, 50, 63, 91
"Little Bear, A" *(Playhouse 90),* 35
Logan, Josh, 4
Lombardo, Nick, 207
London, Jack, 24
Long Gray Line, The, 9
Look Magazine, 75
Lopert, Ilya, 81, 82
Lopez-Dawson, Kamela, 196
Loren, Sophia, 72
Lorimar, 159, 177
Lorre, Peter, 34
Los Angeles Times, 107, 174
Losey, Joseph, 131
Lotus, 100
"Louella Parsons Story, The," *(Climax),* 24
Love, Phyllis, 38
Lubin, Milton, 23
Ludlum, Robert, 167
Lumet, Sidney, 13, 14, 22
Lynn, Diana, 31, 38

MacArthur, James, 27, 29, 30
Mackenzie, John, 169
MacLachlan, Kyle, 190–192
Macready, George, 77
Malamud, Bernard, 107
Malden, Karl, 60, 63–65
Maltz, Albert, 19
Manchurian Candidate, The, 43, 47, 64, 66–73, 75, 113, 114, 169, 183
Mancini, Henry, 137
Mancuso, Frank, 175
Mankiewicz, Don, 32, 34
Mann, Delbert, 36
Manulis, Martin, 21–24, 27, 31, 35, 36, 63, 184
Marathon Man, 149
March, Donald, 161

March, Fredric, 73, 76, 77, 79, 117, 133
Marcoux, Ted, 203
Marshall, E. G., 35, 38
Marshall, Penny, 185
Marvin, Lee, 23, 24, 133–135
Maslin, Janet, 174
Massari, Lea, 131
Mastrosimone, William, 195
Matter of Conviction, A, 49, 51
Matthau, Walter, 24
Maxwell, Richard, 161
McCarthy, Andrew, 181
McCarthy, Eugene, 114
McCarthy, Joseph, 25
McCrea, Joel, 68
McFadden, Tom, 159
McGilligan, Patrick, 142
McGuire, Dorothy, 24, 38
McQueen, Steve, 97
Meeker, Ralph, 121
Meier, Hal, 11, 12
Meisner, Sandy, 50
Mendes, Chico, 195, 196, 198
Mengers, Sue, 147
Merrill, Dina, 49
Metro, —see MGM
Meyer, Irwin, 192
MGM, 63–65, 70, 97, 100–103, 105, 108, 118, 185
Miami Dolphins, 150
Mifune, Toshiro, 100, 160, 161, 163
Milian, Tomas, 195
Millar, Stuart, 27, 29
Miller, Carolyn Diane (former Mrs. John Frankenheimer), 17, 19, 22, 23, 44, 49, 52, 81
Miller, David, 185
Miller, J. P., 35, 63
Miller, Merle, 135
Miller, Penelope Ann, 176, 177
Miller, Robert Ellis, 12
Mitchum, Robert, 67, 184
Moffat, Ivan, 49, 161
Monroe, Marilyn, 47
Montand, Yves, 98, 105
Monte Carlo, 100
Moore, Constance, 34
Morales, Esai, 198
Moreau, Jeanne, 83
Morris, William, 147
Mosel, Tad, 35
Mosley, Nicholas, 129, 131
Mosley, Sir Oswald, 131
Mottola, Tony, 16
Mulligan, Robert, 13

Murnik, Peter, 203
Murrow, Edward R., 13, 14, 25

Nakamura, Atsuo, 161, 163
Nathan, Vivian, 38, 42, 43, 50
NBC, 9, 11, 13, 14, 45, 77
Neighborhood Playhouse, 50
Nelson, Ralph, 31
Nephew, Neil, 49
New York Daily News, 131
New York Times, 107, 174
Newman, Paul, 20, 76
NFL, 150
Nichols, Mike, 42, 43
Nicholson, William, 195
Nickell, Paul, 13
Nickerson, Kate (pseudonym of Walter Bernstein), 18, 19
Nimoy, Leonard, 94
99 and 44/100 Per Cent Dead, 137
Niven, David, 103–105
"No Passport for Death", *(Danger),* 20
"No Stone Unturned" *(Playhouse 90),* 39
Nolan, Lloyd, 24, 35
North, Sheree, 117, 118

O'Brian, Jack, 31, 35
O'Brien, Edmond, 34, 77, 79, 101, 137
O'Brien, Margaret, 23
O'Brien, Robert, 100, 118, 183
O'Neal, Patrick, 9
O'Neil, Sally, 9
O'Neill, Eugene, 133, 135
O'Toole, Peter, 49
"Old Man" *(Playhouse 90),* 35, 38
Olivier, Laurence, 91
Olmos, Edward James, 195, 197, 198
Omnibus, 13
"Our Crowd", 3
Over the Top, 172
Ovitz, Michael, 171

Palance, Jack, 34, 35, 38, 123, 128
"Pale Horse, Pale Rider" *(Climax),* 24
Paley, William S., 25
Palmer, Betsy, 14
Palmer, Lilli, 168, 169
Papp, Joe, 19
Paramount Pictures, 47, 91, 95, 135, 147, 148, 157, 159, 175, 184, 185
Parker, Hutch, 189, 195
Parker, Robert, 165
Parker, Suzy, 34
Parsons, Estelle, 121
Parsons, Louella, 24, 25

Paths of Glory, 77
"Patterns" *(Playhouse 90),* 32
Patterson, Elizabeth, 32
Paulson, Albert, 40
Peabody Award, 40
Peck, Gregory, 58, 121
Penn, Arthur, 9, 36, 79, 81, 82, 187
Penn, Leo, 20, 21
Percy, Lee, 189, 190
Perez, Jose, 195
Perez, Tony, 195
Persoff, Nehemiah, 40
Person to Person, 13, 14
Peticlerc, Denne, 159
Peters, Brock, 40
Philco Playhouse, 13, 36
Phillips, Michael, 165
Picker, David, 185
Place in the Sun, A 184
Playhouse 90, 27, 30–45, 52, 63, 201
"Plot Against King Solomon, The," *(You Are There),* 18
Polk, Bo, 118
Pollack, Sydney, 40, 49, 50, 97
Polonsky, Abe, 19
Porter, Katherine Anne, 24
"Portrait in Celluloid, A" *(Climax),* 24
Prelutsky, Burt, 44
Pressman, Edward R., 181
Preston, Kelly, 174
Price, Vincent, 31
Pride and the Passion, The, 72
Prochnow, Jurgen, 179
Producers, The, 131
Prophecy, 156–159, 175
Prudential Insurance Company of America, 32
Puttnam, David, 195, 202, 207

Racimo, Victoria, 158
Radio and Television Directors Guild, 30
Radio City Music Hall, 118
Rainmaker, The, 164–165
Randle, Nancy, 189
Randolph, John, 57, 92, 94, 95
Rank, 169
Rauss, Meriam, 5
Rawley, Peter, 167
Reagan, Nancy Davis, 135 —see Davis, Nancy
Redford, Robert, 97
Redstone, Sumner, 152
Reed, Carol, 183, 184
Reed, Florence, 95
Rehme, Robert G., 165
Reid, Tim, 176, 179
Remick, Lee, 34

"Rendezvous in Black" *(Playhouse 90),* 31, 32
Renoir, Claude, 144, 145
"Requiem for a Heavyweight" *(Playhouse 90),* 31, 32
Revkin, Andrew, 196
Rey, Fernando, 143
Rich, John, 9
Richman, Mark, 15
Riggs, Elsie Frankenheimer, 182
Riggs, George, 182
Rindt, Jochen, 129
Rintels, David, 201, 202
Ritt, Martin, 19
Ritter, Thelma, 57, 58
Robards, Jason, 39, 41, 133
Robert Montgomery Presents, 11
Roberts, Bobby, 117
Robertson, Cliff, 36, 37, 63
Robinson, Hubbell, 17, 18, 20, 22, 33, 44, 45
Rock, Philip, 103
Rockett, Al, 9
Rooney, Mickey, 34, 103
Rose, Reginald, 35
Rosen, Robert L., 141, 143, 147–150, 153, 157, 161, 177–179, 184
Ross, Kenneth, 147, 179
Roth, Steve, 177, 181
Ruddly, Jonah, 60
Rule, Janice, 40, 42
Ruggieri, Francoise, 92
Russell, Charles, 14, 19, 20
Ryan, Robert, 40, 133, 134, 185
Rydell, Mark, 15, 43

Sabinson, Allen, 201
Sagall, Steven, 162
"Sailor on Horseback" *(Climax),* 24
Saint, Eva Marie, 38, 62–65
Salinger, Pierre, 113, 114
Salkind, Alexander, 131
Sanda, Dominique, 131, 133
Sargent, Alvin, 121
Saulnier, Jacques, 143, 144
Savalas, Telly, 51, 57, 58
Sayles, John, 161
Sbardellati, Jim, 202
Schafer, Natalie, 23
Schaffner, Franklin, 13
Scheider, Roy, 171–174, 179, 191
Schell, Maria, 39, 41
Schell, Maximilian, 40
Scheuer, Phillip K., 76, 85
Schickel, Richard, 148, 150
Schiffer, Bob, 54
Schmidt, Burr, 40

Schmidt, Lars, 45
Schmidt, Wolf, 179
Scofield, Paul, 84, 85, 87, 89, 105
Scorsese, Martin, 184
Scott, John L., 54
Screen Directors Guild, 30
Seconds, 88, 90–95
Secret Service, 113
See It Now, 25
Selleca, Connie, 177
Seltzer, David, 157
Selzer, Milton, 40
Selznick, David O., 45, 47, 49, 171
Selznick, Joyce, 57
Semel, Terry, 177
Serling, Rod, 20, 24, 31–34, 75
Sevareid, Eric, 18
Seven Arts, 77
Seven Days in May, 74–79, 113, 185, 191
Shakespeare in the Park, 19
Sharif, Omar, 123, 125, 127, 128
Shatner, William, 32, 33
Shaw, Jerome, 25
Shaw, Robert, 147–149
Shea, Jack, 9
Shelby, Carroll, 97
Shepherd, Dick, 47
Shire, Talia, 157, 158
Silva, Henry, 66
Simon, Michel, 129
Simon, Norton, 137
Simon, Robert L., 34, 38
Simpson, Don, 157
Sinatra, Frank, 66–73
Sirhan, Sirhan, 114
Smith, Michael, 192, 193
Smith, Steven, 114
"Snows of Kilimanjaro, The," *(Buick
    Playhouse),* 40, 133, 135
Sobol, Ron, 17
Sokoloff, Vladimir, 40
Sondheim, Steven, 11
"South of the Sun" *(Climax),* 22–24
Spain, Fay, 32, 33
Spiegel, Sam, 184
Spivy, Madame, 63, 66
Splendor in the Grass, 64
Stack, Dennis, 88
Stallone, Sylvester, 172
Stanley, Kim, 35, 38
Stanley, Richard, 11
Stanton, Harry Dean, 179, 192
Stapleton, Maureen, 40
Stark, Dick, 15
Stark, Ray, 77

Steiger, Rod, 32, 33, 38
Steppling, John, 171
Stevens, George, 183
Stewart, Jimmy, 4
Stone, Bob, 24
Stone, Lewis, 17, 18
Stone, Sharon, 180, 181
Story of a Love Story, The, 131
Strick, Joseph, 133
Stroud, Robert, 54, 55, 60
Strudwick, Shepperd, 18, 19
Studio One, 13, 49
Stulberg, Gordon, 137
Sullivan, Dan, 65, 134
Sumner, Gabe, 161
Super Bowl, 147, 150
Suspense, 13, 21
Sweeney, Joseph, 38
Sylbert, Richard, 147

Tales From the Crypt, 186–187
Tamiroff, Akim, 24
Tanen, Ned, 165, 177
Taylor, Frances, 118
Taylor-Young, Leigh, 123
Teamsters Union, 171
Tender Is The Night, 47, 49, 171
Tennant, Victoria, 166
Till, Emmett, 32
Time, 100, 118
"To Wake at Midnight" *(Playhouse 90),* 32
Todd, Ann, 40
Tone, Franchot, 22, 32
Torme, Mel, 34
"Town Has Turned to Dust, A" *(Playhouse 90)*
    32, 33
Train, The, 79, 80–88
Trosper, Guy, 52, 53, 55
Trumbo, Dalton, 107, 112, 123, 129, 185
Turkel, Ann, 137
"Turn of the Screw" *(Ford Startime),* 44, 45,
    50
Turner Pictures, 189, 201, 207
Turner, Ted, 201, 209
20th Century-Fox, 40, 49, 63, 131, 135, 137,
    141. —see Fox
24 Hours of Le Mans, —see also Le Mans
Two Minute Warning, 152
Two Weeks in Another Town, 63

Ulysses, 133
Union Corse, 141
United Artists, 60, 67, 70, 72, 79, 81, 86, 183
United Way, 147

Universal Pictures, 165, 169
Utt, Kenneth, 19, 41

Vanity, 174
"Velvet Alley, The," *(Playhouse 90)*, 32
Vidor, Charles, 27
Vidor, King, 142
"Violent Heart, The," *(Playhouse 90)*, 38
Voice of the Turtle, 4
Volkenberg, Jack Van, 12
Voscovek, George, 133
Votrain, Peter, 43

Wager, Alexandra, 45
Waite, Ric, 207
Wallace, Eva, 21
Wallace, Mike, 25
Wallach, Eli, 41, 42
Warden, Jack, 24
Warner Bros., 177, 183, 195, 199
Warner, Jack, 183
Waters, Ethel, 13
Wayne, Fredd, 77
Wayne, John, 24, 25
Weaver, Fritz, 149
Web, The, 13
Weinstein, Henry, 49, 171
Weitman, Robert, 118, 183
Weld, Tuesday, 121, 165
Welles, Orson, 183
White House, 113
Wilder, Billy, 209
Wilderness, 165
Willenkomper, 148

Williams, Andy, 208
Williams, Clarence, III, 175, 186, 187, 191–
     193
Wilmington, Michael, 168, 169
Wilson, Scott, 117, 118
Wilson, Tom, 207
Winant, Bruce, 203
Winant, Ethel, 201, 202, 206, 207
Windom, William, 117
Windust, Bretaigne, 22
Winger, Cliff, 196
"Winter Dreams" *(Playhouse 90)*, 38, 39, 184
Winters, Shelley, 49, 51
Wirtz, Henry, 201, 202
Wizan, Joe, 137, 161
Woolrich, Cornell, 32
Woolsey, Ralph, 135, 137
Wright, Teresa, 24, 25
Wyler, William, 184
Wynn, Keenan, 34
Wynter, Dana, 38, 39

Yeager, Colonel Chuck, 8, 9
Year of the Gun, The, 181, 187
You Are There, 13, 14, 18–20
Young Savages, The, 46–52, 57, 195
Young Stranger, The, 26–30
Young, Nathan E., 75, 83
Youngerman, Joseph C., 30
Youngstein, Max, 183

Zavitz, Lee, 86
Ziesmer, Jerry, 150, 152
Zoltan, 107, 108, 109